Charles Douglas

John Stuart Mill

A Study of His Philosophy

Charles Douglas

John Stuart Mill
A Study of His Philosophy

ISBN/EAN: 9783337073619

Printed in Europe, USA, Canada, Australia, Japan

Cover: Foto ©Thomas Meinert / pixelio.de

More available books at **www.hansebooks.com**

JOHN STUART MILL

A STUDY

OF HIS PHILOSOPHY

BY

CHARLES DOUGLAS, M.A., D.Sc.

LECTURER IN MORAL PHILOSOPHY, AND
ASSISTANT TO THE PROFESSOR OF MORAL PHILOSOPHY
IN THE UNIVERSITY OF EDINBURGH

WILLIAM BLACKWOOD AND SONS
EDINBURGH AND LONDON
MDCCCXCV

PREFACE

THIS book professes to be only what its name suggests — a study of Mill's Philosophy: its aim is to examine some ideas which underlie his work rather than to give a summary of his opinions, or a detailed account of his contributions to the philosophical sciences. In a book addressed chiefly to students of philosophy it seemed best to say little of the life or even of the intellectual development of Mill; and where biography does occur its introduction is largely an accident. If my criticism or interpretation of Mill should seem to suggest philosophy other than his, I hardly feel impelled to apologise for

this; for systems of thought are never understood except in their relations to one another.

References to Mill's works are made to the
most recent Library Editions, except in the cases
of the 'Logic,' 'Political Economy,' and 'Liberty,'
in which it seemed better to refer to the original
People's Editions.[1]

In connection with the special subject of Mill's
Philosophy, I have laid myself under obligations
to the work of those who have preceded me: to
the late Professor Green's Lectures on Mill's
Logic; to Professor Bain's 'John Stuart Mill';
to Mr Courtney's 'Metaphysics of J. S. Mill,'
and to his attractive 'Life of John Stuart Mill';
to Professor Masson's appreciative and pointed
criticism;[2] to Professor Höffding's 'Einleitung
in die Englische Philosophie unserer Zeit'; and
to the late M. Taine's delightful study.[3] Other

[1] Messrs Longmans, Green, & Co.

[2] V. Recent British Philosophy: a Review with Criticisms;
including some Comments on Mr Mill's Answer to Sir William
Hamilton.

[3] Le Positivisme anglais, étude sur Stuart Mill.

and more detailed obligations are acknowledged, so far as possible, where they occur.

The whole of this book has been read in proof by the Rev. A. Halliday Douglas, of Cambridge. Part of it has also been read in manuscript by Professor Andrew Seth, of this University, and all of it by Professor Henry Jones, of Glasgow University, and by Mr J. A. Smith, of Balliol College, Oxford. I am indebted to all these gentlemen for criticisms and suggestions; and my thanks are especially due to Professor Jones, but for whose help my work must have been still more imperfect than it is.

UNIVERSITY OF EDINBURGH,
February 1895.

CONTENTS

CHAPTER I

CHAPTER II

ISOLATION

CHAPTER III

EXPERIENCE

CHAPTER IV

CAUSALITY

CHAPTER V

SELF-CONCERN

CHAPTER VI

LIFE IN NATURE

Contents

CHAPTER VII

DETERMINISM

CHAPTER VIII

FREEDOM

CHAPTER IX

ETHICAL HEDONISM

CHAPTER X

THE WORTH OF CONDUCT

CHAPTER XI

NATURE AND SPIRIT

JOHN STUART MILL

THE work of John Stuart Mill marks an impressive transition in many departments of thought. There is probably no other English writer who has had so definite an effect on the development of so many philosophical sciences; and there is none whose personal philosophy contains more striking evidence of radical changes in the speculative outlook of his generation.

Current ideas of Mill's philosophical work do but scant justice to its nature and proportions. Like many other philosophers, he has been "more criticised than read"; and the criticism

A

to which he has been subjected has generally been rather a controversial disproof of certain theories, common to him with other writers, than an attempt to discover the distinctive ways of thinking to which his philosophy owes its special interest.

We inherit, for the most part, that clerical prejudice against Mill which resulted from his attack on Mansel, in whose Agnosticism distressed but imprudent apologists found temporary shelter ; or we generalise about "lack of ideality," and suggest a "pig-philosophy"; or, if our penetration be somewhat greater, we are still apt to content ourselves with finding Mill to be a "sensationalist."

In all this there is little enough explanation of that in Mill which yet needs to be explained —his real contribution to the development of knowledge and practice ; and indeed this conception of him, which makes him merely an inconsistent and eccentric disciple of Hume, omits all that is most individual in his philosophical attempt. The following pages are intended to show that such an account of his philosophy is misleading and one-sided, and that, even where it has most appearance of truth, it is incomplete.

It is not, indeed, to be denied that Mill is deeply imbued with the sensationalist prejudice, —that he accepts from his English predecessors that conception of knowledge, which makes it a mere complex of sensations and ideas, supposed to be capable of existing in some degree independently of the synthesis in which knowledge consists. He expressly affirms this view of knowledge, and it affects his idea of explanation. It leads him to conceive things as finally reducible to sense-impressions, and even to regard such impressions as the very type or equivalent of reality. It engenders a suspicion of the constructive part which thought plays in experience—a suspicion which betrays itself in Mill's whole account of knowledge and action. He constantly tends to think of things as naturally and really isolated from one another, and to treat the relations in which we know them as fictions, which do not belong to them as they actually are. He is apt to regard thought as merely the effect of things, and to ignore the extent to which the very being of things as we know them consists of relations which reveal themselves in thought.

It is in this spirit that he adopts Hume's conception of the relation of cause and effect—the conception which finds in it a mere succession of subjective states; and his tendency 'to see in knowledge only a series of mental changes connects itself not simply with this theory of causality, but with the more general refusal to regard the relations which thought constitutes and determines as really belonging to the nature of things.

This fictitious isolation of the subject from the object of knowledge, which Mill inherited from his predecessors, plays, as we shall see, a most real part in his logical theory; and it is of hardly less account in his conception of what conduct is and ought to be. It commits him, so far as his explicit theory goes, to thinking that desire is necessarily for personal pleasure; and it makes a hedonistic conception of moral good natural and almost inevitable for him.

This individualism, then, which appears as sensationalism in the theory of knowledge, and as egoism in that of conduct, forms the general groundwork of Mill's philosophical work. It represents the point of view at which he found himself when he began to think, and which he never wholly abandoned. On the other hand, it is matter of common knowledge that this is not Mill's whole philosophy. His account of human life contains elements that are almost explicitly at variance with his inherited creed.

The theory of Induction, for example, which is his most important contribution to the science of logic, avowedly rests upon a doctrine of causality which is not that of sensationalism. He makes use of a conception of the causal relation in which it is regarded not as mere succession of ideas, but as unconditional dependence of fact upon fact. In the same way, his recognition of a self, other than transient states of consciousness, however unsatisfactory the manner of it may be, betrays a consciousness that knowledge is not merely a sequence of ideas. Still more significant of this conflict within his philosophy is the profoundly ethical cast of his Hedonism—his tendency to subordinate the hedonistic conception of moral good to a way of regarding it which makes it consist, not in a mere effect upon feeling, but in objective personal qualities.

These elements in Mill's philosophy have not been by any means unremarked. But they have very generally been regarded as mere eccentricities on his part — as results which he obtained by a leap away from his serious thinking, and to which he was in no sense entitled. Even those whose sympathy with such ways of thinking might be expected to be most active have been disposed to see in them inconsistencies on which an *argumentum ad hominem* against Mill's empiricism might be founded, rather than to treat them with any cordiality or esteem.

It would be idle to deny the justification which exists for such an attitude as this. However poor a virtue consistency may be, in science at all events, the effort to attain it is the condition of all real excellence; and for philosophy, methods must always possess a greater importance than results. "Wolves in sheep's clothing" have been frequent, and the effects of good intentions have been calamitous, in philosophy; mistaken methods and prejudices must not pass unchallenged—*et dona ferentes.*

On the other hand, a straightforward examination of Mill's work seems to me to show that,

both for Mill himself and for the real meaning of his philosophy, these so-called inconsistencies are of no second-rate importance. They
have, at all events, not less to do with his
contribution to knowledge, in logic, ethics, and
politics, than what are generally supposed to
be his more deliberate and serious conclusions.
To leave them out of account in criticising his
work is to do him less than justice.

The suggestion of this aspect of his thought
must not, of course, be understood to mean that
Mill was an idealist. To affirm that he was so
consciously would be to contradict what he has
said about himself; nor can we regard his philosophy as, even unconsciously, idealistic. His
very neglect of metaphysics is in itself inconsistent with a genuine or thorough idealism;
and even apart from this, we could only make
him out to be an idealist by ignoring elements
which permeate his whole philosophical work.
We find, indeed, many important utterances
which are idealistic in spirit and temper, and
which seem to constitute an abandonment of
empiricism; but the general theory of thought
and things is never recast so as to give effect

to these suggestions. His philosophy is certainly not idealism.

With all this, it remains true that the idealistic elements in Mill's thinking are really internal to his point of view, and that they are thus highly significant in the history of empiricism. They are not mere felonious appropriations of desired results produced by the labour of other men. They represent the effect in his own mind of new ways of thinking, to which he was singularly responsive, and by which he was profoundly influenced. If his idealism is "not in word, but in power"—if it appears not so much in definite logical utterance as in the point of view from which he regards the great human interests—it is not, on that account, less fruitful or less real. Its main importance, indeed, consists just in its having been developed within empiricism, and in the growth of positive sciences.

This element in Mill's thought is essentially ethical, both in its interest for him and in its actual development. His view of human activity and its worth is more idealistic than any other part of his philosophy. In his attitude towards his earlier masters, he is much more critical of

Bentham than of James Mill. He is, in fact, profoundly conscious of moral issues; and he finds their complexity to be too rich for the meagre explanation of them in which his predecessors had been satisfied. It is with the force of genuine conviction that he asserts the reality of voluntary choice, and its significance both as a means to human welfare and as the expression of personal life; while it is still more notable that he recognises the social character of moral criteria, that the internal sanctions of morality bulk largely in his mind, and that he is aware of the very limited extent to which the moral good of individuals is indicated by their subjective feelings.

It can hardly be denied that the latent idealism of such convictions implies a conception of man, in his relation to nature and to society, which Mill never worked out. But it is also true that his attempt to explain the legitimacy of his moral faiths, and still more the extent to which they affect his point of view in ethics and economics, produces a real and very considerable effect in his theory. If his view of man and nature is not such as to warrant his ideas of

morality, it is yet profoundly influenced by them,
and all the more influenced because he thinks
himself bound to find a basis in facts for his
interpretation of the moral consciousness. Nor
is there anything that need surprise us in this
metaphysical effect of Mill's ethical idealism.
If he had been more deliberately metaphysical,
that idealism might have penetrated his doctrine
still more profoundly. As it is, he gives no
central or abiding effect to his idealistic tendencies in his explicit theory of thought and
reality.

The very inconclusiveness and tentative character of Mill's philosophical work give it a
peculiar educational usefulness. There is, indeed,
hardly a more instructive, or, to use his favourite
word, a more " fruitful " philosophical writer.
But still greater than his importance in this
respect is the value of the discipline which his
intellectual attitude constantly affords. We find
him always free, fair, candid, without pretence
or fear ; his point of view is singularly objective
and impersonal ; and his severe, delicate reserve
and self-effacement make his work scientific in
its manner no less than in its substance. His

very lack of a coherent system belongs to the sobriety of his thinking—to the serious thoroughness of his mental habit—to his unwillingness to fill up gaps in his knowledge by myths or guesses. These qualities give his writings an enduring usefulness and interest; and they secure for his convictions and his intellectual methods that influence upon the development of thought which more systematic speculations have sometimes failed to obtain : "men will long feel the presence of his character about them, making them ashamed of what is indolent or selfish, and encouraging them to all disinterested labour, both in trying to do good, and in trying to find out what the good is, —which is harder." [1] In this respect, at least, the study of Mill's philosophy brings its own reward. He gives new depth to the conviction that the disinterested pursuit of truth is possible and altogether worthy, and that the desire of "wisdom for life" still plays its own high part in human affairs.

In all this, too, and all the more readily because of his simplicity and candour — because of the freedom with which, on due occasion, he "gives

[1] Mr Morley's Critical Miscellanies, 2nd Series (1877), p. 250.

himself away"—one may learn much from the
incompatibility of various elements in his thinking. A fuller and more concrete idea of human
life, and specially of its moral and social aspect,
forces itself through the individualism of his
inheritance, and the empirical naturalism which
is his normal point of view for mental and
social facts. His examination of moral relations
issues in a way of regarding them which is
idealistic in principle, if not in actual result.
But he never makes clear the connection of this
aspect of his thought with his philosophy as a
whole.

Our task, in studying his philosophical attempt,
is that of disentangling, and relating to each
other, mental tendencies which appear at first
sight to be wholly inconsistent. We shall have
to see how these ways of thinking impede and
modify one another; how Mill's preconceptions
are partly corrected by his half-conscious use of
a more adequate logic; and how, in spite of
this, these preconceptions, of which he is never
wholly rid, foil his endeavours and vitiate his
conclusions.

The lesson which his philosophy teaches, more

clearly perhaps than any other, is the difficulty
of erecting a theory of knowledge and action on
a basis of individualism ; and the large transi-
tions which we find in his way of thinking help
us to estimate the interval that separates the
philosophy and science of our day from those of
the last generation.

CHAPTER II

ISOLATION

MILL'S whole speculative work is vitally affected
by his theory of experience. Every philosophy
derives its character largely from its doctrine of
knowledge; and in modern systems of thought
this element has become even more important
than it was before, not only because knowledge
itself is regarded with greater interest, but,
still more, because all the problems of philosophy are looked at from a logical point of
view. The relation of things to human personality and experience is, for modern philosophy,
their principal characteristic; things are primarily objects of knowledge; and the way in which
thought is regarded thus goes far to determine
the conception of reality. The fact that logic

occupies this central position in philosophy is
specially exemplified in Mill's writings ; for there
is no important part of his philosophical doctrine which is not rooted in the account that
he gives of human knowledge, and all the
elements in that account affect his theory
in various ways. It is therefore expedient
to begin the study of his philosophy by a
survey of some of the more outstanding features of the conception of knowledge which
underlies it.

The avowed basis of Mill's theory of knowledge is an assertion of the separateness of personal life from outward reality—a limitation of
knowledge to the mental states of the individual ;
and this individualistic conception of thought, as
a subjective process, isolated from the real world
of objects, is of the greatest interest, both as a
clue to Mill's philosophical parentage, and in
respect of its significance for his whole idea of
man's place in the world. While the general
effect of his theory of personality is positive and
objective, this affirmation of the limited and exclusive character of human subjectivity forms, as
we shall see, a constant element in his philo-

sophy; and we must give an account of its main outlines.

This aspect of Mill's theory of knowledge is the result of a type of speculative system, and a phase of philosophical development, peculiarly English.

The philosophical activity of Locke and his successors is one of the main developments—and the development that possesses most historic interest—of the work of Descartes. It consists, both in intention and in execution, of a study of human knowledge, taken by itself, as a fact of observation; and it thus depends for the idea of its subject-matter on the distinction which Descartes had drawn between mind and matter —thinking substance and extended substance.

While Locke's work is based, in this way, upon the Cartesian result, it is no less determined, in respect of its method, by that sober view of human knowing-power which characterises all the great English thinkers. Nothing in his mental habit is more impressive than the seriousness and constancy of his endeavour to keep within the bounds of experience, and to limit what he has to say to the facts of mental life as they come under observation. If he finds, even in his theory of knowledge, that the very nature of thought itself forces him to take account of realities as well as of ideas, and if he is thus entangled unwillingly in metaphysical problems he returns with all the greater eagerness to the safe regions of the "historical plain method."

The results of his study of knowledge show that the dualistic conception of reality — the recognition of separate extended and thinking substances—remains a settled fact for Locke, no less than it had been for Descartes. After analysis of things into ideas has gone to the furthest extent that Locke conceives possible, there remain certain qualities of extended or material existence that will not be resolved. Behind ideas lies the source from which they come—a substance of which we have no further knowledge than that which ideas yield us, and which is itself ultimately inaccessible to knowledge, because it cannot be resolved into ideas. The implicit definition of this "unknown somewhat" as material, or not mental, is the main object of Berkeley's attack upon Locke's theory.

Berkeley's polemical attitude towards Locke is

apt to produce a wrong impression of the relation
between the two thinkers. One is liable to be
misled, if one estimates a philosopher's differences
from his predecessors at his own valuation; for
the changes of method or of presuppositions which
a thinker makes—in so far as they are deliberately or consciously made—can hardly fail to
bulk disproportionately in his mind, or to occupy
his attention more than the elements in his theory
that are common to him with others. This is
undeniably the case with Berkeley's relation to
Locke. Berkeley is so keenly aware of the reform that he is making in philosophy, and of all
its uses and consequences, that he hardly pauses
to recognise the extent of his agreement with his
predecessor, both in standpoint and method. One
might thus easily be led to imagine a vastly
greater difference between them than actually
exists.

Berkeley's advance upon Locke's position was
no doubt highly significant. Locke's acceptance
of the Cartesian dualism left the metaphysical
issues undecided and obscure; for however
strongly the manner of his philosophy might
tend to emphasise the mental aspect of all

reality, it did not preclude the possibility of an ultimate or metaphysical materialism, so long as certain qualities of matter, or even an "unknown somewhat," remained independent of conscious life. So far, indeed, as matter was positively conceived, it was reduced to dependence upon knowledge; but the admission of a nonspiritual residue, however indeterminately or negatively it might be thought of, was still a possible ground for the explanation of all reality in terms of this unknown quantity; and it was this possibility of a materialistic solution of the problem of dualism that was met by Berkeley's immaterialism. This immaterialism, however, was only the result of a consistent and deliberate use of Locke's method. Berkeley "had been accustomed by Locke, in the first place, to regard all that exists on its phenomenal or ideal side; and, at least in the 'secondary qualities' of matter, to regard *only* this ideal or phenomenal existence." [1] It was a direct application of this lesson, to reduce, as Berkeley did, all the qualities of matter, and material substance itself, to ideas— to make the existence of matter consist in the

[1] Professor Fraser's Berkeley (Philosophical Classics), p. 29.

possibility of its being perceived, and to regard
it as derivative, or as relative to intelligence.
It is rather in his view of mind than of matter
that Berkeley's originality lies. His negative
criticism of the idea of "material substance,"
while it was his starting-point, did not constitute
his whole philosophy : its interest for him was
a derived one ; and his motive, from the first, was
his positive interest in the assertion of mind or
spirit. The reduction of matter, and so of all
existence, to dependence on mind, constitutes, in
fact, a greater change in the idea of mind than
in that of matter. For the idea of matter, such
a reduction means only the impossibility of using
it as the principle of metaphysical interpretation;
but the idea of mind is more vitally and positively affected. So long as spirit is regarded as
one of two mutually independent substances, it
is necessarily limited ; it explains, at most, only
itself and the ideas in which reflection observes
it. But spirit as the sole substance is the explanation, not only of its own phenomena, but of
matter also, and of the relation of material to
mental facts. It becomes the very principle of
explanation ; and facts are only understood when

they are seen in relation to it. Something of this sort is perhaps conveyed in Berkeley's own intimation that, while "ideas" constitute all our knowledge of matter, we have a "notion" of spirit.

But this positive view of spirit was not worked out by Berkeley; and Hume's interpretation of mind, as nothing but the series of ideas, was the natural sequel to Berkeley's criticism of Locke. However far it might be, in intention, from Berkeley's philosophy, this conception of mind resulted from an application to the idea of mental substance of the same method of criticism which Berkeley had applied to Locke's idea of matter. In his theory of mind Hume gave effect to Berkeley's method, and to his limitation of knowledge to ideas, at the expense of the "notion" of spirit.

The main significance of this formative period of English philosophy consists, undoubtedly, in its well-known historical relation to Kant—in the occasion which it gave for his "criticism" of experience. It led, in this way, to an assertion of the relativity of experience to a "subject"—of the necessity for a spiritual interpretation of reality — of the objective synthesis of judgment against the mere subjectivity of "ideas"—of spirit as an active "subject" rather than a passive "substance." All this might seem, indeed, to be forecast by Berkeley's spiritualism.[1] But it was essentially inaccessible to him, no less than to Locke and Hume: it required a conception of mental life alien to their individualistic abstraction of knowledge from reality—of the subject from the object.

It is thus only natural that the work of Locke, Berkeley, and Hume should also have had historical results entirely different from the critical idealism of Kant. As a matter of fact, it is apt to be forgotten that the most direct—though not the most important—issue of their work was not its effect upon Kant, but its development by English thinkers, for whose speculations it continued to be a positive starting-point. John Stuart Mill is, in a sense, the last of these; and some important elements in his philosophy are inherited from them.

What took place, in the philosophical development which we have been considering, was the

---

[1] Cf. Professor Fraser's Preface to 'Siris,' Berkeley's Works (Clar. Press), vol. ii. pp. 317 ff.

determination of the psychological point of view. The progress of philosophy partly consists in the creation of sciences: it leads to the definition of points of view from which things are regarded, and so to the development of special sciences, which are theories of abstracted portions or aspects of reality. This is clearly instanced in the work of Locke, Berkeley, and Hume. At whatever rate we may estimate the differences between these thinkers, it is impossible to ignore the extent of their agreement; and that agreement consists primarily in their emphasis on the subjective aspect of things. However they may vary in the extent to which they consider explanation to be possible, they agree in thinking that the explanation of things consists in reducing them to "ideas," or states of consciousness. Their whole work is dominated by this conception. Theirs is the philosophy of ideas—a philosophy for which the abstract or unexplained subject is everything, and in which all reality tends to resolve itself into the passing states of the individual consciousness. Its final stage, indeed, is not reached till personal life is so resolved, and becomes, with Hume, only a name for the series of ideas. But the tendency to this result, and even the necessity for it, is present from the beginning. It is bound up with the idea of explanation which directs the work of Locke no less than that of his successors. Philosophy has, for the time being, become psychology; and in this way the psychological standpoint is defined.

Psychology shares with all other special sciences the necessity for abstraction — for a limitation of attention to one part or aspect of existence. Such limitation is the condition of all specialisation of theory; and each science is defined by the form which its abstraction takes. In the case of psychology, the point of view adopted is inevitably subjective; the position of ideas in the subjective process is considered by it, to the exclusion of all other relations that they may have, in the complex of reality. Psychology is thus the science of Individual Mind. Its origin belongs to that deepened consciousness of personal isolation which characterises modern thought and life: it is the science of the isolated or abstracted individual.

The determination, however, of this psychological point of view was the outcome of an attempt to solve philosophical rather than merely scientific problems. The abstraction from outward relations was not, in general, deliberately or consciously made for psychological purposes. The facts of consciousness were regarded as the sole clue to reality itself: the *abstract* subject was taken to be the whole of knowable existence. Such metaphysical use of abstract conceptions is an inevitable accompaniment of the growth of knowledge. It testifies, indeed, to the strength of the demand for metaphysic, that every science tends in this way to become metaphysical—that every aspect of experience, in turn, is taken for the whole, or made to explain the whole. The special metaphysical attempt, which we have been considering, was essentially psychological in its character; and it separated personal life from all other reality, because it made "ideas" the sole object of knowledge. It thus left the individual limited to himself, shorn of his relations to outward objects of knowledge and to other persons, bound hand and foot in the prison-house of his own subjectivity.

This individualism was Mill's philosophical starting-point. He inherited a theory of man's

relation to nature and society which came straight
from the eighteenth century. The doctrine of
man's natural separateness from the world of
things and from other persons has seldom been
accepted with less reserve than in the writings
of Bentham and James Mill; and Mill learned it
from them so thoroughly that he may be said
never to have been able entirely to forget it.
Even when he was most critical of his early
teachers, he continued to regard himself as an
exponent of the "experience philosophy"; and
the groundwork of this philosophy, as he understood it, was the limitation of human knowledge
to "states of consciousness."

It need not surprise us, then, to find, in Mill's
theory of knowledge, elements that embody the
individualism of the "theory of ideas." Mill is
himself aware of the relation of his theory of
knowledge to that of Berkeley, and to some extent
of Hume. He recognises Berkeley's results as "the
starting-point of the true analytic method of studying the human mind, of which they alone have
rendered possible the subsequent developments;"[1]
and he insists on the truth of Berkeley's concep-

---

[1] *Dissertations and Discussions*, vol. iv. p. 157.

tion of knowledge, although he finds it necessary
to do so at the expense of the theological idealism
to which Berkeley's philosophy was meant to lead.

Mill's individualism, however, is really an
integral part of his philosophy: it is connected
with the motive of his thinking no less vitally
than with his inherited bias. The 'System of
Logic' was intended to be a "text-book" of
empiricism—of the doctrine "which derives all
knowledge from experience, and all moral and
intellectual qualities principally from the direction given to the associations;"[1] and Mill's
interest in this theory of knowledge was mainly
due to his conviction, that "the notion that
truths external to the mind may be known by
intuition or consciousness, independently of observation and experiment," is "in these times the
great intellectual support of false doctrines and
bad institutions."[1] But his intention of making
experience the sole source of knowledge is carried
out in his limitation of knowledge to the states of
individual consciousness; and in this way his
individualistic theory of knowledge is connected
with his practical interests.

[1] Autobiography, p. 225.

This aspect of Mill's thought centres in his assertion that "of the outward world we know and can know absolutely nothing, except the sensations which we experience from it."[1] We can trace to this conception a whole system of ideas about knowledge, which play a most important part in Mill's philosophy. Once we take the view that "feeling and thought are much more real than anything else," and that "they are the only things which we directly know to be real,"[2] we are committed to a theory of knowledge. It follows inevitably that "the whole variety of the facts of nature as we know it is given in the mere existence of our sensations, and in the laws or order of their occurrence;"[3] and that "every objective fact is grounded on a corresponding subjective one,"[4] and is merely "a name for the unknown and inscrutable process by which that subjective or psychological fact is brought to pass."[5]

This conception of all reality, beyond subjective states, as merely matter of inference, applies both

[1] Logic, p. 39. [2] Essays on Religion, p. 202.
[3] Examination of Hamilton, p. 257.
[4] Logic, p. 49. [5] Ibid.

to material and to mental facts. A body is simply
"the external cause to which we ascribe our sensations";[1] and "the thinking principle, or mind,
in my own nature, makes itself known to me only
by the feelings of which it is conscious."[2] Of the
inferential character of our knowledge of outward
reality, Mill speaks confidently. He even goes so
far as to suggest that "we have in all probability
no notion of not-self, until after considerable experience of the recurrence of sensations according
to fixed laws, and in groups."[3] Knowledge
begins, in fact, with simple unreferred sensations; and the consciousness of a real world,
the reference of sensations to outward objects,
is a later stage in its development. Things
are merely the causes of our ideas; and we
gradually come to infer their existence from the
presence of their effects. This is no less true of
the relations between the elements of our experience than of these elements themselves. The
relations are themselves simply feelings. "Resemblance is nothing but our feeling of resemblance; succession is nothing but our feeling of

---

[1] Logic, p. 36.   [2] Ibid., p. 40.
[3] Examination of Hamilton, p. 265.

succession."[1]   Relations are feelings that are produced by the relation between feelings. No less
than simple sensations, they are effects upon us
of the order of things—an order which we do not
directly know, but which produces knowledge in
us, and whose reality we are able to infer, although Mill does not explain how the inference
comes about, or how knowledge is produced by
that which has no objective character. On the
whole, as Mill says plainly, "the distinction
which we verbally make between the properties
of things and the sensations we receive from them,
must originate in the convenience of discourse
rather than in the nature of what is signified by
the terms."[2]

It might be suggested that this particular
"convenience of discourse" is in itself a highly
significant fact: the objectification, which is
required for coherent speech, might reasonably
be regarded as more than an accidental excres-
cence upon knowlege. It is at all events proper
that we should examine the validity of a way of
thinking which leads to such practical difficulties
—difficulties which are not accidental, but which

[1] Logic, p. 47.   [2] Ibid., p. 41.

belong inseparably to the attempt to make states of consciousness our ultimate term of explanation.

There are undeniable grounds for making the personal life of the thinking subject our clue to reality. All thought is in the life and development of individual minds : subjective states are the only appropriations of the objective world that can constitute knowledge. But it is none the less misleading to regard objective reality as explained by reducing it to ideas; for the very conception of " ideas " abstracts from their relation to the objective world, and " ideas," in this abstraction, are not knowledge. Knowledge consists, not in ideas *per se*, but in ideas synthesised by and organised into a subject, in which alone they have being and permanence. It is not, in fact, the self taken in abstraction, but the self as it exists in the knowing synthesis, that can be made a term of explanation. To speak of " ideas " or " states of consciousness," however, is to abstract the self from the synthesis of knowledge; and, while this abstraction may be proper to the psychological point of view, it yields a conception of the " self " which is metaphysically useless.

Further criticism of Mill's individualism must be postponed until we come to speak of his own correction of it. It is to be observed, meanwhile, that this view of knowledge really enters into his conception of man's place in the world. He thinks of knowledge and conduct as effects of merely outward reality; and this deterministic empiricism—this idea of thought and action as products of a world which is wholly external— is rooted in the individualism that makes reality not the object but the cause of knowledge, and so subordinates personal life to an order with which it stands in no internal or vital relation. Apart from this individualistic assumption, the view of human life as a causally connected unity, and even as rooted in the natural order, would not lead to that empirical conception of it, as the passive creature of circumstances, which Mill sometimes adopts.

The effect of Mill's individualism on his general view of human life shows his inability to escape from it; and we find further evidence of this in his logical theory. His conception of Logic itself commits him to an abstract or subjective treatment of it. To affirm that "so far as it is a science at all, it is a part or branch of Psychology," and that "its theoretic grounds are wholly borrowed from Psychology,"[1] is to make Logic a science of "mental states"; and this view, which is an obvious sequel to the idea that the objects of knowledge are "in other words" states of consciousness,[2] evidences itself only too freely in Mill's treatment of logical questions.

The theory of judgment which regards it as a coupling of two mental states is a decisive and important instance of the attempt to interpret knowledge psychologically; and this, while it is not Mill's general or leading view, is yet explicitly stated by him, and is by no means without effect in his logical theory. It follows naturally from the treatment of "ideas" in the earlier part of the 'Logic';[3] and it has considerable influence on the subsequent discussion.

This theory of judgment connects itself with the conception of causality which Mill inherited from Hume—the conception which regards it as

---

[1] Examination of Hamilton, p. 461.

[2] Logic, p. 64.   [3] Cf. Logic, bk. i. c. iii.

merely subjective. We need not pause here to discuss the consistency of this doctrine with the place which Mill assigns to causality in his treatment of Induction. The view of the causal relation as simply a mental sequence obviously belongs to that same mode of thought which regards predication as mere coupling of mental states. From the point of view of psychology, causality *is* nothing more than this sequence of ideas, which constitutes a habit of expecting what we call the effect when we find the cause; and Mill's aversion to that idea of a "mystical tie"[1] or "mysterious compulsion,"[2] which seems to him to vitiate other theories of causality, leaves him with a view of the causal relation which gives effect to his individualist leanings—a view which results in the completest possible dissociation of the factors in the relation, and falls in with his conception of knowledge as a coupling of isolated ideas. It need not surprise us that this theory of judgment and of the causal relation modifies his idea of definition and inference.

Whatever view is taken of judgment must affect the idea of definition; for the scope of def-

[1] Logic, p. 548.　　[2] Examination of Hamilton, p. 603.

inition is at all events limited by that of judgment, since we always define by judging. Mill
asserts that definition is purely verbal—"a mere
identical proposition which gives information only
about the use of language."[1] He takes all definition—apart from a postulate which might give
it objective significance—to be merely a declara-
tion of the meaning of a word. Now, the relation of this to the psychological theory of judgment and causality is evident. If judgment be a
coupling of ideas, then the ideas that a *defining*
judgment couples are those of a name and an
interpretation of it. If, on the other hand, we
regard judgment as a statement of the objective
reality of a relation, then definition also will be a
statement about reality: it will be a statement
of the determining qualities of a thing. While
definition is always a hypothetical judgment, it
may still, on this view, be a hypothetical judgment about reality; and it can only be regarded
as essentially verbal on the ground that judgment
itself has no objective reference.

Nominalism is, in fact, a normal element in a
sensationalist theory of knowledge; and there is

[1] *Logic*, p. 94.

nothing mysterious about the persistent connection between these tendencies of thought. In so
far as we limit knowledge to sensations, we are
compelled to regard judgments as concerned
merely with ideas; for if knowledge be not essentially a synthesis, then its real objects are bare
and unrelated particulars, and the connections
between them are nominal and unreal. Mill's
contention that definition is merely verbal, results
naturally from his tendency to regard judgment
as a coupling of mental states, and to make
isolated and unreferred sensations the object of
knowledge.

His theory of inference bears traces of the same
origin. He regards syllogism as a mere mode of
statement, and not a form of proof; and this
view of it depends on his conception of the
elements from which knowledge is built up. If
these elements are isolated states of consciousness, and therefore mere particulars, then it is
no doubt true that the major premise of a syllogism, being simply a general statement about all
such particulars, can never prove anything. But
if the objects of our knowledge are regarded as
realities capable of analysis, then a general state-

ment, which takes to do with their common element and abstracts from their differences, may
have a value, as a means of proof, greater than
that of all the unanalysed instances, on which it is
nevertheless analytically founded. Mill's denial
of the validity of syllogistic proof really suggests
that the truth of argument depends upon its
content, and that its general form can prove
nothing; but he fails to give effect to this suggestion because he conceives the content of judgment in such a way that it cannot be a ground
of proof. To affirm that "the syllogism is not a
correct analysis"[1] of the process of reasoning,
because that process is always "an inference from
particulars to particulars," is to assume that the
particulars in question contain no universal element; and Mill does assume this, in so far as he
identifies the object of knowledge with isolated
sensations.

That the psychological view of knowledge
serves in part to determine Mill's theory of
inference, is also shown, if further proof be
needed, by his identification of the logical theory
of reasoning with the psychological explanation

[1] Logic, p. 128.

by association of ideas,[1] and by his interpretation of logical inference as a "habit of expecting
that what has been found true once or several
times, and never yet found false, will be found
true again."[2]   Whatever validity such explanations may possess as statements of the psychology of reasoning, to make them the basis of
logical theories is to regard logic as the science
of the subjective process; and the propriety of
this depends on that theory of explanation which
makes it consist in reduction to "ideas."

It appears, then, that that conception of the
knowing subject which isolates it from all other
reality plays no small part in Mill's Logic, affecting, as it does, his idea of definition and inference,
as well as of the character and problem of logical
science itself.

[1] Logic, p. 428.   [2] Ibid., p. 204.

CHAPTER III

WHILE Mill's logic contains elements that are due to the individualistic, or psychological, point of view from which he sometimes regards thought, these elements do not constitute his whole theory of knowledge. His individualism has, indeed, a real effect on his logical doctrine: his theories of definition and inference are influenced by his limitation of knowledge to states of consciousness. But he also entertains an entirely different, and even opposite, conception of knowledge; and this conception is the basis of his most distinctive and valuable work as a logician.

The ground of this less abstract idea of experience is to be found in Mill's consciousness of the direct relation of thought to the rest of reality—a consciousness which is expressed primarily in

a denial of the unqualified or absolute isolation of
mental life. He affirms his conviction that "the
conceptions, which we employ for the colligation
and methodisation of facts, do not develop themselves from within, but are impressed upon the
mind from without; they are never obtained
otherwise than by way of comparison and abstraction, and, in the most important and the
most numerous cases, are evolved by abstraction
from the very phenomena which it is their office
to colligate."[1] He insists that "the conception
is not furnished *by* the mind until it has been
furnished *to* the mind."[2] He regards the feeling
of certainty and the necessity that sometimes
belongs to our judgments as due to the impress
of reality upon our mental life, and to the degree
in which our mental habits are fashioned by the
course of things.[3] He makes experience so
direct a rendering of reality that it is "its own
test";[4] and he studies the principles that should
regulate its growth, by inspection of its actual
course of development.[5]

[1] Logic, p. 427.　　　　　[2] Ibid., p. 428.
[3] Examination of Hamilton, p. 328.
[4] Logic, p. 209.　　　　　[5] Ibid., p. 515.

One of the most important instances of this way of thinking is the account which Mill gives of those axioms that lie at the root of knowledge.

He holds that "unless we knew something immediately, we could not know anything mediately, and consequently could not know anything at all;"[1] and he investigates axioms with a distinct consciousness that the account given of them determines the mode in which experience itself is to be conceived. Knowledge depends upon recognition of these axioms, the truth of which is self-evident and immediately known. If they are known *a priori*, then experience contains actual elements which are not empirical in their origin. Mill declares against this view. Axioms, he says, "are experimental truths; generalisations from observation;"[2] and this is not only true of the axioms on which mathematical science depends; those postulates which lie at the root of all knowledge of nature are no less empirical in their origin. "The law of Causation, the recognition of which is the main pillar of inductive science, is but the familiar truth, that invariability of succession is found by ob-

[1] Examination of Hamilton, p. 157.   [2] Logic, p. 151.

servation to obtain between every fact in nature
and some other fact which has preceded it."[1]   It
is, in fact, "such a notion as can be gained from
experience."[1]

In the same way, an experiential origin is
claimed for the idea of the Uniformity of Nature.
"It would . . . be a great error to offer this
large generalisation as any explanation of the
inductive process.   On the contrary, I hold it
to be itself an instance of induction, and induction by no means of the most obvious kind."[2]
The conception of experience which this view of
axioms yields is very obvious.   From its simplest
beginnings to its largest and most general results,
experience is the product in man of the order
of things in which he lives.   That order is re-
produced in him; his thought depends upon
and follows it.

Now, while this way of thinking is in the
highest degree significant, as a correction of that
individualistic limitation of thought to itself
which is an element in Mill's theory of knowledge, it must, at the same time, be recognised
that such a statement of the relation of thought

to reality is equivocal and even misleading. It may mean nothing better than the deterministic empiricism that makes thought the mere creature of a reality conceived as foreign to it; it may subject intelligence to things, in such a way as to render a science of Logic fatuous and impossible; and Mill does actually tend to conceive knowledge in this way. In his zeal for experience, and for the direct relation of thought to things, he barely escapes, if indeed he does escape, the reduction of knowledge to a merely passive process.

On the other hand, it is happily not needful to put such a construction on Mill's theory of experience. That theory may be combined with an idea of Nature which does full justice to the distinctive character of knowledge. If we take such a view of the activity of the thinking subject as is sometimes explicitly stated,[1] and very generally implied, by Mill himself, the assertion of the dependence of every element in knowledge upon experience is no more than every sane philosophy admits. Any kind of "Idealism" which

[1] Examination of Hamilton, pp. 258 ff.; Dissertations and Discussions, vol. iii. pp. 120 ff.

lives by clinging to those conceptions for which no experiential basis can yet be found, must have an increasingly precarious existence; and even Mill's strongest assertions of the dependence upon experienced fact of all conceptions and axioms leave undisputed the dependence of experience itself upon activity. Such assertions form, indeed, no small contribution to the development of a theory of knowledge. They make thought in the fullest sense objective; so that things may be said to think in us, and knowledge is the coming to consciousness of reality itself.

This interpretation of Mill's experientialism is not one which requires to be discovered or invented in his defence. It is only a statement of the significance which his theory of knowledge actually has for him. Objectivity is characteristic of Mill's whole treatment of logic. He regards it as "common ground on which the partisans of Hartley and of Reid, of Locke and of Kant, may meet and join hands";[1] and he does so because he thinks of it as a science of Evidence, the object of which is to investigate

[1] Logic, p. 8.

the nature of proof, and which is therefore not
directly concerned in metaphysical or psychological differences. This view of logic as an objective science of evidence distinguishes Mill sharply
from Comte. Comte made logic a science of discovery, the object of which was to find how the
craving for clear and coherent conceptions could
be satisfied : he did not investigate the methods
of verification and proof. Mill's logic, on the
other hand, is, above all, a study of the conditions of proof—of the mode in which the real
causes of phenomena can be found and verified.[1]
He regards truth as an objective standard, by
which every one means the same thing—" agreement of a belief with the fact which it purports
to represent "[2]—and he makes this the basis of
logic. " If the operation of forming a judgment
or a proposition includes anything at all, it includes judging that the judgment or the proposition is true. The recognition of it as true is not
only an essential part but the essential element
of it as a judgment ; leave that out, and there

[1] Cf. Höffding, ' Einleitung in die Englische Philosophie
unserer Zeit' (German trans.), p. 32.

[2] Dissertations and Discussions, vol. iii. p. 357.

remains a mere play of thought in which no
judgment is passed." [1]   Logic is thus " the science
of the conditions on which right concepts, judgments, and reasonings depend." [2]   It is not merely
the science of formal accuracy or consistency in
thinking ; for " it is only as a means to material
truth that the formal, or, to speak more clearly,
the conditional, validity of an operation of
thought is of any value." [3]   Logic " is the art
of thinking, of all thinking, and of nothing but
thinking." [4]

This assertion of the objective and normative
character which belongs to logic as a science, and
of the idea of truth as the determining idea of
all logical investigation, gives the science a position entirely different from that of a mere branch
of psychology.   Mill adopts a new conception of
logic, at the outset of his discussion of the
" Import of Propositions," when he says that it
" has no concern with the nature of the act of
judging or believing ; the consideration of that
act, as a phenomenon of the mind, belongs to
another science." [5]

[1] Examination of Hamilton, p. 421.   [2] Ibid., p. 464.
[3] Ibid., p. 476.   [4] Ibid., p. 462.   [5] Logic, p. 55.

Such a conception of logic is hardly consistent with the Humian phenomenalism of Mill's theory of knowledge ; it depends rather upon the assumption that the object of knowledge is a real world distinct from the subjective mental processes of the individual. This is an assumption which Mill may have learned from Reid, and of which he seems to be so unconscious that he does not see any necessity for vindicating it. He suggests, indeed, that "if the only real object of thought, even when we are nominally speaking of Noumena, are Phenomena, our thoughts are true when they are made to correspond with Phenomena." [1] The world of Phenomena seems to form, in this suggestion, a sort of *tertium quid* between thoughts and things. In any case " Phenomena " are sharply enough distinguished from " thoughts ": the object of knowledge is regarded as other than states of consciousness. Mill does not escape the antithesis of thought and its object any more than Locke or Kant; [2] and, when he comes to discuss the problems of logic in detail, he finds

[1] Examination of Hamilton, p. 495.

[2] Cf. Professor Andrew Seth's article " Epistemology in Locke and Kant," Philosophical Review, vol. ii. p. 167.

the objective reference of thought to be the aspect of it which requires most emphasis and considera-tion.   The serious and constructive part of his logic is rooted in his demand for proof and veri-fication ; and it thus depends on the conscious-ness of a real world of knowable objects.

This conception of knowledge is not only im-plicitly conveyed in Mill's logical discussions: it is also expressly stated and argued for.   He abandons and criticises the representation of knowledge as an aggregate of unreferred ideas, and recognises that it depends on a consciousness, on the one hand, of the real world, and, on the other hand, of the self.   These, he says, in speaking of developed knowledge, " represent two things with both of which the sensation of the moment, be it what it may, stands in relation, and I cannot be conscious of the sensation with-out being conscious of it as related to these two things." [1]

Mill seems, indeed, to forget much of his own preceding discussion of the " things denoted by Names," [2] when he says of the theory of know-ledge, by which that discussion is really domin-

[1] Examination of Hamilton, p. 266.   [2] Logic, bk. i. c. iii.

ated, " the notion that what is of primary importance to the logician, in a proposition, is the relation between the two *ideas* corresponding to the
subject and predicate (instead of the relation between the two *phenomena* which they respectively
express), seems to me one of the most fatal errors
ever introduced into the philosophy of logic." [1]
But this sweeping statement does not stand alone.
It forms part of a discussion of the " Import of
Propositions," in which the implication in all
judgment of an objective reference is asserted
again and again, unhesitatingly and deliberately.
Propositions " are not assertions respecting our
ideas of things, but assertions respecting the
things themselves." [2] An integral part, too, of
Mill's criticism of Hamilton's Logic is expressed
in his desire to hear " less about Concepts and
more about Things, less about Forms of Thought
and more about grounds of Knowledge." [3] He
insists, against the subjective or formal conception of logic, that " the judgment is not a recognition of a relation between concepts, but of a succession, a coexistence, or a similitude, between

[1] Logic, p. 57.   [2] Ibid., pp. 56 ff.
[3] Examination of Hamilton, p. 622.

facts,"[1] and that. "judgment is concerning the
fact, not the concept";[2] and he adduces Hamilton's own contention that new truths are discovered by reasoning, to disprove his assertion
"that reasoning is the comparison of two notions
through the medium of a third.[3]

It cannot be doubted that this, which has now
been stated, is Mill's real view of knowledge. It
is the conception that underlies his interest in
Induction, and in the actual scientific procedure,
upon which his theory of Induction is based ; and
it is the conception to which his assertion of the
empirical character of all knowledge leads naturally and almost inevitably. Mill's acceptance of
this objective theory of logic is so frank and so
thorough that he says, of logical laws, that "since
they are laws of all phenomena, and since
Existence has to us no meaning but one which
has relation to Phenomena, we are quite safe in
looking upon them as laws of Existence."[4] Such
an utterance as this is conceived, indeed, in the
spirit of the same resolute empiricism which
prompts Mill's limitation of knowledge to the

[1] Examination of Hamilton, p. 426.　　[2] Ibid., p. 421.
[3] Ibid., p. 415.　　　　　　　　　　　　[4] Ibid., p. 492.

subjective process, and makes him regard logic
as a branch of psychology—*sed quantum mutatus
ab illo.*

Within the limits of the "experience philosophy," Mill's limitation of knowledge to mental
states has given place to a conception of it which
makes it an apprehension of the fulness of concrete reality. His consciousness of the objectivity
of knowledge is grown so definite that it leads him
to regard logic as a science not of abstract or subjective thought but of existence. Logic becomes,
on such a view of it, the science of certain ultimate
relations of things. The existence of these relations may indeed be dependent on the relativity
of all being to thought; but they belong none the
less but all the more on that account to the constitution of reality, and are not merely subjective
modifications of conscious life. At such a point
as this Mill is much more nearly idealistic than
he can be said to be in that subjectivist phenomenalism which is sometimes, strangely enough,
regarded as an idealistic element in his thinking.[1]

It connects itself with this assertion of the
objective validity of logical laws, and still more

[1] Cf. Mr Courtney's Metaphysics of J. S. Mill. p. 35.

directly with the idea of logic as a science of
truth, that Mill makes judgment the unit of
logical theory.[1]   As he says himself, "The answer
to every question, which it is possible to frame,
must be contained in a Proposition, or Assertion.
Whatever can be an object of belief, or even of
disbelief, must, when put into words, assume the
form of a proposition.   All truth and all error
lie in propositions.   What, by a convenient misapplication of an abstract term, we call a Truth,
is simply a True Proposition; and errors are
false propositions."[2]   Judgment is, in fact, the
simplest possible form of objective thought: apart
from it, there is no belief and no knowledge.
Reference to reality exists only in judgment:
if it appears to belong to concepts, it belongs
to them simply in virtue of the judgments by
which they have been constructed.[3]   But since
objective reference and the possibility of truth
are thus present for the first time in judgment, it is with judgment that we have to
do in logic.   "Logic does not undertake to
analyse mental facts into their ultimate ele-

[1] Cf. Mr Bradley's Principles of Logic, book i. c. i.
[2] Logic, p. 12.   [3] Examination of Hamilton, pp. 419, 420.

ments."[1] It does not investigate the mode in which knowledge originates historically. It is the science of the objective reference or the validity of knowledge; and so it has to consider judgments and not concepts. Its starting-point is in the judgment, since it has to do, not with the existence, but solely with the use of concepts.[2] Concepts have no meaning for it, as they have none for knowledge, otherwise than in the objective synthesis of judgment. In his discussion of judgment, Mill is so free from the influence of epistemological individualism that he denies the very existence of concepts. He regards the concept as a mere abstraction, made for the purpose of judgment. It has "merely a fictitious or constructive existence,"[3] and is differentiated from the rest of the mental complex, to which it actually belongs, only by "a special share of attention guaranteed to it by special association with a name."[3] This fictitious or constructive character of the concept makes it an impossible basis or starting-point for logic.[3]

[1] Logic, p. 66.
[2] Cf. Mr Bradley's Principles of Logic, book i. c. i.
[3] Examination of Hamilton, p. 402.

Mill's suggestion, that it would be better to
say that we think by means of general names
than by means of concepts,[1] is a remarkable
instance of his tendency to nominalism. It
affords, however, a less useful and less consistent correction of the formal conception of
logic than his own statement and assumption
that logic has to do only with judgment, and
that neither ideas nor things have any place in
knowledge otherwise than in the synthesis of
judgment. Mill is only carrying this view a
stage further when he suggests, in explanation
of the importance of hypothetical · propositions,
"that what they predicate of a proposition,
namely, its being an inference from something
else, is precisely that one of its attributes with
which most of all a logician is concerned."[2] Logic
is, in fact, primarily a science of inference or
proof; and the inferential relations of judgments
are those with which it takes to do. What is
relevant for the logician is the way in which a
proposition "may be made available for advancing
from it to other propositions."[3] On the other hand,

---

[1] Examination of Hamilton, p. 403.

[2] Logic, p. 54.   [3] Ibid., p. 76.

judgments are in themselves real; they constitute knowledge; and they are capable of truth and falsehood. It is thus at once possible and necessary for logic to find its starting-point in them.

This conception of logic as the science of judgment and reasoning is so central to Mill's theory, that his view of the meaning of general names is partly determined by the necessities of judgment. " Propositions and Reasonings," he says, " may be written in extension but they are always understood in Comprehension;"[1] "all judgments, expressed by means of general terms, are judgments in comprehension."[2]   In the proposition, *e.g.*, " The summit of Chimborazo is white," " the meaning of the proposition . . . is that the individual thing denoted by the subject has the attributes connoted by the predicate."[3]   This is the view which is required in order to make reasoning intelligible;[4] and the fact that judgment and reasoning are only explicable on the understanding that the meaning of general names is fixed by their connotation, has probably much to do with Mill's acceptance of that theory.

---

[1] Examination of Hamilton, p. 437.   [2] Ibid., p. 501.
[3] Logic, p. 62.   [4] Ibid., p. 75.

This view of the meaning of general names—
that it "resides in the connotation "[1]—is one
which Mill consistently and unhesitatingly maintains, in opposition to the theory that the extension or denotation of names is their meaning.
" In predicating the name," he says, " we predicate only the attributes ; and the fact of belonging to a class does not, in many cases, come into
view at all."[2]

Now this assertion that " attributes " are the
subject-matter of judgment and reasoning, raises
an important issue for Mill's theory of knowledge, an issue which is significant in connection
with his refusal to regard the distinction between sensations and properties of things as
anything more than a " convenience of discourse."[3]

Abstinence from a distinction between sensations and qualities of things is, of course, apt to
be a one-sided bargain, since it is very generally equivalent to a reduction of the objective
world to states of consciousness.   But Mill's
assertion of the objective reference of knowledge
leads us to expect a recognition of attributes or

[1] Logic, p. 59.   [2] Ibid., p. 76.   [3] Cf. chap. ii.

qualities of things as other than mere mental
states; and such an expectation does not remain
wholly unfulfilled. Mill's account of judgment,
as an ascription of attributes to reality, contains
a view of attributes which is not really consistent
with their identification with states of individual
consciousness. He does not, indeed, expressly
qualify his denial of the distinction in question.
But, on the one hand, he distinguishes sharply
between objects, or phenomena, and the ideas of
them; while, on the other hand, he connects the
idea of phenomena, characterised by attributes,
with that of an order of nature. It remains possible, of course, still to maintain that these
phenomena, and nature itself, cannot be distinguished from feelings or subjective states. But
such a refusal to recognise an objective order of
things would render Mill's brave words about
the objective reference of judgment wholly idle
and unmeaning. Why should we take pains to
insist that judgment is about things, and not
about ideas, if, all the while, there is no real
ground for distinguishing things from ideas at
all ?

That Mill recognised the attributes of things,

as belonging to the real world, is borne out by
his actual use of them: the idea that they are
not mere mental states, but determinations of
objective reality, evidences itself in his theory
of classification.   He recognises the legitimacy
of various subjective modes of classification,
which are "all good, for the purposes of their
own particular departments of knowledge or
practice."[1]   But he insists, none the less, on
the reality of "natural groups," whose individual
members are bound together by the common pos-
session of certain characters.   Now such "natural
groups" "are constituted in contemplation of, and
by reason of, characters."[2]   Their resemblance—
their agreement in certain attributes or characters
—forms the ground of the relation between the
individuals which constitute the group.   "The
kind, to us, *is* the set of properties by which it
is identified."[3]

Attributes or qualities of things thus form the
basis of objective classification—of the classification of things according to their own nature. Such
classification is not, indeed, determined by "resemblance to a type," but only by the presence of

[1] Logic, p. 468.   [2] Ibid., p. 472.   [3] Ibid., p. 379.

characters which serve to differentiate things which possess them from things which do not. Still the idea of classification according to Natural Kinds implies a system of objective natural relations. It involves the existence of classes which are " distinguished from all other classes by an indeterminate multitude of properties not derivable from one another,"[1] and between which, consequently, "there is an impassable barrier."[2] The problem of fixing the conception of a kind is " to find a few definite characters, which point to the multitude of indefinite ones."[2] Kinds are thus constituted by a standard, reference to which determines whether objects belong to them or not;[3] and Mill recognises that such kinds— classes of phenomena bound together by relation to an intellectual standard — are objectively present in nature.

The theory of kinds, we learn from Mill, was added to the Logic " suggested by otherwise inextricable difficulties";[4] and that it originates, in this way, in the necessities of his treatment of

[1] Logic, p. 81. [2] Ibid., p. 471.
[3] Cf. Mr Bosanquet's Logic, vol. i. pp. 125 ff.
[4] Autobiography, p. 181.

induction, is a significant fact. In itself, however, the theory is, in the highest degree, important. Such a conception as it implies, of the intelligibility of nature—of the degree in which reality expresses and embodies principles that are not alien to our reason—is a suggestive element in Mill's Logic. It conveys the idea of nature as a rational system; and this constitutes the logical significance of Mill's contention that natural or objective classifications, no less than those which are devised in various subjective interests, are based upon characters of things. Since these characters are simply attributes or qualities, and since they are, at the same time, the ground of an objective or natural classification of things, attributes come to have in this connection the objective significance which belongs to them in Mill's theory of judgment, but which is not made clear in his discussion of attributes themselves.

CHAPTER IV

CAUSALITY

MILL's assertion of the existence of Natural
Kinds — his belief in an objective method of
classification—implies a conception of nature, as
an objective system, which goes far to correct
his phenomenalist theory of knowledge; and this
conception is specially inconsistent with the
psychological doctrine of causality which he
sometimes affirms. Mill inherited from Hume
that idea of the causal relation which makes it
simply a subjective habit of expectation, induced
by frequent repetition of a sequence of mental
states; and he does not openly abandon this way
of regarding causality. But the conception of
nature, as a system of objective things, whose
attributes determine one another, has no vital
connection with this purely psychological account

of the relation of cause and effect; and it need
not surprise us if we find, in Mill's explicit doctrine of causality, elements which are not consistent with that mode of conceiving the relation
which he derived from Hume.

Such elements are not far to seek. Even
when Mill makes consciousness of change the
motive of the search for causes,[1] he does so in a
spirit akin to that rather of Lotze than of Hume.
What seems to him to need explanation is the
"changeable element," which is recognised to be
"in phenomena";[2] and the idea of the causal
relation, as one which belongs objectively to
things as we know them, is still more definitely
suggested in the statement that "the cause . . .
is the sum-total of the conditions, positive and
negative, taken together."[3] Such an account of
causation presents the idea of known reality as a
single developing process, whose later stages
grow out of its earlier, and in which various
elements conspire to produce each new manifestation of its nature. But this is a way of thinking for which the relations that characterise

[1] Examination of Hamilton, pp. 366, 367.
[2] Ibid., p. 367.   [3] Logic, p. 217.

reality in our knowledge are, virtually at all events, even if not explicitly, objects of constructive thought, rather than mere states of subjective feeling. If we make nature a system of things, then causality becomes merely the most abstract way of conceiving their systematic or rational connection.

The same tendency shows itself in Mill's assertion that, in the investigation of causes, "the Plurality of Causes is the only reason why mere number is of any importance." [1] The causal relation is not constituted by the mere frequency of any particular sequence: it is in the nature and not the constancy of the sequence that it really consists; and the demonstrative use of a number of instances depends merely on the fact that they furnish a rough substitute for analysis of the phenomena.

These elements in Mill's theory of causality convey the idea that the causal relation is not a mere habit of expectation, but an objective determination of things. But this idea of causality is most definitely expressed by Mill in his statement that the causal relation is distinguished from

[1] *Logic*, p. 287.

the relation of mere sequence by being unconditional. "Invariable sequence, therefore, is not synonymous with causation, unless the sequence, besides being invariable, is unconditional."[1] It is to express this unconditional relation that the words "cause" and "effect" are required; and Mill criticises Comte's refusal to use these words mainly on the ground that this refusal indicates the absence of an idea of unconditional relation.[2]

The significance of such an interpretation of causality can hardly be overstated. It means, for Mill himself, that the causal relation is a necessary one;[3] and this conception of the relation is a real departure from Mill's own assertion of the absence of "necessity" from the action of causes.[4] That assertion, however, is the inevitable issue of the reduction of the causal relation to a habit of expectation, or a mere sequence of ideas; for if the causal relation is unconditional, it is not any kind of subjective sequence. Mill's statement that causality is a necessary relation is thus decisive for his account of it.

---

[1] Logic, p. 222.
[2] Auguste Comte and Positivism, pp. 57-59.
[3] Logic, p. 222.   [4] Ibid., p. 548.

This conception of causality as an unconditional relation of things is Mill's most positive idea on the subject; although he does not clear it of certain confusions, which are bound up with the theory that serial order is the essence of the causal relation—that sequence is its primary characteristic. His tendency, for example, to separate "uniformities of coexistence" from the principle of causality,[1] may be traced to the presupposition that the causal relation is essentially serial—that it is a relation involving temporal sequence in its terms, and that an interval of time elapses, as it were, between the cause and the effect. Now, such a view is really a return to the psychological conception of causality; and it must, in the long-run, bring about a reduction of causality to mere change or sequence, and a failure to conceive it as the principle involved alike in change and in permanence. But that "unconditional" relation, in which Mill finds the essence of causality, involves the unity of cause and effect. If, as he says, the cause "is the sum-total of the conditions positive and negative taken together," [2] then the cause

[1] *Logic*, pp. 381 ff.   [2] *Ibid.*, p. 217.

cannot be present without the effect; for "the
sum-total of the conditions" constitutes the very
presence of the effect itself. Mill tries to make
the idea of causality, conceived as mere sequence,
do duty for that of the whole system of categories,
which all relation may be said to imply, but to
which even the fullest and most concrete interpretation of causality is not adequate. The
abandonment, however, of the view that the
causal relation is essentially serial is really implied in regarding it as unconditional. Now
the idea of the causal relation as unconditional
—as a unity—is that which Mill actually makes
use of; and it is his use of the idea as the
ground of induction that must decide his interpretation of it, since his interest in it is purely
logical, and he considers it simply as a principle of knowledge or explanation relative to
experience.

Causality is, for Mill, the ground of all induction. He suggests that "M. Comte's determined abstinence from the word and the idea of
Cause had much to do with his inability to conceive an Inductive Logic, by diverting his attention from the only basis upon which it could be

founded;"[1] and his own discussion of the Inductive Methods rests consistently upon the
view, which he announces, that "the validity
of all the Inductive Methods depends on the
assumption that every event, or the beginning
of every phenomenon, must have some cause,
some antecedent, on the existence of which it
is invariably and unconditionally consequent."[2]
It is to be observed that, even in this statement, Mill continues to speak of causality as
if it were a principle regulating change and
change only. In so far as he does so, he
deprives the causal relation of that unconditional character which makes it the basis of
induction. It is no doubt true that there are
many uniformities of coexistence which we are
unable to trace to causal conditions; and our
knowledge of such uniformities is, as Mill suggests, merely empirical;[3] for an inductive knowledge of things only exists in so far as we
trace them to their conditions. But the suggestion of uniformities of coexistence for which
no real conditions exist implies a co - ordinate

[1] Auguste Comte and Positivism, p. 59.
[2] Logic, p. 369.   [3] Cf. Logic, book iii. chap. xxii.

possibility of unconditioned events; and the attempt to limit the law of causality, or unconditional relation, to successions of events must inevitably issue in its complete abrogation. Causality, in the sense in which it is the ground of inductive reasoning, and of guaranteed knowledge, is simply the most abstract unconditional relation. The cause is the ground or explanation of the effect;[1] and it is in this sense that the law of causation is the *prius* of Inductive reasoning. Induction goes on the supposition that everything _is completely caused, or is ideally capable of being presented as an effect or product of conditions.

Stated in this way, the law of causation becomes equivalent to the principle of the Uniformity, or, more correctly, the Unity, of Nature, in the sense in which that principle is "the fundamental principle, or general axiom, of Induction,"[2] and must "be regarded as our warrant for all the others." It is to be observed that this principle, taken in the sense in which it is the *prius* of Induction, is not really the

---

[1] Cf. Mr Bosanquet's Logic, vol. i. pp. 264 ff.

[2] Logic, p. 201.

result of Induction at all. When Mill suggests
in one sentence that the Uniformity of Nature
is a result arrived at by complex and developed
Induction, and in the next that every Induction really assumes this principle, he takes the
principle in different senses. Our developed
idea of Nature, as a uniform whole, is certainly
the result of reflection upon experience. But
experience itself, in the only sense in which it
is a source of knowledge, consists in a consciousness of objective relations, which implies the
real unity of known reality.

Now, it may be proper to call this consciousness,
of things as real, the potentiality of the complete
knowledge of nature as an orderly system with
uniform laws; and in the same way, the conception of the Uniformity of Nature is the ideal
of all the generalisations by which knowledge
progresses towards it. But to identify the mere
consciousness of an objective world with the
fully developed notion of the Uniformity of
Nature is to make the whole labour and progress of knowledge unmeaning and useless; and
this is what Mill means by his denial of the
a priori character of the principle that the

course of nature is uniform.[1] It is not really inconsistent with this denial to make the consciousness of nature as an objective unity the implicit ground of knowledge. The appearance of contradiction between the statements is due to Mill's failure to distinguish between the explicit conception in which our knowledge of nature is supposed to be completely realised, and the point of view which is implied in every stage of that knowledge—between the results and the constitution of experience.

What is involved in the possibility of knowledge is the consciousness of an object: of relations whose reality does not depend upon our recognition of them; of the unity or self-consistency of the world of fact; and this is what is meant by making unconditional relation, or the uniformity of nature, the ground of induction. There is, in fact, only one intuition — if we choose to call it so—the intuition of the whole; and no truth is necessary, except the whole truth. The ground of all knowledge is necessity, objectivity of relations, the presence in things themselves of those connecting bonds

[1] Cf. chap. iii.

which our knowledge seeks in them. This
is the one necessity of thought. Without it,
knowledge cannot be; but experience itself,
determined by this point of view, is the source
of all those complex presentations which constitute our knowledge. That the experience
which furnishes knowledge is determined by
consciousness of the objective world does not
mean that knowledge contains elements not
produced by experience.

The idea of causality as an unconditional
relation, which belongs to Mill's assertion of the
objective reference of knowledge, determines his
conception of Inductive Reasoning. But not
only does induction rest, in this way—as all
knowledge may be said to rest—upon the law
of causation: it is also the special development
of knowledge which investigates causes. "To
determine the effect of every cause, and the
causes of all effects, is the main business of
Induction;"[1] "the problem of Inductive Logic
may be summed up in two questions: how to
ascertain the laws of nature; and how, after
having ascertained them, to follow them into

[1] *Logic*, p. 247.

their results."[1]   Induction is thus primarily a
regress from complex things to their conditions: to the simpler elements which constitute
them; to the factors of which they are products. The kind of explanation that induction
gives of any phenomenon consists in pointing
out "some more general phenomenon, of which
it is a partial exemplification; or some laws of
causation which produce it by their joint or
successive action, and from which, therefore, its
conditions may be determined deductively."[2]
The problem of induction is, in fact, that of
analysis: it breaks up the complexity of individual concrete facts into simpler and ultimately into the simplest and most general facts.
This is the resolution of experience into its low-
est terms—into its most general truths. It is
the interpretation of every whole in terms of its
parts—of every complex fact or event in terms
of facts or events which are less complex.[3]

Now, such a view of induction implies that the
conception of Causality on which it rests is not
that of temporal sequence but that of unconditional relation; it assumes that things are capable

---

[1] Logic, p. 208.   [2] Ibid., p. 311.   [3] Ibid., p. 307.

of analysis into those conditions, the discovery of which constitutes its problem.

While Mill's logic is vitiated by his failure to recognise the reality of any relation more complex or more concrete than that of cause and effect, it should still be observed that the idea of relation implied in his theory of Induction might be made to authenticate a doctrine of Definition and Deduction widely different from his.

The theory of Definition which is associated with Mill's name is based upon his psychological view of the causal relation. But by this revised conception of causality Definition is made a possible result of induction. The idea that things are capable of expression in terms of their conditions makes real definition of them possible instead of mere description, or statement of the meaning of their names. Such true definition would be an account of the determining conditions of the thing—of the real elements to which its character must be referred. Definition, in this sense, is definition in terms of causes; it expresses discovery, and is not simply a statement of conventions; it may be a hypothetical judg-

ment, assuming the reality of the thing which
is defined; but it is a statement about the thing,
and not simply about its name; and such definition of things—impossible so long as they are fixed
in abstract isolation from other things, and so from
real conditions—becomes a possibility, and the
goal of inductive science, when once it is understood that the nature of things can be expressed
in terms of their causes. This statement of the
nature of phenomena is what Mill represents as
the aim of induction; and his refusal to recognise
it as *definition* of things is part of his failure
to give effect to his own correction of the psychological way of regarding knowledge.

Mill's theory of Deductive Reasoning, no less
than of definition, might be revised, in the light
of that conception of causality which determines
his view of induction. To make the nature of
things consist in the conditions of their existence
—to regard an account of their causal relations
as the explanation of what they are—is to recognise an universal element in the knowledge of
objective reality; for such a conception of things
completely does away with that abstract view of
them which makes them merely particular and

separate and regards their relations as external
to their nature; and the recognition that relations are objectively characters of things gives to
the universal element, that is present in all predication, a legitimacy which it does not otherwise possess. Some such view of the causal relation as that which is suggested by Mill's assertion of its "unconditional" character is, in
fact, the only ground upon which the assertion
and proof of general truths can be justified. The
truth of general statements implies the presence
of a necessary or universal element in things,
the objectivity of relations, the validity of causal
explanation.

It cannot be said that Mill makes clear the
significance, for the theory of reasoning, of his own
doctrine that causality is an unconditional relation. But his assertion that inference is primarily "from particulars to particulars" accommodates itself to a less abstract conception of
"particulars" than that which the statement
naturally implies, and which belongs to Mill's
sensationalist account of knowledge.

He recognises that knowledge involves elements which are general — that all real judg-

ment asserts with some degree of generality. For example, "it is only by means of general names that we can convey any information, predicate any attribute, even of an individual, much more of a class."[1] Judgment is essentially generalisation. It refers to the objective world some general character. No "attribute," as judgment ascribes it, can ever be regarded as merely particular; and the ideal character of judgment is betrayed by the impossibility of eradicating generality from the relations which it affirms.. Mill goes still further in the same direction when he asserts that every inference to a particular implies a general truth. "Whenever the evidence, which we derive from observation of known cases, justifies us in drawing an inference respecting even one unknown case, we should on the same evidence be justified in drawing a similar inference with respect to a whole class of cases. The inference either does not hold at all, or it holds in all cases of a certain description; in all cases which, in certain definable respects, resemble those we have observed."[2]

---

[1] Logic, p. 436.   [2] Ibid., p. 186; cf. p. 129.

All this connects itself with the view of relations, and primarily of causality, on which
Mill's theory of Induction is founded; but the
actual significance of that view is not given
effect to by Mill in his doctrine of Syllogism.
He does indeed admit the practical expediency
of generalising all conclusions so as to test their
legitimacy;[1] and he also defends the utility of
general propositions, on the ground that, " though
in strictness we may reason from past experience to a fresh individual case without the intermediate stage of a general proposition, yet
without general propositions we should seldom
remember what past experience we have had,
and scarcely ever what conclusions that experience will warrant."[2] But such a statement
hardly suggests the practical necessity which
exists for the form of syllogism; and it does
nothing to indicate the real worth which, on
Mill's own showing, syllogistic argument might
be held to possess. Rooted in his doctrine that
the causal relation is unconditional, the idea that
knowledge depends upon universal elements is
explicitly conveyed in his assertion of the general

[1] *Logic*, p. 129.   [2] *Ibid.*, p. 435.

character of all predication. Even when inference appears to be from particular to particular, these particulars are not really so absolute, or self-contained, or separate from one another, as their name suggests. If they were wholly exclusive and disconnected, no inference from one to the other would be possible: if there were no relation actually between them, none could be constructed to connect them from without. But the existence of such relation rids them of their absolute particularity; and inference from one to the other is legitimate, simply because they are not mere abstract particulars, but have a common element: it is this common element that renders the transition possible, and enables us to infer. Inference from one particular to another is thus secondary to, and dependent on, inference from particular fact, to a general law which expresses the ground of proof.

On such a view of inference—and it is a view which Mill does more than merely suggest—the worth of syllogism is much more internal to knowledge than Mill conceives it to be; for if inference is made possible by the presence of universal elements in knowledge — by its im-

plied generality — then the selection of those
elements, by which inference is determined, is
at the root of the whole matter. Now, the
function of syllogism is to make the determining qualities of things the ground of inference.
The major premise is not, as Mill assumes, a
mere collective statement of a definite or indefinite number of cases taken in extension. It
is, as he himself might suggest, a judgment as to
relations of attributes: it is the statement of
a law. The object of syllogism is to infer the
character of a particular fact, from a law which
is recognised as applying to it; syllogistic argument is the determination of a concrete case
by an abstract principle; it is the proof of a
fact by its conditions. Mill's own conception of
causality as an unconditional relation might, if
he had given effect to it, have formed the basis
for some such theory as this: it might have led
him to ascribe to syllogism—as the expression of
inference from laws or causes—a worth and an
importance which he nowhere vindicates for it.

Mill himself recognises the necessity, for inference, of that abstraction which it is the
function of syllogism to effect. "The voluntary

power," he says, " which the mind has of attend-
ing to one part of what is present to it at any
moment, and neglecting another part, enables us
to keep our reasonings and conclusions respecting
the class unaffected by anything in the idea or
mental image which is not really, or at least which
we do not really believe to be, common to the
whole class." [1]

Reasoning is always hypothetical. " An Inference is nothing but a necessary truth ; " [2] or,
as Mill says, " the only sense in which necessity
can be ascribed to the conclusions of any scientific investigation, is that of legitimately following from some assumption, which, by the conditions of the inquiry, is not to be questioned." [3]
The hypothesis on which inference rests is the
limitation of attention to the common element in
the particular facts ; and syllogism is the definite
expression of this hypothesis. In this way, by
expressing and defining the abstract relation,
syllogism secures its relevancy for purposes of
proof ; and it seems reasonable to regard the syllogistic procedure, which performs this function,

[1] *Logic*, p. 425 ; cf. p. 148.
[2] Mr Bradley's *Principles of Logic*, p. 221.   [3] *Logic*, p. 149.

as more than a merely formal or external expression of thought: syllogism is, in fact, as
Aristotle held, the normal and complete expression of reasoning.

Syllogism gives effect to the point of view
which is implied in all reasoning. Reasoning
implies systematic connection of things; for it
affirms their connection, in virtue of common
elements, and primarily in virtue of their causal
relations; but the causal relation, and indeed all
relation, implies system, since it implies a unity
of things which is articulated in their various
concrete and defined connections; and this unity
of things means that they are elements in a
system, or are related to one another according
to a principle. Now, syllogism expresses this
systematic character of reasoning, since it makes
inference depend upon the common relation of
particulars to a principle which determines their
connection. Its function is to represent the relation between things as necessary; and this is a
function which is so far from being accidental
or external to inference, that it constitutes the
very essence of all reasoning.

Mill's Logic is thus very far from being a con-

sistent whole. The constructive treatment of Induction, which is his most signal achievement as
a logician, depends on a view of thought which
does not affect his theory of definition and syllogism as it might do. His doctrine that definition
is purely verbal, or refers only to names, and his
assertion that the syllogistic form of inference
has no demonstrative but only expository value,
depend upon his psychological conception of
causality. But he suggests ideas of judgment
and inference which go far to correct his theory
of definition and deduction, and which imply the
inadequacy of a purely sensationalist account of
relation. He does not, indeed, give effect to these
ideas; and their place in his theory of reasoning
hardly entitles us to say more than that certain
elements in that theory are at variance with the
psychological conception of knowledge which is
its avowed basis. It is not to be denied, however,
that his Logic contains a view of judgment, and
of the causal relation, which cannot be reconciled
with his sensationalism; and this view is at the
root of the most important part of his theory—
his doctrine of Induction.

CHAPTER V

SELF-CONCERN

MILL's limitation of knowledge to subjective mental states evidences itself in his theory of conduct no less than of knowledge. His individualism affects his idea of desire, just as it moulds his conception of the character of definition and inference. We have already seen that his view of experience as simply a complex of sensations is at the root of his logical nominalism. The same view of experience lends itself to his assertion that pleasure is the sole object of desire, and that all action is determined by the idea of pleasure.

Psychological Hedonism is not a new acquisition with Mill: it forms part of his heritage of "experience-philosophy." Apart from its influence in ancient philosophy, it had been made an integral part of the basis of ethics by Hobbes, and, after him, in the 'Système de la Nature,'[1] and in the beginnings of English Utilitarianism. It formed an essential, though disguised element, in Paley's doctrine of obligation;[2] and it was the dominant conception of James Mill's ethics.[3] It received, however, its most definite expression in Bentham's assertion that "Nature has placed mankind under the governance of two sovereign masters, *pain* and *pleasure*. It is for them alone . . . to determine what we shall do. On the one hand the standard of right and wrong, on the other the chain of causes and effects, are fastened to their throne. They govern us in all we do, in all we say, in all we think: every effort we can make to throw off our subjection, will serve but to demonstrate and confirm it. In words a man may pretend to abjure their empire: but in reality he will remain subject to it all the while."[4]

Such a statement as this left nothing to be

[1] Système de la Nature (1781), vol. i. p. 268, quoted by Professor Sorley, Ethics of Naturalism, p. 23.

[2] Paley's Principles of Moral and Political Philosophy, bk. ii. chap. ii.

[3] James Mill's Analysis of the Human Mind, chap. xxii.

[4] Bentham's Principles of Morals and Legislation, chap. i.

desired or achieved in the way of definiteness and thoroughness : Mill found psychological hedonism ready to his hand. Yet it hardly needs to be pointed out how inevitably this doctrine connects itself with the individualism of Mill's theory of knowledge. If nothing can be directly known but subjective states, then nothing else can be desired; for desire is limited, in respect of its objects, by knowledge; and we can desire only what we can think. If our knowledge of things in their relation to our activity is limited to the pleasure and pain effects that they produce in us, plainly we can desire only the production and avoidance of these effects, and our actions must be determined wholly by the idea of them.

While, however, psychological hedonism is thus rooted in a sensationalist account of knowledge, it also exemplifies another aspect of individualism. It depends on an abstraction or separation of the thinking subject not merely from the world of objects, but also from the moral world of other persons. It expresses a complete limitation of the interests of each individual to the closed circle of his own feelings. In so far as other persons enter into the calculations of the agent, they are regarded, according to this theory, merely as circumstances. They themselves—their interests and rights—are in no sense ends. If they are considered, it is because their advantage is a means to that of the agent himself—because he conceives that he will gain a greater balance of pleasure by serving them than he can obtain otherwise. They form part of the environment, and so they must be taken into account; but as ends they are ignored wholly.

This opinion is frankly accepted by Mill. "There is in reality nothing desired," he says, "except happiness. Whatever is desired otherwise than as a means to some end beyond itself, and ultimately to happiness, is desired as itself a part of happiness, and is not desired for itself until it has become so."[1] The object of desire, for Mill, is a state of feeling. It can be nothing else, since no individual can know anything beyond his feelings. It is to be observed that this does not simply mean that action takes the direction most pleasant for the agent,[2] or that pleasure

[1] Utilitarianism, p. 57.

[2] Cf. Mr Stephen's Science of Ethics, p. 50; Professor Sorley's Ethics of Naturalism, pp. 23-25.

actually results from the satisfaction of desire by action.[1] Such interpretations are not, indeed, excluded by the ambiguous statement " that desiring a thing and finding it pleasant, aversion to it and thinking of it as painful, are phenomena entirely inseparable, or rather two parts of the same phenomenon."[2] But Mill's use of this and other statements consists in making them a ground for finding the springs of conduct in desire for feelings of pleasure. It is his whole intention to make out that desire is primarily for pleasant feeling, and that other things, including morality and social wellbeing, come to be desired by being associated with the idea of pleasure.[3] This is the view of which he makes actual use in his hedonistic ethical construction ;[4] and it is the view which naturally follows from his individualistic account of thought.

Mill's treatment of Political Economy contains elements which give effect to this conception of the individual. His ethical ideas in general stand in the closest reciprocal relations with his

---

[1] Cf. Green's Prolegomena to Ethics, pp. 163-177.
[2] Utilitarianism, p. 58.   [3] Cf. ibid., p. 60.
[4] Ibid., p. 58, &c.

economics; and his psychological hedonism, in
particular, connects itself with certain assumptions which are common to him with other
economists. These assumptions find their most
definite expression in the idea of what is known
as the "economic man"—the view of human
nature which forms the starting-point of economic theory. Mill defines this view so clearly
that his statement of it is worth quoting at
some length: "Political Economy does not treat
of the whole of man's nature as modified by the
social state, nor of the whole conduct of man
in society. It is concernéd with him solely as
a being who desires to possess wealth, and who
is capable of judging of the comparative efficacy
of means for obtaining that end. It predicts only
such of the phenomena of the social state as take
place in consequence of the pursuit of wealth.
It makes entire abstraction of every other human
passion or motive, except those which may be
regarded as perpetually antagonising principles to
the desire of wealth, namely, aversion to labour,
and desire of the present enjoyment of costly
indulgences. . . . Political Economy considers
mankind as occupied solely in acquiring and con-

suming wealth; and aims at showing what is the course of action into which mankind, living in a state of society, would be impelled, if that motive, except in the degree in which it is checked by the two perpetual countermotives above adverted to, were absolute ruler of all their actions." Mill regards Political Economy as completely defined by the statement that it is "the science which traces the laws of such of the phenomena of society as arise from the combined operations of mankind for the production of wealth, in so far as these phenomena are not modified by the pursuit of any other object." He points out that Political Economy presupposes "an arbitrary definition of man, as a being who invariably does that by which he may obtain the greatest amount of necessaries, conveniences, and luxuries, with the smallest quantity of labour and physical self-denial with which they can be obtained in the existing state of knowledge."[1]

It must of course be kept in mind that Mill explicitly regards this assumption as an arbitrary one; and we shall have to consider presently

[1] Unsettled Questions of Political Economy, pp. 137-144.

the extent and significance of his corrections of
it. But he asserts that it is essential to the
very existence of Political Economy as a science,
and that it is a legitimate and useful abstraction; and his economic work is also powerfully
affected by a view of wealth which is closely
related to this abstract hypothesis—the "notion
sufficiently correct for common purposes," which
identifies wealth with value in exchange.[1] It
cannot be doubted, in view of his actual corrections of the economic abstraction, that his acceptance of it as a working hypothesis is partly determined by its congruence with the doctrine of
psychological hedonism; and it is also probable
that the influence, through his economic studies,
of the abstract theory of Ricardo may have
helped to strengthen the hold which psychological hedonism had upon his mind. While the
economic abstraction may be thought legitimate,
apart from any special theory of desire, it undoubtedly gains considerable *prestige* from a
hedonistic psychology; and the habit of using
the individualistic hypothesis, on which Political
Economy has been made to depend, constitutes

[1] Political Economy, pp. 1-4.

a real predisposition to adopt an individualistic view of conduct; for such a view of conduct goes far to clear away the difficulties which are apt to arise from the abstract character of the economic hypothesis.

It thus appears that three elements at least, in Mill's philosophical heritage, conspired to bias him in the direction of individualism. He had inherited, from his predecessors in psychological and metaphysical speculation, a theory of knowledge which limited it to the subjective states of the individual consciousness, from which an external or objective world could only be doubtfully and indirectly inferred. He was thus committed, by his philosophical education and antecedents, to a conception of man as isolated from the real world and incapable of knowing anything beyond the limits of his own mind. He had also learned, from Bentham, to regard subjective states of mind—pleasant feelings—as the only possible objects of desire; and the individualistic sensationalism of his philosophical upbringing made it impossible for him at first to criticise this theory. The "Principles of Morals and Legislation" came to him, as it

were, as "a friend with whom his education had
made him long familiar"; and he was thus led to
conceive man as bound over to the moral isolation of self-concern, as well as to separation from
the world of objective knowledge. With these
two elements we must also include the influence
of the Ricardian economics, which formed part
of his philosophical creed, and gave him a sphere
for applying, as well as grounds for supporting,
his individualistic conception of human desire
and of personality in general.

But however powerfully Mill may have been
influenced by the individualism of these theories,
it did not retain any final or absolute hold upon
his mind. He did not, in fact, continue to be
merely the disciple or exponent of those from
whom he received the tradition of empiricism.
Empiricism underwent, in his hands, a real
development; and the significance of his philosophy consists less in the limitations which he
inherited than in the presence of other tendencies, which may be inconsistent with his avowed
principles, but which are genuinely characteristic
of his thinking. He never, certainly, realised
how far his positive investigation had led him

from the theory of knowledge on which he continued explicitly to base it. But however little he
might be aware of the inadequacy of his philosophical creed, or able to make clear to himself
the logic of another theory of knowledge and
conduct, Mill did, in vitally important respects,
shake off the individualism of the empiricist
tradition. His thought remains coloured by it:
it forms, as we have seen, an element in his
speculative result ; but there are also in his
philosophy other elements which constitute a
departure from it.

The essence of that individualistic bias, which
Mill inherited from his predecessors, is the assertion of an abstract subjectivity as absolute and
complete reality. It is the conception of individuality as an exclusive or repellent rather
than a synthetic or uniting principle. The idea
of human personality on which it depends is
that of an isolated, inaccessible, and impene-
trable subject.

Now it is at all events a partial correction of
this mistake to regard man, with all his functions,
as an element in the real world ; and this is how
Mill actually thinks of human life. The very

essence of his work as a philosopher is that he makes man an object of inductive study, and accepts human life and conduct as a part or aspect of reality. He considers man as an element in nature, and makes not only organic life, but mental change too, in all its aspects, an object of experience among other objects, and related to them as fact to fact. He regards human personality as part of that succession of changes which we call nature, and the conception of man's relation to nature is vital to his point of view.[1]

This objectification of human personality removes the abstraction of individualism. For scientific investigation of anything—the attempt to discover what it is, or to define its nature—is a study of relations. It is an inquiry into resemblances and differences, causes and effects; and to attempt such an inquiry into any object is to assume its real relatedness to other objects. As Mill himself says, " we cannot describe a fact without implying more than the fact. The perception is only of one individual thing; but to describe it is to affirm a connection between it

[1] *Vide* chaps. vi. and vii.

and every other thing which is either denoted or
connoted by any of the terms used."[1] In making man an object of experience, then, and of
science, which is simply developed and special-
ised experience, we regard him as related to
other facts, and part of the order of nature.
Mill's most characteristic philosophical quality
is a real consciousness of man as an object of
knowledge; and this is radically inconsistent
with the individualistic view of man as simply
"subject." This "naturalistic" character of
Mill's philosophy is his unconscious correction
of the abstract logic of individualism.

This objective view of human life connects
itself, as we shall see, with the "positive" or
scientific character of Mill's philosophical interests. He does not aim at the construction of
a philosophy, in the sense of a system of principles. His philosophy is all contained in his
scientific treatment of certain classes of facts.
He philosophises, simply as occasion serves or
compels him, in the course of his exposition of
logic, psychology, ethics, or politics. Just on
this account, his nominal adherence to the in-

1 *Logic*, p. 422.

dividualism of his predecessors finds comparatively little to evidence it in his real thinking.
The objectivity of science is, in fact, inconsistent
with such abstraction. In serious thinking about
things as they are, the individualistic standpoint
cannot be maintained: the logic of mere identity
breaks down. Every act of predication is a
practical denial of the separateness of individual
things, and an affirmation of their ultimate unity
of relation; for if things were "cut off with a
hatchet," predication would be falsification, and
science would be impossible. We cannot think
facts in terms of abstract identity or of mere
difference; for the very essence of thinking is
synthesising; and the legitimacy of this depends
on the real relation of things to each other. It
was in the prosecution of his scientific task—in
his attempt to know the human interests—that
Mill's individualism fell away from him, and left
him face to face with the order of nature and the
issues of life.

But if Mill, in this way, outgrew the limitations of his early sectarianism, in the course of
his effort to investigate knowledge and conduct,
he was influenced in the same direction by con-

tact with other minds, of a different order from those by which his early education had been moulded. His gradual emancipation from the influences under which he grew up culminated in entire dissatisfaction with the hunger-bitten philosophy of his teachers, and left him open to impressions of another kind. He found himself dissatisfied not simply with the speculative basis, but, still more fatally, with the practical ideals of his juvenile Radicalism; and his intellectual life lost, for a time, that philanthropic impulse which was required to make it fruitful.[1] This internal failure of his philosophy taught Mill the importance (even from a purely hedonistic point of view) of some kind of disinterestedness;

---

[1] Autobiography, p. 133. "It occurred to me to put the question directly to myself : 'Suppose that all your objects in life were realised ; that all the changes in institutions and opinions which you are looking forward to, could be completely effected at this very instant : would this be a great joy and happiness to you?' And an irrepressible self-consciousness distinctly answered, 'No!' At this my heart sank within me : the whole foundation on which my life was constructed fell down. All my happiness was to have been found in the continual pursuit of this end. The end had ceased to charm, and how could there ever again be any interest in the means? I seemed to have nothing left to live for."

and it impressed him with the necessity for a
cultivation of emotional as well as of active and
intellectual life.[1]

It was in this state of mind, and at this "crisis
in his mental history," that Mill read Words-
worth,[2] and discovered his "healing power";
and the satisfaction which he got from Words-
worth's expression of "states of feeling, and
of thought coloured by feeling, under the excite-
ment of beauty,"[3] was a decisive factor in his
development.   It not only restored him to a
more tranquil state of mind, so that he felt
himself "at once better and happier";[3] but it
also quickened his intellectual sympathies, and
transformed his dissatisfaction with his former
aims and beliefs into a serious effort to appreciate those of another school of philosophy,
towards which he had hitherto adopted an
attitude merely of antagonism.   His intimacy
with Maurice and Sterling, which this change
of attitude made possible, introduced him to
the philosophical writings of Coleridge; and by
the influence of Coleridge and Carlyle, and,

---

[1] Autobiography, pp. 142, 143.
[2] Ibid., pp. 146 ff.   [3] Ibid., p. 148.

through them, of German thought, his philosophical standpoint was profoundly modified, so
that Carlyle said, "Here is a new Mystic,"[1] and
Mill's former associates observed the change
in his opinions with the gravest apprehension.
His political ideas were at the same time con-
siderably affected by those of St Simon and his
school.

Mill's subsequent attitude towards Bentham
shows the extent of this change in his intellectual
sympathies. While he retains the highest respect
for the strength, directness, and systematic quality
of Bentham's intellectual methods,[2] as well as for
his work as a reformer,[3] he misses in him much
that he has learned to demand and appreciate.
He finds in him too much of a "resolute denial
of all that he does not see,"[4] and a fatal "defici-
ency of Imagination."[5] To this lack of imagination, indeed, Mill attributes Bentham's want of
sympathy with ages and characters other than
his own, and the fact that he sees in man "little

[1] Autobiography, p. 174.
[2] Ibid., p. 214 ; Dissertations and Discussions, vol. i. p. 382.
[3] Dissertations and Discussions, vol. i. p. 333.
[4] Ibid., p. 356.　　　　　　[5] Ibid., p. 353.

but what the vulgarest eye can see."[1] Mill even finds "ignorance of the deeper springs of human character"[2] in Bentham's failure to recognise, as he should do, not only desire of perfection, sense of honour, and love of order, of beauty, of power, and of action, but also the influence of art in fashioning and transforming human life.[3] But far more definite than any of these criticisms, as a proof of Mill's real abandonment of Benthamism, is his attack on Bentham's neglect of the moral consciousness itself as a fact in human nature. "Man is never recognised"- by Bentham, he says, "as a being capable of pursuing spiritual perfection as an end ; of desiring, for its own sake, the conformity of his own character to his standard of excellence, without hope of good or fear of evil from other source than his own inward consciousness. Even in the more limited form of Conscience, this great fact in human nature escapes him. Nothing is more curious than the absence of recognition in any of his writings of the existence of conscience, as a thing distinct from philanthropy, from affection for God or man, and

---

[1] Dissertations and Discussions, vol. i. p. 355.
[2] Ibid., p. 389.   [3] Ibid.

from self-interest in this world or in the next. There is a studied abstinence from any of the phrases which, in the mouths of others, import the acknowledgment of such a fact."[1]

It is a highly significant element in Mill's attitude towards ethical and political questions that he attaches, in this way, much greater importance than his predecessors to the possibility of unselfish motives. He points out that "mankind are capable of a far greater amount of public spirit than the present age is accustomed to hold possible;"[2] and his disbelief in universal selfishness is so complete that he has "no difficulty in admitting that Communism would even now be practicable among the *élite* of mankind, and may become so among the rest."[3] He asserts, in the most unequivocal way, the immediacy, naturalness, and force of social feeling. "The social state is at once so natural, so necessary, and so habitual to man, that, except in some unusual circumstances or by an effort of voluntary abstraction, he never conceives himself otherwise than

[1] Dissertations and Discussions, vol. i. p. 359.

[2] Political Economy, p. 127.

[3] Representative Government, p. 55.

as a member of a body;"[1] and the feelings that
arise from this organic relation to society are so
strong and so persistent that they constitute a
" firm foundation " for morality. The " feeling of
unity " with others may become so strong as to
prevent the individual from desiring any benefit
for himself in which they are not included.[2] " To
those who have it, it possesses all the characters
of a natural feeling. It does not present itself to
their minds as a superstition of education, or a
law despotically imposed by the power of society,
but as an attribute which it would not be well
for them to be without."[3]   Mill joins with
Comte, therefore, " in contemning, as equally
irrational and mean, the conception of human
nature as incapable of giving its love and de-
voting its existence to any object which cannot
afford in exchange an eternity of personal enjoyment."[4] He affirms that the Religion of Humanity fulfils the essential condition of a genuine
religion — " strong and earnest direction of the
emotions and desires towards an ideal object,
recognised as of the highest excellence and as

[1] Utilitarianism, p. 46.   [2] Ibid., p. 48.
[3] Ibid., p. 50.   [4] Auguste Comte and Positivism, p. 135.

rightfully paramount over all selfish objects of desire;"[1] and he considers that the danger of such a religion, as a motive power, is "not that it should be insufficient, but that it should be so excessive as to interfere unduly with human freedom and individuality."[2]

We need not pause to inquire into the truth of this high doctrine. However far it may seem from us, "in the time of the present distress," we cannot doubt the serious intention with which Mill asserted his faith in such a possibility. To entertain such hopes for mankind could not seem a light thing to him; and that he did entertain them there is no room for doubt. His ethical convictions are rooted in them, and even his conception of economic method accommodates itself to their presence.

His estimate of the significance of social feeling affects Mill's theory of economics in a twofold way.

In the first place, he insists, as his predecessors had not done, on the hypothetical character of Political Economy.[3] He points out that its

---

[1] Essays on Religion, p. 109.   [2] Utilitarianism, p. 49.
[3] Cf. Professor Ingram's History of Political Economy, p. 155.

deductions are based on an abstract or hypothetical conception of human nature.   He is
aware, as Ricardo was not, of the distinction between the "economic man" and actual
human persons.   He knows the reality and importance of altruistic motives.

But, in the second place, Mill even takes a
further step, under the influence of his belief
in unselfish desires.   His recognition of the real
prevalence of motives other than the greed and
indolence of the "economic man" renders him
sceptical of the utility and even the legitimacy of
the economic abstraction.

The complexity of all causation prejudices
Mill against belief in the utility of formulæ and
deductions in general:[1] he understands that
omissions in the premises lead to errors in the
results of an investigation.[2] His partial antagonism to Benthamism, too, deepens his sense of
the multiplicity of causes in social life.   His
assertion of the real extent of disinterested feeling and action makes him realise how much is
left out of account in rigid adherence to economic
method.

---

[1] Dissertations and Discussions, vol. i. p. 208.   [2] Ibid., p. 349.

He does, indeed, as we have seen, defend the procedure of economics on the ground of the hypothetical character of the science, and the possibility of correcting empirically the hypothetical result. But the case against this method of investigation has never been stated more pointedly and definitely, in its practical aspect, than by Mill himself. "There is little chance," he says, " of making due amends in the superstructure of a theory for the want of sufficient breadth in its foundations. It is unphilosophical to construct a science out of a few of the agencies by which the phenomena are determined, and leave the rest to the routine of practice, or the sagacity of conjecture. We either ought not to pretend to scientific forms, or we ought to study all the determining agencies equally, and endeavour, so far as it can be done, to include all of them within the pale of the science; else we shall infallibly bestow a disproportionate attention upon those which our theory takes into account, while we misestimate the rest, and probably underrate their importance." [1] Mill's views on this point are, in fact, not such

[1] Logic, p. 583.

as to form a consistent doctrine. He is prevented from accepting the method of economics,
as he finds it and defends it, because those
factors, from which the economic point of view
abstracts, bulk so largely in his conception of the
causation of conduct that their omission goes far
to render economic calculation worthless.

It is part of this sceptical treatment of the
economic abstraction that Mill endeavours to
substitute, in his actual discussion of the problems, the idea of a "standard of comfort" for
that of the "economic man." His emphasis on
this idea, which was itself derived from Ricardo,[1]
is an important change in the method of economics. The idea plays a much more considerable part with Mill than with his predecessors,
and its employment is a real advance in con-
creteness. It constitutes a substitution of real
factors — states of actual desire and will — for
the abstract or hypothetical "economic man,"
whose desire and indolence are purely indefinite,
determined in their effects simply by the con-

---

[1] Cf. Ricardo's 'Principles of Political Economy,' ch. v.,
quoted by Professor Marshall ; *vide* Professor Marshall's 'Principles of Economics' (2nd ed.), vol. i. pp. 551-553.

ditions in which he happens to be placed. This
clearer recognition of actual human character,
with all its varied desires and tendencies, as
one of the factors in economic processes, constitutes an abandonment of the point of view
which had limited economics to the abstract
consideration of purely commercial motives and
their effects.[1]

This altered conception of economic method is
beyond doubt partly due to Mill's belief in the
influence which so-called "non-economic" motives exert; and nothing could more strikingly
illustrate the hold which that belief has upon
his mind. In view of such an estimate of the
possibility of disinterested social feeling as is
indicated both in his explicit utterances and in
the adaptation of his economic method to include it as a factor, it is not easy to attach much
importance to his adhesion to the doctrine of
psychological hedonism. The doctrine has come
to mean so little that what is left is hardly worth
criticising; and even this residue seems to be
given up in the admission that "when the will

[1] Cf. Appendix to Professor Bain's John Stuart Mill: a
Criticism, by J. E. Cairnes.

is said to be determined by motives, a motive
does not mean always, or solely, the anticipation
of a pleasure or of a pain."[1]   The impossibility
of desiring anything except pleasant feeling does
not seem to count for much in the assertion of
cases in which "action itself becomes an object
of desire, and is performed without reference to
any motive beyond itself,"[2] or in the demand
that virtue should be "desired disinterestedly,
for itself."[3]

Such utterances really constitute an abandonment of the doctrine of inevitable self-concern.
It may remain true that a man can only act
as he pleases ; and indeed it is not easy to see
who can have any interest in disputing a proposition which is at once so innocent, so self-
evident, and so uninforming: but this harmless
necessary remnant of psychological hedonism
does not isolate human desire either from the
actual things in which the joy of life is found,
or from those social feelings which men have
sometimes tried to regard as a mere artificial
perversion of self-love.

It cannot be said that Mill explicitly abandons

[1] *Logic*, p. 551.   [2] *Ibid.*   [3] *Utilitarianism*, p. 54.

psychological hedonism. His belief that pleasure alone is desired is his express ground for asserting that it alone is desirable. He retains the form of the doctrine, and uses it as the basis of his ethical theory. But his corrections and limitations of it are so considerable and so vital, that he thinks of man, not as an isolated subject buried in his own self-concern, but as, in his own nature, heir to the riches of the world, and a member of society.

CHAPTER VI

LIFE IN NATURE

THE vexed question of Mill's relation to Positivism has a real and not_merely an antiquarian
interest in the study of his philosophy; for, in
some important respects, his work has the character to which the name "positive" is generally
applied. He is justified, indeed, in his protest
against being considered a Positivist, in the nar-
row or technical sense of the term; but it is
none the less true that the intention and the
subject-matter of his investigations are such
as to connect his work with the positive
philosophies.

Positivism is essentially a theory of practice.
Comte's saying, "*Voir pour prévoir, prévoir pour
pourvoir*," expresses the Positivist conception of

science; and this way of regarding knowledge is strikingly exemplified by Mill: the motive of his philosophy is mainly ethical; his aim is that of a reformer; he prosecutes the work of science for the sake of practice, as part of an effort to secure the means of human wellbeing. Every science interests him primarily as a study of the conditions of some practical benefit.

Logic, for example, is the science of evidence; it is the theory of correct thinking; its object is to investigate the methods of discovery and proof; it is the science on which the art of right thinking is based; and every other part of Mill's philosophical activity bears an equally direct relation to some practical ideal. Speculative results hardly possess for him an independent value. Their interest is mainly secondary: they are chiefly important as reasons for conduct, or statements of the effect of actions or circumstances on the interests of human life. Even when Mill is not arguing definitely for a reform, or a practical improvement, the consequences of his theories are never wholly absent from his thoughts. The utility of a way of thinking is always, with him, an important argument in its favour. His mind inclines steadily to those beliefs—whether scientific, moral, or religious—whose usefulness is evident.

The practical or humanistic bent of Positivism determines its scientific character. Because its interest centres in practice, it makes human life its object and investigates the conditions of human development and satisfaction. In this respect also Mill exhibits positivist tendencies. His humanism limits his interest to the sciences of human life. Man, in his varied relations and endeavours, is practically his sole topic. Whatever problems he finds in nature or in the abstract conditions of existence, he interprets in terms of human interest and effort.

No less akin to Positivism is the connection between Mill's practical standpoint and his view of the limits of science—the view that regards ultimate causes as radically inaccessible to human knowledge, and confines investigation to phenomena. This limitation of knowledge to phenomena is a theoretical expression of the fact that Mill investigates primarily the conditions of human satisfaction; and this relation to his positive interests is its chief significance in his philosophy. It belongs to the complete restriction of his interest to human wellbeing and the modes of its production. It is not rooted in any metaphysical agnosticism; such assertive agnosticism was profoundly repugnant to Mill; and even his polemic criticism of "metaphysical" conceptions is only an incident in the defence of what he conceives to be a more excellent way of studying human advantage. The motive of his aversion to metaphysic is his belief that the scientific or analytic investigation of human life and its conditions is best calculated to lead to real improvement.

In his philosophy, then, Mill's deepest and most persistent interest—his practical aim—is expressed in his "naturalism." His constructive work is largely determined by this point of view; and his interest in defending it is also the ground of his negative attitude towards metaphysics. Our review of his philosophy must include a statement of some of the leading conceptions in which its naturalistic side is developed.

The essence of Mill's naturalism consists in his making man an object of inductive study. He is dominated by a consciousness of man's place among the objects of experience. He considers every human activity as a cause of effects and an effect of causes, and so a part of "nature" in that wide sense of the word in which it means simply the object of knowledge—the "*facies totius universi*."

In this use of the word "nature" to mean the entire system of things (which Mill regards as "the true scientific sense"),[1] the inclusion of man in it is presupposed by every serious attempt to understand him. So much of "naturalism" there is in every theory of human life. In some form, and at some degree of removal, the facts of man's life — his "nature" — must form the basis of every such theory. The difference of philosophical opinion, and the real difference of method corresponding to it, lie in the answers given to the question how man is related to the world of non-human nature.

Mill's answer to this question evinces his naturalism in a more definite way than the mere fact of his scientific study of human life can be held to do. We shall have to see, in our survey

[1] *Essays on Religion*, p. 7.

of what we may call Mill's "Anthropology"—
his theory of man's actual constitution and functions—how close and binding he conceives the
relation to be between man and the world in
which he lives. Meantime we may note that
this more strict and definite "naturalism" is by
no means unconnected with that objective and
inductive way of studying man which is so
characteristic of Mill.

Analysis is, for Mill, the essence of knowledge. The aim of all science, as of observation itself,[1] is to resolve complex realities into
their component parts. Scientific progress—
growth in the knowledge of things — consists
in the progressive "mental decomposition of
facts."[2] Science, that is to say, is a search for
the constituent elements, or factors, of the products which it investigates: its problem is the
resolution of complex realities into their simplest
elements. Now, in connection with this scientific
ideal it is significant for Mill's view of the relation of human life to nature that he insists that
explanation must be in terms of real factors: it
cannot consist merely in hypotheses whose sole

[1] Logic, p. 248.   [2] Ibid., p. 249.

claim on our acceptance is their power of explaining the known phenomena.[1] On the other hand, it is no less significant that he always regards "the swathes and bands of ordinary classification" as a tentative and temporary shift, by which our "discriminating faculty" must not be imprisoned. He demands a perpetual readiness to carry analysis beyond any point at which its progress may seem to have been arrested;[2] and even when two phenomena are found to be irreducibly distinct, he still thinks it possible to regard them as causally connected.[3]

On such a view as this of the nature of explanation, and the directions which it may and must take, the discovery of a real connection of human life and society with the natural order becomes at once possible, and, in a sense, necessary: possible, because all conventional limits to analysis have been set aside, and the singleness of reality has become an expected result; necessary, because intellectual clearness demands at once a complete analysis and an analysis into real factors. It is only natural after this that Mill should think it a merit in De Tocqueville's

[1] Logic, pp. 328, 329.   [2] Ibid., p. 249.   [3] Ibid., p. 516.

work that he "applied to the greatest question in the art and science of government those principles and methods of philosophising to which mankind are indebted for all the advances made by modern times in the other branches of the study of nature."[1] It is not even surprising to find that he regards the methods of physical and moral science as essentially one, and that he sees no impossibility in purely naturalistic interpretations of moral and social life, or in the recognition of a causal relation between mind and matter. Mill's naturalistic account of man—his tendency to explain man in terms of nature—is thus no less rooted in a logical demand than we have already seen it to be in a practical ideal. It depends upon his conception of scientific explanation as an analysis of phenomena.

This attempt to explain human in terms of natural relations is not, of course, new with Mill: we have only to do with an interesting and highly suggestive development of one of the permanent directions of human thought. Mill would have recognised the application to his

[1] Dissertations and Discussions, vol. ii. p. 4.

own naturalism of his remark about "Positivism": that "the philosophy called Positive
is not a recent invention of M. Comte, but a
simple adherence to the traditions of all the
great scientific minds whose discoveries have
made the human race what it is."[1] But it is
none the less true that Mill's account of man's
relation to nature has special characteristics,
which are due to the influences under which it
was developed. Mill is, in fact, chiefly to be
understood, in this connection, as the successor
and spiritual descendant of the English psychologists, and especially of Hartley and James Mill.

Naturalistic psychology was systematised by
Hartley much more fully than by any previous
writer. It became in his hands an attempt to
give an analytic account of the mental process,
as an orderly and sequent unity, dependent for
the very conditions of its existence upon its
relation to organic states, and so to the external
world; and Mill's idea of mental life and its
relation to nature is largely formed upon Hartley's. Specially in his resolution of all mental
development into Association of Ideas, Hartley

[1] Auguste Comte and Positivism, p. 9.

has a quite decisive influence upon Mill's view of knowledge. This conception of Association, as practically the sole principle of mental growth, systematically stated by Hartley, and developed by James Mill, forms the main term of psychological explanation for Mill.[1]

Apart, however, from any definite psychological theory which Mill may have learned from his predecessors, it is significant of the English derivation and character of his positivism that he asserts the possibility and usefulness of psychology itself. In this important assertion he is in direct opposition to the positive philosophy of Comte. Comtism is, as it were, a Catholic positivism, making little of the individual. Mill's positivism, on the other hand, is English and Protestant, full of the consciousness of the individual, and resolute in the attempt to know human nature on its subjective side. Mill regards Comte's denial, and consequent omission, of Psychology as "not a mere hiatus in M. Comte's system, but the parent of serious errors in his attempt to create a Social Science."[2]

[1] Dissertations and Discussions, vol. iii. p. 108.
[2] Auguste Comte and Positivism, pp. 66, 67.

The difference is in fact of greater importance
than might appear at first sight. It means
that Mill's view of man includes an element
of which Comte, while he does not deny its
reality, takes no scientific cognisance; and it
constitutes a difference in the estimation of personal life which goes far to account for the
divergence of the ethical theories of Mill and
Comte.

But, even in his assertion, against Comte, of
the possibility and usefulness of knowing conscious states by direct observation, Mill holds no
truce with dogmatic spiritualism. He asserts,
indeed, strenuously and consistently, the impossibility of substituting physiology for psychology.[1]
Psychology is limited by the possibility of introspection. From whatever sources, or in whatever ways, the knowledge may be obtained, of
facts that are used in psychological explanation,
these are psychologically relevant only in so far
as they can be related to facts that are known
introspectively. Direct consciousness of mental
states gives the only clue to the psychological
interpretation of whatever facts may be other-

[1] Logic, p. 556.

wise observed. Mere description, however, of
mental states cannot be regarded as in any degree a solution of the problem of psychology;
and Mill's belief, that direct self-observation is
essential to psychology, does not prevent him from
recognising the distinction between descriptive
classification of mental states and genuine analysis of them. Nothing short of such analysis,
however, can give a real account of mental life.

The problem with which Mill has thus to deal
is that of the possibility of psychology—whether,
namely, within the limits of psychology, a
thorough analysis of mental states can be
achieved. This analysis can only be regarded
as complete when the "mental decomposition" of
mental processes is carried so far that their complexity is resolved into a series of changes which
are self-evident and, for our knowledge, necessary.
Now, conscious states, taken by themselves, do
not furnish the spectacle of such a series as this:
psychology, in so far as its results are furnished
by simple introspection, is merely empirical.
Psychological analysis reveals, in fact, only an
actual sequence of presentations. It may be supposed to yield more than this, by a confusion of

the relation between cognitive states with that
which obtains between the objects that are known ;
but mental life itself is, for our observation, discontinuous. The stages of the mental series do
not follow one another " unconditionally." When
we take them by themselves, we do not discover
a self-evident connection between them. The analysis of mental facts into simpler mental facts
can never be carried so far as to yield the knowledge of a causal relation between the elements
of mental life itself. It is therefore necessary to
ask whether that relation, and the continuity
which it gives, can be seen to belong to mental
facts, when we remove the abstraction in which
psychology regards them.

From one obvious way out of this difficulty
Mill is debarred by his " positive " or phenomenalist view of mental life. The explanation of
mental changes as results of the activity of a non-
phenomenal Self—of a subject which is not a set
of psychical events or factors—is impossible for
him. The implication of such a Self in all knowledge he does indeed admit;[1] and we shall
afterwards have to consider the importance of

[1] Examination of Hamilton, pp. 247 ff.

the admission for his whole theory of experience. But he recognises no *phenomenal*
reality of mental life, other than the series of
mental states; and psychology is a science of
phenomena—an explanation of known realities
by known realities. It is an instance of Mill's
refusal to adopt this mode of completing the
psychological explanation, that he will not
account for the more obvious gaps or breaches
in the continuity of the mental process by the
hypothesis of " unconscious mental modifications."
This hypothesis, primarily designed to meet the
more considerable failures of strictly psychological analysis in the attempt to discover a
continuous mental process, might, if its validity
were admitted, be regarded as an explanation of
the phenomenal mental life itself. It is therefore
an important element, in Mill's criticism of
Hamilton, that he declines this way out of the
difficulty of psychological analysis: [1] in doing so,
he simply affirms, in a definite instance, that
limitation of the knowledge of mind to conscious
states which he elsewhere generally asserts. To

---

[1] Examination of Hamilton, pp. 355 ff. ; cf. James Mill's
Analysis, note on chap. v.

affirm "unconscious mental modifications" as an explanation of the course of the conscious process, is really to make the non-phenomenal subject a term of psychological explanation.

The very words in which the hypothesis is, perforce, expressed, indicate its futility for the purposes of observational psychology. For such psychology, the "mental" is simply consciousness, and the "unconscious" is, in its very essence, not mental. The hypothesis constitutes a departure from the psychological point of view, and it furnishes no other. In point of fact, the non-phenomenal Self—the self regarded as essentially other than conscious states—is unavailable as a term of scientific explanation. Just because all mental states are inevitably characterised by their relation to the "subject," that relation cannot be treated as a mere factor in their development. It makes no difference between mental phenomena, because it belongs to all alike.

The essential incompleteness of psychological analysis is by no means clearly realised by Mill. He remains in great measure unaware of it, because his thought is largely governed by the assumptions of his psychological predecessors.

He is content to assume, with them, "sensations" out of which the complex unity of conscious life is built up. He does not state definitely whether these "sensations" are psychical or merely physical facts; nor does he appear to realise how powerfully the answer to this question affects the nature and limits of psychological analysis; but it is probable that he regards sensations in general, just as James Mill did, as mental units out of which perceptions are built up. In so far as he does so, he simply adopts from his predecessors that hypothesis to which the illusory appearance of completeness in their psychological analysis is mainly due. It cannot, however, be too definitely understood that "sensation," regarded as mental fact, is purely hypothetical. As Wundt says, "The . . . conception of sensation arises only from the necessities of psychological analysis. Simple sensation is never given to us in isolation, but is the result of an abstraction to which we are driven directly through the complex nature of all inner experiences."[1] Sensa-

<hr>

[1] Wundt, Physiologische Psychologie, third ed., vol. i. p. 289. Cf. Professor Seth's Scottish Philosophy, Lecture iii.

tion does not exist in consciousness, otherwise than in the synthesis of the perceptive act; and the analogy of chemical elements, by which Wundt and others seek to defend the use of the hypothetical unit in psychology, is really not a correct one; for the very essence of the matter is that the psychological unit cannot exist in isolation, as the chemical element can and does. In so far as Mill is content to accept the hypothetical sensation unit, and to regard psychological analysis as effected when an explanation is obtained in terms of such sensation, he abandons his own demand for an analysis into "real" factors, and resorts to such a use of hypothesis as we have already found him condemn. But when he is aware of the absence of a purely psychical continuity — and at all events in those cases in which more metaphysical psychologists resorted to the hypothesis of "unconscious mental modifications"—he proposes a way out of the difficulty. He finds "unconscious modifications of the nerves" to be the only thinkable form of the "latent" process.[1]

This method of explaining the psychical result

---

[1] *Examination of Hamilton*, pp. 355-357.

involves conceptions of psychological explanation
that might have meant more than they do for
Mill's theory. If he had been less satisfied with
the tradi\.ional assumptions of psychology, he
might have made much more than he actually
does of the relation of mental to organic states.
In so far as he recognises the internal incompleteness of psychological analysis, he resorts, for
its completion, to physiology; and in so doing, he
makes use of factors that are no longer hypothetical but definitely real; for even when sensations, or rather impressions, are psychologically
nothing, they are everything for physiology.
Nothing can be more real than the transmission
of nervous impressions from the periphery to
the cerebral cortex. But in these real stages
of the physiological process there is a positive
continuity: in them we have to do with a
discoverable causal series. Relation to the organic process is thus a quality of mental life
in virtue of which it can be studied as a continuous whole. Nor, it may be suggested, is
there anything arbitrary or strange about the
fact that mental processes can be explained in
this way. Our consciousness *is* in relation to

the physical process in question; and, since its existence and character belong to it in this relation, there is nothing singular in the necessity for interpreting it in the light of the physical process.[1] Relation to organic change is a real quality of mental life as we know it; and, if this be recognised, it cannot appear unreasonable that this quality should give to mental life whatever continuity it may have for our knowledge, or that the analysis of mental facts should be capable, through their real relation to organic states, of a completion that is not possible when they are regarded in an isolation which is, after all, fictitious and abstract.

Mill is too well satisfied with psychology, as he finds it, to recognise fully the dependence of its ultimate explanations upon physiology, or to see how largely "unconscious" factors contribute to every psychical result. But this certainly arises from no jealousy of the recognition of material conditions. On the contrary, once the reality and distinctiveness of mental facts have been admitted, he argues for the thorough concomi-

---

[1] Cf. Mr Bradley's Appearance and Reality, chap. xxiii., esp. pp. 337-342.

tance of mental and bodily states.[1] He points out that "if it be materialism to endeavour to ascertain the material conditions of our mental operations, all theories of the mind which have any pretension to comprehensiveness must be materialistic;"[2] and while he recognises that "the relation of thought to a material brain is no metaphysical necessity, but simply a constant co-existence within the limits of observation,"[3] he yet insists that the influence of physiological factors is "one of the most important departments of psychological study."[4] The development of Mill's psychological position issues in a thorough-going incorporation of man in nature, a conception of the laws of mind as possibly "derivative laws resulting from laws of animal life,"[5] and a definite assertion that mental life is related to material conditions within the organism.

[1] Essays on Religion, pp. 198 ff.
[2] Dissertations and Discussions, vol. iii. p. 109.
[3] Essays on Religion, p. 199.
[4] Logic, p. 556.   [5] Ibid.

I

CHAPTER VII

DETERMINISM

MILL's naturalistic conception of human life appears more decisively in his deterministic view of activity than in any other part of his philosophy; determinism is, in fact, the main outcome of his inclusion of man in nature, and the central doctrine of his scientific theory of human thought and conduct.

Mill's interest in determinism is mainly logical. The doctrine is forced upon him by his objective treatment of man, and required as the presupposition of his attempt to construct a science of social relations. That his belief in it is brought about rather by logical than by ethical requirements is shown indirectly by the extent to which he qualifies his statement of it, by his emphatic assertion of the reality of choice and volition; and no stronger evidence could be desired of the degree in which he was aware of the moral difficulties of the theory than his own account of his desire to evade it.[1]

The deterministic idea of human conduct belongs, in fact, to the manner of Mill's attempt to investigate human life : it simply expresses, for him, the view that man is a possible object of inductive study. Induction depends for its possibility upon the existence of causal relations, since it is essentially an inquiry into causes.[2]

---

[1] Autobiography, pp. 168 ff. "For example, during the later returns of my dejection, the doctrine of what is called Philosophical Necessity weighed on my existence like an incubus. I felt as if I was scientifically proved to be the helpless slave of antecedent circumstances ; as if my character and that of all others had been formed for us by agencies beyond our control, and was wholly out of our own power. I often said to myself, what a relief it would be if I could disbelieve the doctrine of the formation of character by circumstances ; and remembering the wish of Fox respecting the doctrine of resistance to governments, that it might never be forgotten by kings, nor remembered by subjects, I said that it would be a blessing if the doctrine of necessity could be believed by all *quoad* the characters of others, and disbelieved in regard to their own. I pondered painfully on the subject till gradually I saw light through it."

[2] Logic, pp. 247 and 369 ; Auguste Comte and Positivism, pp. 59 ff.

The existence of causal relations, therefore, in
human personality, conditions the possibility of
making an inductive study of man's conduct, and
of knowing his life objectively. [Determinism
means for Mill, primarily, the existence of causal
connection within personal human life, in the
same sense in which it obtains in the world of
external nature.[1]] In the case of action it means
that " a volition is a moral effect, which follows
the corresponding moral causes as certainly and
invariably as physical effects follow their physical causes." [2]   In the case of knowledge (though
Mill does not explicitly connect this with his determinism) it means that the associative sequence
of ideas is invariable and unconditional.   In either
case, determinism may be taken to affirm simply
an " abstract possibility of being foreseen," [3] for
every voluntary act, and every sequence of presentations.   " Correctly conceived, the doctrine
called Philosophical Necessity is simply this:
that, given the motives which are present to an

---

[1] Logic, pp. 547 ff.; Examination of Hamilton, pp. 576 ff.,
and 603.
[2] Examination of Hamilton, p. 578.
[3] Ibid., p. 603.

individual's mind, and given likewise the character and disposition of the individual, the manner
in which he will act may be unerringly inferred;
that if we knew the person thoroughly, and knew
all the inducements which are acting upon him,
we could foretell his conduct with as much certainty as we can predict any physical event." [1]

This general conception of human personality
as an orderly or causally connected complex
simply expresses, as we have seen, the possibility
of making it a subject of investigation. But
besides this, and even apart from the question of
man's relation to the external world, Mill's determinism contains a definite view of the nature of
moral causation. "Those who say that the will
follows the strongest motive, do not mean the
motive which is strongest in relation to the will,
or in other words, that the will follows what it
does follow. They mean the motive which is
strongest in relation to pain and pleasure; since
a motive, being a desire or aversion, is propor-
tional to the pleasantness, as conceived by us, of
the thing desired, or the painfulness of the thing
shunned." [2] The form of this statement is con-

[1] Logic, p. 547.   [2] Examination of Hamilton, p. 605.

nected with Mill's psychological hedonism: it involves his doctrine of the relation of desire and pleasure. But this doctrine is not really essential to his determinism: his deterministic theory of volition turns less upon his view of the object of desire than upon his idea of the relation of desire to volition. That "will is the child of desire"[1] is really all that the theory needs to assert psychologically; and it is by this view of the causation of actions that Mill distinguishes his determinism from fatalism; since he maintains that, while a man's character is formed by his circumstances, "his own desire to mould it in a particular way is one of those circumstances, and by no means one of the least influential."[2]

Apart from certain individualistic assumptions, which do not necessarily belong to it, this aspect of Mill's determinism is simply a resolute assertion of the inner unity of the mental process: what he contends for is the real relation of acts of will to the whole mental life of the individual. This is the significance, for example, of his assertion that "the difference between a bad and a good man is not that the latter acts in opposition to his strong-

[1] Utilitarianism, p. 60.   [2] Logic, p. 550.

est desires; it is that his desire to do right, and his
aversion to doing wrong, are strong enough to over-
come, and in the case of perfect virtue, to silence,
any other desire or aversion which may conflict
with them;"[1] and it is the ground of his statement
that consciousness does not witness "that I could
have chosen one course while I preferred the
other"[2] of two alternatives. Mill does not conceive
of the will as an isolated "faculty." He means by
it nothing more than the facts of consciousness
which are called volitions; and these are so dependent upon the whole conscious life of the agent
that, while "I can indeed influence my own volitions . . . by the employment of appropriate
means," "direct power over my volitions I am
conscious of none."[3] Its dependence on other
elements in consciousness is so integral to the
volition itself, that it cannot be affected otherwise
than through them.

Such a conception of the integrity of mental
life is at the root of the idea of "character,"
which plays so large and useful a part in Mill's
theory of conduct. Character he defines, with

---

[1] Examination of Hamilton, p. 585.

[2] Ibid., p. 582.　　　　[3] Ibid., p. 377.

Novalis, as "a completely fashioned will";[1] and
it is in the light of this conception of character
that Mill's determinism has its chief importance.
Will "passes out of the dominion of its parent (desire) only to come under that of habit;"[2] and "a
habit of willing is commonly called a purpose."[1]
Purposes, or volitional habits, must be regarded,
in this way, as the effect of volition; and it
is in the formation of purposes not directly
dependent on immediate inclinations that the
development and confirmation of character consist. Character is thus the effect of past volitions; but it is, for Mill, no less the source
than the product of voluntary conduct; and it
is this interdependence of volition and character
that gives his deterministic theory of will its
main interest for him.

The connection in which Mill's most deliberate
statement of his determinism occurs is in itself
suggestive of the place of the theory in his philosophy. It forms the prelude to his discussion of
the "Logic of the Moral Sciences,"[3] and is the
basis of the contention "that there is or may be

---

[1] Logic, p. 552.   [2] Utilitarianism, p. 60.
[3] Logic, book vi. chap. ii.

a science of human nature." [1] The significance of
determinism consists in the fact that it is involved in every attempt to study human personality inductively, and is thus the only hypothesis
on which Ethology—the science of character—can
even be attempted. This makes it an essential
presupposition of social science, the possibility of
which Mill regards as bound up with that of
Ethology. The use of the determinist theory,
for Mill, thus consists in its being required to
make Social Science legitimate.

In Mill's opinion, social science rests on Ethology. "Human beings in society have no properties but those which are derived from, and
may be resolved into, the laws of the nature of
individual man." [2] This is his reason for in-
sisting, against Comte, on the necessity for
Psychology. There can be no science of character that is not based upon observation of
mental life; and without a science of character
there can be no science of society. This emphasis
on individual human nature as the explanation
of social life is the key to Mill's conception of
social science, and to his criticism of Comte's

---

[1] Logic, book vi. chap. iii.   [2] Ibid., p. 573.

sociological attempt. The 'Politique Positive' is
an account of the life and growth of society which
abstracts, all but completely, from the fact that
society consists of persons; and Mill asserts the
importance of this omitted element. He demands,
therefore, "a science of Ethology, founded on
the laws of Psychology."[1] He contends that
there are "universal laws of the Formation of
Character,"[2] and that these are primarily psychological laws. He regards them also as the ultimate laws of social development.[3]

This assertion of the relation of Psychology to
Social Science is really useful and important.
Psychology forms an element in every science
whose subject-matter is mental. Ethics, Politics,
Æsthetics, and the Science of Religion, for example, are sciences of special relations of mind;
and none of them can be dissociated from psychology, which is simply analysis of the mental
function implied in them all. The complete development of any of these sciences involves an
analysis, a cleared conception, of mental action
itself: that is a psychology. Just as all natural
sciences imply physics—an analytic statement

[1] Logic, p. 570.   [2] Ibid., p. 564.   [3] Ibid., pp. 595, 596.

of material relations as such—so do all spiritual sciences imply analysis of mental relations. No natural science can give a result, or assume a process, that contradicts the physical possibilities, or is irreducible to those processes in which physical change is found to consist. Similarly, no spiritual science can violate, by its results, the known modes of mental action—can represent mental processes as occurring in a manner inconsistent with what we know of mental function. Psychology is thus regulative of spiritual sciences as physics are of natural sciences; and this is the real meaning of Mill's contention that a psychological ethology is the necessary basis of social science. The absence of such a basis must mean, according to him, a social science which takes no heed of the individuals who make up society, and which is therefore unauthorised and insecure.

The possibility of a science of individual character is thus of no small importance to Mill's philosophy; and his belief in it is quite definite. He admits, indeed, that "there are reasons enough why the moral sciences must remain inferior to at least the more perfect of the phys-

ical: why the laws of their more complicated
phenomena cannot be so completely deciphered,
nor the phenomena predicted with the same
degree of assurance."[1] But these reasons consist
simply in the greater complexity of the phenomena with which the moral sciences have to do,
and not in any abstract impossibility of knowing
or investigating moral facts; so that, "though we
cannot attain to so many truths, there is no reason that those we can attain should deserve less
reliance, or have less of a scientific character."[2]

Mill's estimate of the accuracy which is possible for a science of human nature results, in
fact, from his demand for a resolution of its
empirical laws into the laws of the causes on
which they depend. Because its explanations
are of this derived kind, such a science cannot
give a complete analysis of all the partial and
limited influences by which character is affected: it will give an account of "the main
phenomena, but not the perturbations."[3]

The degree of precision which Mill thinks
attainable in a science of human nature connects
itself in this way with the psychological char-

---

[1] Logic, p. 395.   [2] Ibid.   [3] Ibid., p. 554.

acter of the ultimate laws of such a science; and this degree of precision corresponds no less fully to the end for which the science is required. "Whenever it is sufficient to know how the great majority of the human race, or of some nation or class of persons, will think, feel, and act," the general propositions of ethology "are equivalent to universal ones. For the purposes of political and social science, this *is* sufficient," "that which is only probable when asserted of individual human beings indiscriminately selected, being certain when affirmed of the character and collective conduct of masses."[1] Mill is satisfied, in fact, with that degree of accuracy, in the science of character, which enables it to serve as a basis for Social Science.

It can hardly be denied that the project of a science of character, as Mill conceives it, is one which is beset with difficulties, and which it is not easy either to connect with psychology or to make use of in the study of social phenomena.[2] Apart, however, from the question how

[1] Logic, p. 554.

[2] Cf. an article by Mr Ward on "J. S. Mill's Science of Ethology," International Journal of Ethics, vol. i. p. 446.

far such a science is possible, or likely to be useful, Mill's demand for it has a twofold significance
in his philosophy: it explains his interest in
determinism; and it indicates his sense of the
need for an interpretation of personal life.
His belief in ethology also suggests a way of
regarding personality which he actually adopts,
when he comes to investigate the conditions of
human development.

One of the most general and important problems of a science of character—a problem, too,
the manner of whose solution affects the interpretation of determinism in the most vital way—
is that of the relation of human character to the
external world. Mill is emphatic in his assertion of man's dependence upon nature—of the
ethical and economic significance of the external
world of circumstance. He does not hesitate to
affirm "that Nature is to the greater number a
severer taskmaster even than man is to man."[1]
Circumstances impose on man necessities that
guide and form his life; and the conditions that
affect him most are of natural and not human
origin. This is a view of man's relation to

---

[1] *Dissertations and Discussions*, vol. i. p. 27.

nature which Mill develops in more than one instance.

His appreciation of Malthus's doctrine of population, for example, must be understood in this way. He regards the necessity for limiting population as due to natural rather than to social causes. " The niggardliness of nature, not the injustice of society, is the cause of the penalty attached to over - population ":[1] it is because nature limits the productiveness of labour that population cannot increase indefinitely without harm. Man is, in fact, an organism, and subject, as all organisms must be, to the world from which he draws his life and supplies his needs. Production, Mill points out, is limited and determined by natural conditions. It is not arbitrary : its conditions are not fixed, and cannot be altered, by human will. Its possibility depends on the presence of natural resources : it is limited in its amount, and determined in its character, by these. Man must seek his livelihood from nature on terms that are of nature's fixing. An improvement of his powers, or a husbanding of his acquired resources, may increase his gains ;

---

[1] Pol. Econ., p. 118.

but even to this nature sets limits. Man lives, as it were (a lesson that Mill learned from the Physiocrats), partly by the bounty of nature, which multiplies for him the results of his labour. The productiveness of labour depends upon nature, and is governed by laws that man cannot change.[1]

This is less true of the distribution than it is of the production of wealth; for the distribution of what nature yields is a matter in which man can to some extent choose and arrange, and its laws are "partly of human institution."[2] Here also, no doubt, there are necessities to be discerned; for the effects of "human institution" "are as much a subject of scientific inquiry as any of the physical laws of nature."[3] But the laws that determine the effects of distributive arrangements are laws of character itself; and Mill makes much of the distinction, between distributive arrangements, which man can regulate, and conditions of production, which are fixed, and with which he cannot interfere.[4]

This dependence of production upon natural

---

[1] Cf. Pol. Econ., pp. 13 ff., 63 ff., 264.   [2] Pol. Econ., p. 13.
[3] Ibid., p. 14.   [4] Ibid., p. 264.

conditions is of quite crucial importance; for nothing is more certain than the vast significance, in all human development, of the economic factor. No other condition exerts so much influence on the formation of character as the mode in which nature can be made to yield a livelihood. The economic significance of nature, as a factor in production, makes nature the greatest of ethical factors also. This is the main explanation of the influence on character of climatic and other natural conditions. In proportion as they compel and reward labour, by producing in response to it an improvement in comfort, they develop character, not simply in its economic utility, but in many other respects as well.[1]

Of more direct influences of the external world on character Mill is no less aware than of that which it exerts in virtue of its economic significance. He never tires of affirming "the extraordinary susceptibility of human nature to external influences,"[2] whether such influences are of human or of directly natural origin. The effects of pain, privation, occupation, and all the

---

[1] Cf. Pol. Econ., bk. i. c. vii.
[2] Subjection of Women, p. 40.

K

circumstances that belong to man's struggle with nature, and to the relations of social life, appear to him to be the determining forces that bring about changes of character.[1] Progress is not a law of human nature with Mill; he regards it as brought about by the force of circumstances; he conceives of man as forced forward by economic necessities, rather than by any essentially progressive tendency in himself.[2]

Moral ideas and feelings, no less than developments of character, appear to him to be the result of circumstances. "Laws and systems of polity always begin by recognising the relations they find already existing between individuals. They convert what was a mere physical fact into a legal right."[3] In this way Mill explains the sentiment of justice itself. In its retributive aspect, it is simply a developed expression of the natural feeling of retaliation: it is "a spontaneous outgrowth from two sentiments, both in the highest degree natural, and which either are or resemble

[1] Pol. Econ., bk. ii. c. xiii.; bk. v. c. viii.; and Essay on De Tocqueville, Dissertations and Discussions, vol. ii.

[2] Dissertations and Discussions, vol. ii. p. 71.

[3] Subjection of Women, p. 8.

instincts ; the impulse of self-defence, and the feeling of sympathy." [1] It is thus of purely natural origin : it is an instinctive feeling ; and the direction which it takes is determined by the form which circumstances give to the individual's relation to his fellows.

Suggestive as are these indirect evidences of Mill's tendency to exalt the power of nature over human character, we are yet not wholly dependent on them for our knowledge of his way of conceiving man's relation to the world. He expressly interprets thought and conduct as effects in man of the course of things.

This is the meaning of his emphasis on " the law of association as the governing principle, by means of which the more complex and recondite mental phenomena shape themselves, or are shaped out of the simpler mental elements." [2] He finds in Hartley's Associationism, for the first time, a real analysis of mental function ; [3] and he accepts it as an account, not merely of the thinking process taken by itself, but also of the

[1] Utilitarianism, p. 76.
[2] Dissertations and Discussions, vol. iii. p. 108.
[3] Autobiography, p. 68.

relation of thought to the world. He states his
father's " fundamental doctrine," in psychology, as
" the formation of all human character by circumstances, through the Universal Principle of Association ; " [1] and the place given to Association, by
Mill, in conformity with the traditions of English
Psychology, does, in fact, imply more than merely
a causal connection within mental life, and a consequent possibility of investigating it. It implies,
besides, the complete and direct subjection of the
mental process to the course of external events.
It means that consciousness is essentially passive,
and merely receives and reproduces impressions
from the outer world—that the order and connection of our ideas, no less than the elements
which make up their complexity, come entirely
from without. Such a view is not merely implied, but is even explicitly advanced by Mill.
He says that " the conceptions . . . which we
employ for the colligation and methodisation of
facts, do not develop themselves from within,
but are impressed upon the mind from without ; " [2] and that " the conception is not furnished
by the mind, until it has been furnished *to* the

[1] Autobiography, p. 108.   [2] Logic, p. 427.

mind; and the facts which supply it are sometimes extraneous facts, but more often the very
facts which we are attempting to arrange by it." [1]

How far this view of thought is consistent
with other elements in Mill's philosophy is a
question which we shall have to discuss at a later
stage, when these elements come to be considered.
But it constitutes an important part of his positivist or naturalistic theory of human life, and
it leads directly to his idea of the formation of
character. "Our character," he says, "is formed
by us as well as for us; but the wish which in-
duces us to attempt to form it is formed for us;
and how? Not, in general, by our organisa-
tion, nor wholly by our education, but by
our experience—experience of the painful consequences of the character we previously had." [2]

It is to be observed that this way of conceiving the relation of character to the outer world,
while it is perhaps a natural sequel to the determinism which Mill required as a scientific postulate, is yet not necessarily implied in that theory.
It is possible to believe that human character
and experience are capable of analysis into con-

[1] Logic, p. 428.   [2] Ibid., p. 550.

nected processes, and even that they are objectively related to the natural order of things, without thinking of them as directly and passively subject to the external world.[1] We shall see that the freedom of personal experience is suggested by Mill's own questions as to the finality of phenomenalist psychology; but his failure to develop this idea constructively, in his account of character and its conditions, leaves him, in his investigation of human experience, committed to the view that it is nothing more than an incident in the course of nature.

[1] Cf. James's Principles of Psychology, c. xxviii.

CHAPTER VIII

FREEDOM

WE have seen that Mill's theory of knowledge, in some of its most important developments, contains a recognition of objective existence, such as his inherited sensationalism can hardly be said to justify: a reality which is not merely mental states is implied, in his theory of judgment, to be the object of knowledge; and this reality is definitely conceived, in his constructive logical theory, as a system of unconditional relations.

This idea of an objective world has for its correlative Mill's conception of a subject, or self, other than mere states of mind. The consciousness of objective reality involves the consciousness of a knowing subject; and the idea of objects as other than mere subjective states of individuals makes it impossible to regard such states as the subject that knows. Mill does indeed affirm that "the Mind is only known to itself phenomenally, as the series of its feelings or consciousnesses,"[1] and that "the feelings or consciousnesses which belong or have belonged to it, and its possibilities of having more, are the only facts there are to be asserted of Self—the only positive attributes, except permanence, which we can ascribe to it."[2] But this does not prevent him from admitting the necessity for another conception of the Self.

The way is left open for such a conception by Mill's recognition of the phenomenal limits and incomplete character of all inductive explanation. "What is called explaining one law of nature by another," he tells us, "is but substituting one mystery for another, and does nothing to render the general course of nature other than mysterious: we can no more assign a *why* for the most extensive laws than for the partial ones;"[3] and the limitations of scientific theory are hardly less definitely expressed in his statement that no

---

[1] Examination of Hamilton, p. 263.   [2] Ibid.
[3] Logic, p. 310.

mere summation of the actions of its elements
"will ever amount to the action of the living
body itself."[1] Such suggestions make it possible
to maintain that the self is not completely expressed in mental states, while at the same time
these states are regarded as all that can be
known of it.

The recognition of a subject which is not
simply states of consciousness is forced upon
Mill by his assertion of the objectivity of knowledge ; for experience only yields a knowledge of
actual things in virtue of its inner continuity.
A mere series or succession of unconnected
mental states could never amount to a knowledge of objective reality ; and Mill sees that the
conception of mental life as such a series, which
is the only one that the experienced facts yield, is
inadequate to explain the essential objectivity of
thought. He finds the empiricism, which is
normal to the scientific problem, to be metaphysically incompetent. Experience explains
everything but itself.

Mill does not, indeed, admit "that the mere
impression on our senses involves or carries with

[1] Logic, p. 243.

it any consciousness of a Self."[1]   But memory
and expectation belong to all knowledge; they
are essential to the objectivity which characterises it; without them, the phenomena of mind
would be discontinuous, and there would be no
knowledge of a world.   Memory and expectation, therefore, must be explained by any theory
which is really to give an account of knowledge;
and it is thus a fact of real significance, that they
"are attended with the peculiarity, that each of
them involves a belief in more than its own
present existence."[2]   This characteristic of memory and expectation compels Mill to admit "that
the mind, or *Ego*, is something different from any
series of feelings, or possibilities of them,"[3] in
order to escape "the paradox, that something
which, *ex hypothesi*, is but a series of feelings,
can be aware of itself as a series."[3] | This is the
ground of Mill's belief in a self. | "In so far,"
he says, "as reference to an *Ego* is implied in
Expectation I do postulate an *Ego*."[4]   Memory
and expectation involve a self which is not
merely a series of phenomena: the dependence

---

[1] Examination of Hamilton, p. 262.   [2] Ibid., p. 247.
[3] Ibid., p. 248.   [4] Ibid., p. 258.

of knowledge on them is thus really equivalent to the relativity of things to a thinker.

For Mill, this necessity of a non-phenomenal self is merely "inexplicable"; and his inability to explain its relation to other elements in his theory of knowledge instances the inadequacy of his avowed logic to his real thinking. The admission is really "a trap - door opened by Mr Mill himself in the floor of his own philosophy."[1] But that Mill should have stumbled over the idea of a "subject," and should have been unable to reduce it to a series of "states of consciousness," is no mere personal accident or momentary weakness. For metaphysical empiricism, indeed, such a "subject" is a mere anomaly; but no consistent empirical philosophy would have admitted the necessity for it. From an empirical standpoint, this way of regarding knowledge seems a most needless lapse on Mill's part: Mr Bain, for example, "never could see where his difficulty lay."[2] But the idea of the "subject" belongs, in no external way, to Mill's

---

[1] Professor Masson's Recent British Philosophy, third ed., p. 215.

[2] Professor Bain's John Stuart Mill : A Criticism, p. 121.

theory of knowledge; and his recognition of " the
organic union [1] . . . which connects the present
consciousness with the past one "[2] is not an isolated *aperçu*, nor a mere exception in an otherwise consistent theory. Mill's guarded but undis-
guised admission of the necessity, for knowledge,
of a subject, "different from any series of feelings, or possibilities of them,"[3] does not stand
alone; it is simply the central and crucial instance of an element in his thinking which is
exemplified in many other cases, whose practical
importance, though not their logical significance,
is perhaps greater than that of this conception.
When Mill finds a "subject" to be involved in
knowledge, and asserts "that there is something
real in this tie, real as the sensations themselves,
and not a mere product of the laws of thought
without any fact corresponding to it,"[4] he is
only developing, in relation to the subjective
aspect of knowledge, a conception to which his
theory of induction gives effect in relation to the

---

[1] A phrase which Mill accepted from Professor Masson's
criticism of him ; *vide* Recent British Philosophy, third ed.,
p. 213.

[2] Examination of Hamilton, p. 262.

[3] Ibid., p. 248.   [4] Ibid., p. 262.

world of known reality. His assertion of the
unity and reality of the knowing subject connects itself with his view of knowledge as constructed out of judgments about things.

That Mill's idea of the self is vague and
incoherent need hardly be insisted on, in view
of his most modest pretensions in the matter.
His suggestion that "mind may be described as
the sentient *subject* (in the German sense of the
term) of all feelings,"[1] indicates only too truly
the slight and second-hand character of his
acquaintance with German thought; and it is
not difficult to suppose that, if he had made
himself at home in German philosophy, as
Sterling urged him to do,[2] he might have come
to a clearer understanding with himself on this
and other matters. He had little craving for
system; and when the facts of life forced upon
him ideas that did not tally with his theories, he
accepted the results frankly enough, but he left
them often unexplained. In the present instance, it may be suggested that his assertion

---

[1] In the earlier editions of the Logic, p. 68.

[2] Cf. Mr W. L. Courtney's Life of John Stuart Mill (Great
Writers), p. 76.

of "something I call Myself"[1] is wiser than many pretentious theories; but it can hardly be maintained that this or any other of Mill's statements about the self can be made to convey a clear account of it. In point of fact, the self is genuinely "inexplicable" to him. However much it may be involved in his recognition of objective reality, he does not discover it as so involved. He may rather be said to stumble upon it unexpectedly; and his idea of it is proportionately negative and obscure. He thinks of it as a mere residue from psychological analysis—an element in the mental complex that cannot be resolved; his conception of it is psychological; and however far such a result may be from his intention, the idea of the self which he actually conveys is much more that of a "substance" than of a "subject." He is thus compelled to find in it not an explanation of things but a baffling and incomprehensible problem — an inexplicability added to the mystery of knowledge.

Now, the form of knowledge is certainly not "explicable" in the sense in which objects of

---

[1] *Logic*, p. 10.

knowledge are so; but neither is it at all relevant
to speak of it, in Mill's way, as "inexplicable."
There are excellent reasons for our inability to
explain it as a separate or abstract fact; for even
to demand such explanation of it is to miscon-
strue it altogether. Self - consciousness is the
very term of all explanation; and all knowledge
is in a certain sense of it as well as by it. But
the attempt to know it in isolation is essentially
unreasonable, since it is only real in experience;
and to abstract it from the synthesis of knowledge, or to make it the unexplained residue of a
merely subjective process, is to reduce it, and
with it all reality, to a dead level of unreason.
Mill's conception of the self as "inexplicable" is
thus part of a confusion, which arises from his
failure to conceive it as the subject of knowledge.

But if Mill's assertion of /the dependence of
knowledge upon a subject is not made in such a
way as to do justice to all the issues that are
involved in it, we may still regard it as part of a
theory of experience which forms a highly suggestive correction of his deterministic account of
man's relation to the world.

The connection is not far to seek between the

discovery that self-hood, or personality, is the
basis of all knowledge, and Mill's recognition of
the part which emotional interest plays in the
construction of experience. As Volkmann says,[1]
"Everything interests me of which I can say I
am in it." Interest expresses the relation of its
object to the needs of personal life; and it is
therefore significant of Mill's emphasis upon the
personal element in experience that he makes
much of subjective interest in his account of the
development of knowledge. Interest, for example, promotes that synthesis which is the
main element in knowledge: we know things as
wholes, and not in their mere details, because
"in our perceptions of objects, it is generally the
wholes, and the wholes alone, that interest us."[2]
In the same way pleasure and pain are referred
to the subject rather than to the object, because
their interest is mainly subjective; because they
are of comparatively little importance to us as
qualities of the objective world of things, and

---

[1] Lehrbuch der Psychologie, third ed., vol. ii. p. 203; quoted
by Professor Baldwin in his Handbook of Psychology : Feeling
and Will, p. 148.

[2] Examination of Hamilton, p. 325.

interest us primarily as elements in conscious life.[1] In its more developed stages, too, experience depends for its coherence upon the existence of emotional interest: a capacity of feeling is required in order that there may be a motive for the pursuit of truth.[2] The effort to know things depends upon a sense of their importance—upon the interest which their relations possess for us.

The same sense of the inner unity of personal life, and of the dependence of experience upon this unity, is expressed in Mill's assertion of the relation of activity to the growth of knowledge. The fundamental position, for example, which he assigns to experiences of resistance in his derivation of our conception of matter,[3] makes activity an essential element in the consciousness of an outer world; for "resistance is only another name for a sensation of our muscular frame, combined with one of touch;"[3] but this recognition of a mere contribution, however important, which experiences of activity make to our knowledge of

---

[1] Examination of Hamilton, p. 268.
[2] Dissertations and Discussions, vol. i. p. 92.
[3] Examination of Hamilton, p. 270.

reality, is of subordinate interest, compared with
Mill's admission of the active character of experience itself. This is an idea which does not
affect, in any vital way, Mill's own systematic
treatment of psychological problems; and he regards it as a new development of empirical psychology, when Mr Bain affirms the essentially
active character of conscious life. Still, it is a
development of doctrine which he welcomes with
real cordiality, and which he regards as not only
true but also of the highest importance. "The
mind," he says, "is active as well as passive;
and the apparent insufficiency of the theory to
account for the mind's activity, is probably the
circumstance which has oftenest operated to
alienate from the Association Psychology any
of those who had really studied it."[1] This is
an account of mental life which can hardly
be combined in any organic way with that
complete subjection of thought to things which
Mill elsewhere asserts.[2] To make experience
an activity—an expression of personality—is to
abolish the direct causal relation between out-

---

[1] *Dissertations and Discussions*, vol. iii. p. 120.
[2] Cf. chapter vii.

ward things and the knowledge which experience gives; for if experience is an activity, and
is formed and characterised by the personal life
which makes it real, then it is no longer possible
to regard its results as due to mere unknown
things. Things only affect the growth of experience as they become objects of knowledge; but
objects of knowledge are characterised by their
relation to the activity of the knowing self; and
this essential element in their very being is left
out of account when knowledge is regarded as
simply an effect of things. The relation of personal activity to the world of fact need not be
denied: man's hereditary continuity with nature
is a matter which does not really concern us in
this connection. Every material element in
personality has, no doubt, its conditions in the
world of impersonal existence; but to call personality an effect of these conditions is still
irrelevant and impossible. For, after all has
been said, an essential characteristic of personal
activity is self-consciousness; and to call self-
consciousness an effect of anything is to use
words without meaning. Thought is thus no
more effect of things. The activity of experience

—its dependence upon the constructive action of personal life—is, in fact, only another name for the dependence of knowledge upon a subject: it means that self-consciousness cannot be ignored in giving an account of the ideas of things which experience yields us.

Mill's failure to embody his belief in the activity of experience in a systematic theory, does not mean that this belief is without effect in his way of conceiving human knowledge and conduct. That sense of the reality and significance of personal life, which appears in his defence of introspective psychology, betrays itself in various other ways.

His vindication of the worth of hypothesis in scientific investigation suggests the extent to which his conception of scientific method is affected by his belief in the importance of intellectual motives and interests: he regards voluntary thought as essential to the development of knowledge by investigation.[1]

But a more crucial instance of his recognition of personality is his estimate of the nature and importance of voluntary choice. He asserts the

---

[1] *Logic*, p. 326.

reality of choice in the most definite way. Belief
in it is, in fact, a necessity of that moral interest
which determines his philosophical work.[1] He
seems to miss the idea of it in deterministic
theories ; and he suggests that " the freewill doctrine, by keeping in view precisely that portion
of the truth which the word Necessity puts out
of sight, namely, the power of the mind to co-
operate in the formation of its own character,
has given to its adherents a practical feeling
much nearer to the truth than has generally (I
believe) existed in the minds of Necessitarians."[2]
[Choice is, to begin with, a genuine fact of psychic
life ; and it is a mental function which is of central, and not merely accidental, importance.] " The
human faculties of perception, judgment, discrim-
inative feeling, mental activity, and even moral
preference, are exercised only in making a
choice."[3] Conscious life is, in fact, summed up
in the act of choice : it expresses not simply a
part, but the whole, of the mental activity of the
individual. In it, and in it alone, his mental life
becomes effective : it is the ultimate expression

[1] Autobiography, p. 169. [2] Logic, p. 551.
[3] Liberty, p. 34.

of that life, and the denial of it would amount to a dissolution of personality.

But choice is not only itself real. It is also a factor in the formation of character; and "what is really inspiriting and ennobling in the doctrine of freewill, is the conviction that we have real power over the formation of our own character; that our will, by influencing some of our circumstances, can modify our future habits or capabilities of willing."[1] This is really the important issue for Mill. His interest in the question is a practical one. He is beset with the difficulty "of thinking one doctrine true, and the contrary doctrine morally beneficial";[2] and he requires a solution which will satisfy the demands of both theory and practice. His statement of the reality and effectiveness of choice must be made in such a way as not to contradict his naturalistic conception of human action as part of the causally connected order of events; and his assertion of the absolute correlation of conduct and character makes this difficult, since it is not open to him to suggest either that the act of choice may be independent of the character

---

[1] Autobiography, p. 169.　　[2] Ibid., p. 170.

of the agent, or that that character is itself independent of the causal order.

In face of such perplexities, Mill affirms that the fact of a man's character " being, in the ultimate resort, formed for him, is not inconsistent with its being, in part, formed by him as one of the intermediate agents " ; [1] and he points out that, although character is formed by circumstances, " desire to mould it in a particular way is one of these circumstances, and by no means one of the least influential." [1] This is all that seems to him to be required as a vindication of moral freedom : " this feeling, of our being able to modify our own character *if we wish*, is itself the feeling of moral freedom which we are conscious of. A person feels morally free who feels that his habits or his temptations are not his masters, but he theirs." [1] What Mill argues for, in fact, is the freedom of character itself, against particular impulses and passions. The unity of character, and the possibility of its being in its entirety the source of action, is what he means by moral freedom.

It is not to be expected that such a conception

[1] *Logic*, p. 550.

of freedom will satisfy those who insist that the possibility of moral life depends upon a freedom of the self and of action from or against the actual character, in which Mill finds the explanation of conduct. On the other hand, it must be remembered that those / who separate the self from character, in this way, are apt to "go out for wool and come home shorn"; for, after all, much more depends morally upon the unity of conduct and character than upon the freedom of a psychological abstraction. There is little gain in such freedom, and much loss; for to make self-conscious action in any degree independent of character is to make self-consciousness and character separate things; and this abstract separation of self-consciousness from character leaves character impersonal and mechanical. But to sacrifice the idea of the freedom of character itself is to pay too dearly for the conviction that action is rendered incalculable by the presence of a "surd." Mill's assertion of the determination of conduct by character is an element of strength in his theory; and he is saved from many of the difficulties of determinism by his recognition of the part which volition plays in the formation of character itself.

On the other hand, it must be admitted that Mill is not in a position to express, in any adequate way, that freedom which moral experience demands. He is left amid the antinomies of determinism and indeterminism, because his conception of the self is inadequate and irrelevant. His idea of the self, or subject, is arrived at, as we have seen, simply by his failure to analyse the subjective process of knowing, and not in relation to the objective synthesis, which constitutes knowledge. The idea is thus a psychological one; and, in so far as it is positive, it is little better than that notion of the self which Hume had failed to find any impression to justify. Self-consciousness is, indeed, more than this for Mill; but his idea of it is never free from traces of its psychological origin. It remains for him an object, rather than the very condition, of experience; and it is therefore conceived as separate from character, and so capable of being brought into antagonism with it and subjection to it. In so far as his idea of self-consciousness is vitiated in this way, Mill's theory of volition is a mere

determinism: it must inevitably make self-consciousness, and voluntary action, an effect of
alien things. | This separation of the self from
character, which is common to Mill with some of
his opponents and critics, makes freedom, in any
worthy sense, impossible.　It is at the root of
Mill's curious denial of the possibility of altering
character by direct volition.　"We are exactly as
capable," he says, "of making our own character,
if we will, as others are of making it for us."[1]　A
man can only change his character, in fact, by
changing his circumstances: this is all his power
over his own development.　He can only alter
his character in the same sense, and in the same
degree, in which other people can alter it.

Such a view of the way in which character
is changed betrays an abstract and mechanical
conception of it; and it ignores the fact that the
will to be different is itself a change of character—that character is modified from within, by
the volitions which express it.　The very idea of
character is apt, in truth, to be a misleading abstraction.　In speaking of character, we abstract
from self-consciousness: we leave out of account

[1] *Logic*, p. 550.

the fact that those actions which we ascribe to
character are self-conscious. But to do this is
to omit the most significant element in the case.
The real agent is not character, taken in abstraction from the self-consciousness which is its
most distinctive quality: such character is, in
truth, a mere hypothesis, which neither exists
nor acts. The real agent in human conduct is
personal—character which is self-conscious, or
self-consciousness which is realised and individ-
ualised in the detail of character. Neither an
abstract self apart from character, nor an equally
abstract character apart from self-consciousness,
is an actual or complete personality; and to
make either of these abstractions the source of
conduct is to separate action from its real conditions. Mill's idea of character undoubtedly
tends to leave out of account the self-consciousness which makes it human and personal; and
his derivation of conduct from this impersonally
conceived character makes freedom an impossible
idea for him. He does not conceive action in
such a way that it cannot be made the effect
of impersonal causes; and he does not conceive
human personality in such a way that its self-

development is possible. But these are the very essentials of freedom. Negatively and positively, it must be so conceived. It must mean absence of external or alien causation ; and it must mean the possibility of self-development.

Mill's assertion of choice, and its effect upon character, is thus not made in such a way as to constitute a theory of freedom. It indicates only a dissatisfaction with determinism, which arises from his consciousness of personal life and its issues. The intensity of that consciousness is attested by Mill's effort to conceive action as free, and to regard character as self-determined. His failure in these respects suggests the real incompatibility of moral freedom with his philosophical presuppositions, and especially with his idea of self-consciousness.

But however unable Mill may be to express his conviction of moral freedom in a consistent theory, his assertion of it is no mere compromise or weakness on his part. It is not an isolated concession to custom or prejudice ; it belongs to his mental habit, and connects itself with important elements in his theory of human life.

In economics, for example, Mill insists on the

actual effectiveness of human character and choice. He distinguishes sharply between production and distribution, on the ground that, while production is determined by natural agencies and circumstances, distribution is "a matter of human institution solely." "The rules by which it is determined, are what the opinions and feelings of the ruling portion of the community make them, and are very different in different ages and countries; and might be still more different, if mankind so chose."[1] This determination of distribution by human will makes choice a vitally important factor in economic conditions; and the central position which Mill gives in this way to choice and character, is further asserted in his qualification of his naturalistic account of production. While he adheres to that account in its main outlines, he modifies it by affirming the dependence of production upon character and thought. "No limit," he says, "can be set to the importance, even in a purely productive and material point of view, of mere thought."[2] Intellectual work, mere speculation itself, is productive labour.[3] Mental

---

[1] Political Economy, p. 123.   [2] Ibid., p. 27.   [3] Ibid.

and moral qualities are required for production, and both its nature and its amount depend on them.[1] The growth of knowledge is a development of man's power over nature; and the limitless possibilities of discovery afford the prospect of an equally unbounded development of productive industry.[2] Productiveness depends, too, upon the "energy of labour"; and this is conditioned by the presence of wants and ambitions fitted to call it forth.[3] The education and development of human character is thus, in the fullest sense, a productive industry: it is an indirect, but most real, contribution to the increase of material wealth.[4]

Still more definitely does character condition the right use of wealth when it is produced: the main hope of economic wellbeing lies in the education of feeling and opinion and the growth of self-restraint. The Standard of Comfort, which determines the distribution and consumption of wealth, depends for its maintenance and development upon self-restraint, and upon the education of impulses and wants. It represents, really, the

---

[1] Political Economy, pp. 115, 116.   [2] Ibid., p. 422.
[3] Ibid., p. 65.   [4] Ibid., pp. 25, 26.

economic effect of character. While external causes may raise it for a time, the level at which it is maintained must always depend upon mental and moral qualities.

This conviction of the economic significance of character is the ground of Mill's strenuous assertion of the necessity for education as the only means to social wellbeing. His belief in democracy gives way, in some degree, to grave apprehensions of "the ignorance and especially the selfishness and brutality of the mass."[1] He sees clearly that all social transformation requires "an equivalent change of character,"[2] and that "the primary and perennial sources of all social evil are ignorance and want of culture."[3] Self-dependence and self-protection form the only security of human beings;[4] and "the wellbeing of a people must exist by means of the justice and self-government, the δικαιοσύνη and σωφρο-σύνη, of the individual citizens."[5] "The laws of national (or collective) character are by far the

---

[1] Autobiography, p. 231. [2] Ibid., p. 232.
[3] Dissertations and Discussions, vol. i. p. 28.
[4] Representative Government, p. 55.
[5] Political Economy, p. 458.

most important class of sociological laws,"[1] not
only on account of their direct interest, but also
because it is character that mainly determines
other conditions and guides the development of
society.

In a like spirit, Mill finds the cause of social
development in the growth of thought. " As
between any given state of speculation," he
says, " and the correlative state of everything
else, it was almost always the former which
first showed itself; though the effects, no doubt,
reacted potently upon the cause."[2] In spite of
its relative weakness, intellectual activity is
the mainspring of progress. In it alone man
frees himself from the incubus of the past
and the present. It determines moral and
physical conditions;[2] and its development " is
at the root of all the great changes in human
affairs."[3] Thought is, in fact, man's chief qualification for progress, because in it he " knows the
end from the beginning," and sees the goal of
effort. It emancipates him from his past: it
makes the present a means to his ends. His

---

[1] Logic, p. 590.   [2] Ibid., p. 605.
[3] Auguste Comte and Positivism, p. 104.

active life is liberated by it from habit and routine, and set free to adapt its effort to new needs. This simple and straightforward faith in the worth and weight of ideas is no small part of Mill's heritage from the intellectualism of the eighteenth century. The men of that clear-headed and cold-hearted time had a faith in knowledge and enlightenment for which no esteem can ever be too high; and, even when he forsakes their results, Mill holds by this faith which he received from them. It is the permanent faith of all philosophy—belief in ideas.

It is part of this belief in the worth of thought that Mill makes much of individual initiative and incentive in all reform.[1] Because all improvement depends upon ideas, it must come from individuals; and the most real and secure improvement—that of men themselves—consists in their adoption of new and better ways of thinking.

Personality is thus, for Mill, the very centre of human affairs. Human progress depends, not only upon natural conditions, but still more upon

[1] Cf. Liberty, p. 39, &c.; Dissertations and Discussions, vol. ii. pp. 72 ff.

choice, and thought, and character, and qualities
of personal life. If Mill is committed by his
presuppositions to another way of conceiving
man's relation to the world, yet this assertion of
the fundamental importance of personality forces
itself through his empiricism, and modifies the
strictness of his theory.

CHAPTER IX

ETHICAL HEDONISM

BOTH the strength and the weakness of Mill's idea of conduct appear in his theory of its moral aspect.

It is because conduct consists of acts of personal choice that it is possible to subject it to a moral criterion, and so to form judgments of moral value; and Mill's assertion of the volitional aspect of conduct—its relation to self-consciousness—makes ethics possible for him. He estimates conduct and character, not simply in respect of their effect on human happiness, as any other facts or events can be estimated, but also in relation to the self-consciousness of the agent; and he is able to take this moral view of conduct, because his assertion of choice, and its relation to character, affirms a real connection between conduct and personality. Moral judgment, with the feelings that are appropriate to it, depends upon this personal aspect of conduct, for it constitutes an application to actions of a standard which the agent himself is assumed to be capable of recognising and applying; and this means that moral judgment must assume that a personal or self-conscious being is the cause or source of the actions judged, since only a self-conscious being could recognise the application of an ideal standard. Mill's moral criticism of conduct is thus relevant in virtue of that actual relation of conduct to self-consciousness which is asserted in his emphasis upon voluntary choice.

On the other hand, Mill's deterministic abstraction of character from self-consciousness makes the end or standard by which conduct is judged external to conduct itself. His misleading conception of self-consciousness separates it from character; and, because he regards character as the source of conduct, he is unable to give any coherent expression to that relation of self-consciousness to conduct which he asserts or requires in his doctrine of volition. Conduct is thus not

determined by self - conscious personality : its
whole explanation is in character, which is conceived impersonally. But the worth of conduct,
as Mill conceives it, is relative to personal thought
and desire ; and the end which conduct ought to
realise thus stands in no real or vital relation to
conduct itself.

Conduct and character, taken in this fictitious
isolation from self-consciousness, are in no sense
ends : they are only means to an end, which does
not belong to them in any vital way, and to which
they stand in a merely external relation. "Questions about ends are," as Mill says,[1] "in other
words, questions what things are desirable ;" ends
are thus essentially determined by self-consciousness ; and the separation of the source of conduct
from self-consciousness is, consequently, an exclusion of acts from the end in relation to which
they are judged. The relation of the moral end
to action is thus external or contingent : the end
becomes simply an effect upon feeling, and cannot be realised in the acts themselves. Such is
the connection between hedonism and a psychological idea of self - consciousness, through the

---

[1] Utilitarianism, p. 52.

impersonal conception of character to which that idea leads.

The explicit ground of Mill's hedonistic ethics is " that happiness is desirable, and the only thing desirable, as an end; all other things being only desirable as means to that end." [1] His proof of this depends on his doctrine that only pleasure is desired; and that doctrine combines with his abstract conception of character to determine his acceptance of a hedonistic criterion. Mill points out, indeed, that " questions of ultimate ends are not amenable to direct proof;" [2] and he does not affect to give a demonstration of hedonism. But he also recognises that " there is a larger meaning of the word proof, in which this question is as amenable to it as any other of the disputed questions of philosophy." [2] " Considerations may be presented capable of determining the intellect either to give or withhold its assent to the doctrine; and this is equivalent to proof." [3] The ground of Mill's hedonistic conception of the moral end is not an intuition,[2] but consists in his theory of desire — the doctrine of psychological hedonism. " The only proof capable of being

[1] Utilitarianism, p. 52.   [2] Ibid., p. 6.   [3] Ibid., p. 7.

given that an object is visible, is that people actually see it. The only proof that a sound is audible, is that people hear it: and so of the other sources of our experience. In like manner, I apprehend, the sole evidence it is possible to produce that anything is desirable, is that people do actually desire it. If the end which the utilitarian doctrine proposes to itself were not, in theory and in practice, acknowledged to be an end, nothing could ever convince any person that it was so. No reason can be given why the general happiness is desirable, except that each person, so far as he believes it to be attainable, desires his own happiness. This, however, being a fact, we have not only all the proof which the case admits of, but all which it is possible to require, that happiness is a good: that each person's happiness is a good to that person, and the general happiness, therefore, a good to the aggregate of all persons." [1] This claim that happiness is one of the ends of conduct is transformed by psychological analysis into the statement, " that there is in reality nothing desired except happiness. Whatever is desired otherwise than as a

[1] *Utilitarianism*, pp. 52, 53.

means to some end beyond itself, and ultimately
to happiness, is desired as itself a part of happiness, and is not desired for itself until it has become so." [1]

We need not pause, meantime, to examine the
validity of Mill's transition, in the above passages, from private to general happiness. What
we have to note is, that the only real proof of his
Utilitarianism is the doctrine that pleasure is
the sole object of desire; and that his ethical
theory is thus governed by his psychological
presuppositions.

It is not to be denied that Hedonism emphasises a real aspect of moral good. In making the
end of conduct consist essentially in satisfaction,
it affirms a genuine characteristic of it; for a good
which is not a satisfaction of desire is quite unin-
telligible; and such a good, if we suppose it to be
possible, could not, at all events, be a moral ideal
or end. The objectivity of moral judgments involves the authority of the end or law which they
apply to conduct; and this means that the moral
end must be realisable in and by acts of will; for if
it is not realisable, it cannot be binding or obliga-

[1] Utilitarianism, p. 57.

tory ; and to be realisable means here to be realisable in acts of will, since these are the subject of moral judgment. The moral end, then, must be capable of being willed : it must be a possible object of desire; for it can only be realised by being willed and desired. The moral end must be adapted to the nature of man ; for it is a " human good," and must be so conceived as to be capable of realisation in the facts of human character. If the moral consciousness is not to be an impossible, and therefore unauthoritative, demand, its *dicta* must be relative to the human possibilities. Moral rightness is that particular end or good which human actions are intrinsically capable of realising. Satisfaction is thus a necessary element in moral good; and, in asserting this, Hedonism calls attention to a characteristic of the moral end which is of real significance.

On the other hand, while the interpretation of the moral end as personal happiness emphasises an aspect of moral experience which ethical theory cannot afford to ignore, it is also true that the assertion of this aspect is apt to be made in a one-sided way. In so far as the hedonistic theory of morality is based upon the doctrine

that pleasure or happiness is the sole object of
desire, it expresses an abstract or individualistic
conception of personality. That desire is for
things which are expected to produce pleasure
may perhaps be accepted as a summary statement of certain characteristics of desire regarded
as a mental fact. But, apart altogether from the
question of the completeness or validity of such
a statement, taken in a purely psychological sense,
to derive from it a theory of the moral end is to
make a constructive use of the abstract point of
view required for psychology, in a domain to
which it is quite inapplicable. The laws of
mental life cannot, indeed, be ignored in forming a theory of the moral end, for that end must
be realised by mental life ; and it must not, therefore, be conceived in such a way as to make its
realisation inconsistent with what is known of
mental processes. The psychological results
cannot be left out of account : morality must
be conceived in accordance with them. But the
function of the psychology of conduct, in relation
to a theory of the moral end, is purely regulative :
it cannot be made to determine the end positively,
as it does when a direct passage is made from the

psychological formula that desire is for pleasure to a hedonistic theory of the moral end. To make the formula of psychological hedonism determine the moral point of view is to introduce into ethics an individualistic way of thinking, which is essential and proper to psychology, but which is irrelevant to the theory of morality, because it deliberately leaves out of account those relations to things and persons in which alone morality can exist.

Mill's idea of conduct is based on his psychological conception of knowledge and desire : it is derived from his limitation of consciousness to its own states. His theory of desire depends upon an isolation of personal life from the real world ; and the abstraction of the subjective process from reality, in which his doctrine of conduct is thus rooted, betrays itself in the ethical consequences of the doctrine. The formal statement that desire is always for pleasure or happiness ignores all the particular interests and objects by which desire is actually determined and characterised. It thus makes possible no distinction between actions on their inner or conscious side : in respect of their motive they all become alike and morally

indifferent. Mill does actually recognise a variety
of motives; but this recognition avowedly counts
for nothing in his criticism of conduct. Motives
only acquire ethical importance for him, by a
separation of character from conduct, which is
contrary to his own better judgment in the
matter: they affect the moral worth of the agent,
but not the morality of his actions.[1] Now this
purely external conception of the worth of conduct—this refusal to judge it otherwise than by
its outward results — is an obvious and direct
consequence of the attempt to base ethics upon
the formula that pleasure is the sole object of
desire. The conception of desire which makes a
state of personal feeling its only possible object
can have no ethical meaning but this. It separates conduct from its end, and makes the end a
merely external effect.

Even within the limits of his hedonism, Mill
finds that this external conception of the relation
of conduct to its end issues in a dissolution of
practical life. One of his most searching discoveries, in the time of his doubt and distress,
was the fatuity of the quest of personal happi-

[1] Utilitarianism, p. 26.

ness. "Those only are happy (I thought) who
have their minds fixed on some object other than
their own happiness; on the happiness of others,
on the improvement of mankind, even on some
art or pursuit, followed not as a means, but as
itself an ideal end."[1] If only for its own sake,
happiness must be allowed to come unsought.
Those who aim at something else "find happiness
by the way;"[1] but when it is sought it is not
found. "The conscious ability to do without
happiness gives the best prospect of realising
such happiness as is attainable."[2] That such
admissions as these are a surrender of the doctrine that only happiness can be desired, is a
point on which it is hardly needful to insist. It
is more interesting to observe that they are
a powerful commentary upon Mill's ethical
theory. Moral life ceases to be a unity for him,
because he separates means and end in it, and
makes the standard of conduct a mere outward consequence. We have just seen that
Mill's failure to make the inner aspect of conduct morally significant leads him to ignore that
relation of conduct and character which it had

---

[1] Autobiography, p. 142.   [2] Utilitarianism, p. 23.

been his strength and excellence to assert. This abstraction from each other of related elements in the unity of moral life finds a fitting sequel in the conclusion to which Mill is driven, when he asserts that the ideal end which action must realise can never be made its motive. The external character of the relation between action and its end or criterion makes practical life unreasonable.

Such difficulties as these belong to the inconsistency of the elements in Mill's theory of action. If he had adopted a consistent deterministic account of conduct, and had been satisfied with such external criticism of it as determinism makes possible, his perplexities need never have occurred. They are the outcome of his attempt to fuse the ethical consequences of his mechanical theory of conduct with a criticism of action which implies its relation to self-consciousness. We have seen that Mill's attempt to reconcile his assertion of voluntary choice with his determinism is beset with difficulties; but these difficulties are greatly complicated and intensified when he tries to combine not simply his divergent ideas of conduct, but the ethical conceptions that grow out of them.

This constitutes the dramatic and speculative interest of Mill's ethical theory. It is an attempt to find, within the limits of empiricism, a place for naïve and undistorted moral experience; and Mill is distinguished from his empiricist predecessors by the serious and resolute nature of this attempt: he recognises the moral facts as they had failed to do. Mill's Utilitarianism might, in fact, almost be signalised as a return of modern hedonism to the ethical point of view. It is something of a concession to regard Benthamism as a theory of " Morals "; it is a theory of nearly everything in morals except the distinctively moral element; and Bentham's empiricist predecessors, though some of them were more theologically minded than he, were really no nearer to the ethical conception of conduct. With Mill this is changed, and we have a real attempt to express the results of moral experience. He is not satisfied with a discovery of the means by which each individual's attempt to secure his own happiness, in the present or in a future life, may be turned to account for the general good. He attaches much more importance than previous hedonism had done to the internal sanctions of conduct—to the estab-

lishment of a relation between the hedonistic end
and the desires of the individual. We shall have
to see, at a later stage, in what directions Mill's
Utilitarianism is modified by his attempt to make
out a real identity of private with general interest. But, in so far as his theory of the moral
end consists in making it simply the satisfaction
of actual desire, or the production of pleasant feeling, his main difficulties in working out that
theory arise from his attempt to combine with it
the idea of a less external relation between conduct and its criterion.

Mill makes utility a really moral principle.
He affirms that " the principle of utility either
has, or there is no reason why it might not have,
all the sanctions which belong to any other
system of morals." [1] His main effort, indeed, is
to clear it from the charge of selfishness, and to
idealise it by connecting it with man's whole
spiritual meaning. He insists on the prominent
place which may be assigned, on purely utilitarian grounds, to virtuous conduct. The utilitarian doctrine, he says, " maintains not only
that virtue is to be desired, but that it is to be

---

[1] *Utilitarianism*, p. 40.

desired disinterestedly, for itself;"[1] and the utilitarian standard "enjoins and requires the cultivation of the love of virtue up to the greatest
strength possible, as being above all things important to the general happiness."[2] The hedonism of Mill's ethical theory does not, in fact,
express moral laxity or selfishness: the theory
is conceived in no spirit of concession to self-
regard or human weakness.

Mill's education had been the work of a stern
schoolmaster. What we know of James Mill
makes it very credible "that his moral teaching
was not likely to err on the side of laxity or indulgence:"[3] we learn that "his moral feelings
were energetic and rigid on all points which he
deemed important to human wellbeing;"[4] and
that his "moral inculcations were at all times
mainly those of the '*Socratici viri*'; justice,
temperance (to which he gave a very extended
application), veracity, perseverance, readiness to
encounter pain and especially labour; regard for
the public good; estimation of persons according
to their merits, and of things according to their

---

[1] Utilitarianism, p. 54.   [2] Ibid., p. 57.
[3] Autobiography, p. 51.   [4] Ibid., p. 107.

intrinsic usefulness; a life of exertion in contra-distinction to one of self-indulgent ease and sloth." [1]

It would have been surprising if Mill, brought up on such ethical doctrine as this, had relapsed into a theory of morals conceived in a less arduous spirit; for all the newer influences of his youth, and his growing sympathy with the idealism of some of his contemporaries, could only serve to intensify his appreciation of the serious side of life. There is nothing which should lead us to expect in his hedonism any failure to do justice to the claims of morality or of social relations; and, in point of fact, the most obvious moral quality of the theory is its emphasis upon benevolence. In its assertion of the obligation of justice, and in its demand for reasonable self-sacrifice, Mill's Utilitarianism shows no lack of moral sinew—betrays no weakness or frigidity of moral motive.

Nor, again, is the hedonistic cast of the theory to be explained by any kind of sensuousness in Mill, or in those from whom he learned his ethics. In such men as Bentham and James Mill there

[1] Autobiography, p. 47.

is little enough of the "artistic temperament"; and the art of enjoyment is one in which Mill finds himself fatally lacking.[1] From such men the real temper of hedonism is conspicuously absent. Theirs is not the mood of the epicure. Love of pleasure is, at all events, not their beset- ting sin. They are reflective rather than sensi- tive; and there is in them more of the sage than of the voluptuary. Hedonism, in any ordinary sense of the term, sits strangely enough upon such men as these; and Mill's hedonism is not such as can reasonably be ascribed to any constitu- tional overestimate of even the most refined indulgences.

The philanthropic or humanitarian bent of his mind had probably much more to do with Mill's hedonism than any enthusiastic personal appreci- ation of pleasure. This is a real element in his outlook upon life. He is, above all things, inter- ested in human wellbeing; and his emphasis on happiness connects itself, undoubtedly, with this side of his character. The most obvious evils of human life are its dulness and its misery; and no normally constituted and sympathetic observer

---

[1] Autobiography, p. 143.

can fail to see in these, and especially in the actual pains that men undergo, the most clamant
wrongs that await redress. The saint and the
prophet may perceive, with truer insight, that a
more real tragedy is the failure of life from within
—the weakness that consents to evil, the cowar-
dice that courts defeat, the selfishness that separates every man from his neighbour. But the
needless pain and sorrow of mankind are more
visible evils; and there has been no real philanthropy that has not been alive to their presence,
and urgent for their removal. Mill's consciousness of them colours all his thought about human
conduct. When he insists that "the greatest happiness of the greatest number" is the criterion of
morality, he is the spokesman of those to whom
life brings too much pain. In their behalf he
affirms the equal rights of all human beings; and
it is the spectacle of their misery that makes his
claim seem valid and needful. If Mill's utilitarianism has been of more real and direct service, in
its effect upon social ideals and practice, than
other, and perhaps more accurate, ethical theories,
it has only fulfilled, in this, his main intention.
It derives its character from his sympathy with

the pains of humanity : his hedonism is rooted in moral and humane interests.

Mill himself, in his review of Whewell's ethical writings, asserts, in the most unqualified way, his belief in the moral validity of his own theory. " We are as much for conscience, duty, rectitude," he says, " as Dr Whewell. The terms, and all the feelings connected with them, are as much a part of the ethics of utility as of that of intuition. The point in dispute is, what acts are the proper object of those feelings ; whether we ought to take the feelings as we find them, as accident or design has made them, or whether the tendency of actions to promote happiness affords a test to which the feelings of morality should conform." [1]

In this passage, however, it is to be observed that Mill makes more of the logical than of the ethical aspect of the principle of utility ; and it is beyond doubt that his acceptance of this principle was mainly determined, at all events in the first instance, by his sense of its logical usefulness. "My zeal," he says, speaking of his early Benthamism, " was as yet little else, at that period of my life, than zeal for speculative opinions. It

---

[1] Dissertations and Discussions, vol. ii. p. 459.

had not its root in genuine benevolence, or sympathy with mankind; though these qualities held their due place in my ethical standard."[1] The logical unity, or coherence, of the utilitarian theory was what first commended it to Mill. He saw men's moral judgments determined by traditions, caprices, and prejudices; and he desired to substitute for these a logic of practice. He criticises Whewell's 'Elements of Morality' as "nothing better than a classification and systematizing of the opinions which he found prevailing, among those who had been educated according to the approved methods of his own country; or, let us rather say, an apparatus for converting those prevailing opinions, on matters of morality, into reasons for themselves."[2] Mill regards utilitarianism as the only escape from confused and arbitrary moral conceptions; and he accepts it primarily as the only ethical system which gives a real deduction of moral rules from a single principle. This is the secret of his enthusiasm for Bentham's ethical work. He had been too thoroughly "rooted and grounded" in indi-

[1] Autobiography, p. 109.
[2] Dissertations and Discussions, vol. ii. p. 453.

vidualism to detect the abstraction which under-
lay Bentham's whole conception of conduct; and
when he read the 'Principles of Morals and
Legislation' all his previous ideas became an
orderly and complete system of ethics. "The
feeling rushed upon me," he says, "that all previous moralists were superseded, and that here
indeed was the commencement of a new era in
thought."[1]   The principle of utility "fell exactly
into its place," he adds, "as the key-stone which
held together the detached and fragmentary component parts of my knowledge and beliefs. It
gave unity to my conceptions of things."[2]

For Bentham himself the interest of utilitarianism had been primarily logical: it gave him
a principle for the theory of legislation, just
as his psychological hedonism and his theory of
the "sanctions" of morality summed up, in a
convenient formula, the means by which human
conduct can be influenced; and Mill defends
Bentham's ethical theory on the ground of its
scientific or logical value. "It is by his *method*
chiefly," he says, "that Bentham, as we think,
justly earned a position in moral science analo-

[1] Autobiography, p. 65.   [2] Ibid., p. 66.

gous to that of Bacon in physical. It is because
he was the first to enter into the right mode of
working ethical problems, though he worked many
of them, as Bacon did physical, on insufficient
data." [1] Except in the case of a conflict of moral
rules, which must be settled by reference to first
principles, the utilitarian controversy is " a question of arrangement and logical subordination
rather than of practice; important principally
in a purely scientific point of view, for the sake
of the systematic unity and coherency of ethical
philosophy." [2] That morality should be " referred
to an *end* of some sort, and not left in the
dominion of vague feeling or inexplicable internal
conviction, that it be made a matter of reason
and calculation, and not merely of sentiment, is
essential to the very idea of moral philosophy;
is, in fact, what renders argument or discussion
on moral questions possible." [1]

This logical character of the importance of the
utilitarian principle does not make it less significant, in Mill's eyes, for the practice of morality.
" The contest," he says, " between the morality

[1] Dissertations and Discussions, vol. ii. p. 462.
[2] Ibid., vol. i. p. 385.

which appeals to an external standard, and that
which grounds itself on internal conviction, is the
contest of progressive morality against stationary
—of reason and argument against the mere deification of opinion and habit."[1] He makes this, in
fact, his chief apology for utilitarian ethics, that
the utilitarian principle is one by which concrete
acts and general moral rules can be judged and
determined. He points out that certain of the
consequences of an action can generally be foreseen,[2] and that it is the function of a science of
ethics to criticise these consequences in terms of
the end which it assumes.[3] He urges, in favour
of utilitarianism, that the principle which it
makes use of can be made a criterion of the consequences of action, and therefore a ground for
rules of conduct: utilitarianism is, in this way,
a real theory of right and wrong in conduct [4]—
a theory fitted to guide action. It is thus mainly
as an assertion of the moral significance of consequences that Mill defends hedonism. He shares

---

[1] Dissertations and Discussions, vol. ii. p. 472.

[2] Ibid., vol. i. p. 142.

[3] Logic, p. 620.

[4] Dissertations and Discussions, vol. i. pp. 384 ff.

Bentham's contempt for the authority of those unjustified sentiments of sympathy and antipathy which are apt to be regarded as the ultimate court of appeal in moral questions.[1] He points out that " to all those *à priori* moralists, who deem it necessary to argue at all, utilitarian arguments are indispensable ; "[2] Whewell "deduces his secondary principles" from the hedonistic end, and defends them on hedonistic grounds ;[3] and Kant finds in experience and preference the real ground of his criterion.[4] The utilitarian principle is thus an essential element in the method of ethics.

Mill finds the peculiar excellence of Bentham's utilitarianism in two characteristics of his method.

In the first place, Bentham's method is inductive and analytic. More than any previous moralist, he seems to Mill to have the scientific quality—the power of going behind abstractions and generalities, and dealing with things in the concrete reality of their details.[5]

[1] Dissertations and Discussions, vol. ii. p. 499.
[2] Utilitarianism, p. 5.
[3] Dissertations and Discussions, vol. ii. p. 496.
[4] Utilitarianism, p. 6.
[5] Dissertations and Discussions, vol. i. pp. 341-346.

In the second place, Mill praises the constructiveness of Bentham's work. "With him," he says, "the first use to be made of his ultimate principle, was to erect on it, as a foundation, secondary or middle principles, capable of serving as premises for a body of ethical doctrine not derived from existing opinions, but fitted to be their test."[1] His work is positive, and not merely destructive or critical; and its value is therefore permanent. This constructive utility of Bentham's ethical theory, which had been part of its original attraction for Mill, continued to appeal to him, even when he was most aware of Bentham's shortcomings; and his sense of it helped the individualistic presuppositions of the theory to retain that hold upon Mill's mind which they never entirely lost.

But, with all his belief in the logical value of the principle of utility, and with all his appreciation of the force and skill with which Bentham had developed and applied that principle, Mill is keenly aware of the limitations of Bentham's system of morality. He criticises it with all the energy of a former disciple. He points out that

[1] *Dissertations and Discussions*, vol. ii. p. 461.

Bentham makes no contribution to the science of
personal morality, since his theory "does not
pretend to aid individuals in the formation of
their own character;"[1] and he insists that without an ideal of personal life, "the regulation of
. . . outward actions must be altogether halt-
ing and imperfect."[2]

In such criticism of Bentham's ethical thinking Mill shows a sense of its outwardness and of
its failure to meet the facts of moral experience,
which belongs to his own deepened consciousness of the spiritual significance of conduct.
When he says that Benthamism "will do nothing
. . . for the spiritual interests of society,"[3] he
betrays a consciousness of an ideal which is not
expressed in his hedonism. The mere summation
of pleasures has become in a high degree irrelevant. Mill is thinking of moral life in terms
of an idea of character, to which no justice is
done when it is criticised merely as a means to
the production of pleasant feeling. He expresses,
in this renunciation of Bentham's theory of life,
the demand for a direct relation between the

---

[1] Dissertations and Discussions, vol. i. p. 363.
[2] Ibid., p. 364.   [3] Ibid., p. 365.

moral end and the conduct which realises it. Such a demand — inconsistent with a purely hedonistic theory of the moral criterion, and with the determinism which is natural to such a theory — connects itself with Mill's belief in the reality and importance of voluntary choice, and is fulfilled by a conception of moral goodness as a real quality of self-conscious action.

Mill's idea of conduct as a spiritual function, however he may fail to give it coherent expression, issues in a view of morality which stands in no very positive relation to his hedonism. It betrays itself in the social character of his conception of the moral end, in the extent to which he qualifies his assertion of the worth of pleasure, and in the importance which he attaches to the inward aspect of the moral life. We shall have to see, in the next chapter, how largely these ways of thinking modify the complexion of his utilitarian ethics.

CHAPTER X

THE WORTH OF CONDUCT

It has already been suggested that Hedonism is a theory which makes morality relative to the interests of personal life; and it is especially characteristic of Mill that he emphasises this personal aspect of moral good. His sense of the value of conduct is not diminished by his belief in the possibility of giving a naturalistic account of its development;[1] and, with all his experientialism, he retains the strongest and sanest conviction of the worth of practical ideals.[2] His conception of such ideals, and of the value which they express, makes them relative to the needs of individual persons.

[1] Cf. Autobiography, p. 151.
[2] Cf. Dissertations and Discussions, vol. iii. p. 16.

Against all abstract conceptions of value, and against the materialistic interpretation of it which is more often implied in habits of thought and conduct than theoretically expressed, he maintains the relativity of every kind of good to personal consciousness and experience. Human desire is the source of the value of things: their worth consists in the satisfaction of desire which they afford. The people of a country, for example, " are that for the sake of which its wealth exists;"[1] and social institutions, and economic conditions, are criticised in relation to the good of individuals. Popular, and even scientific, critics of utilitarianism are apt to do but scant justice to the unqualified assertion which the theory makes of the worth of the human interests. Mill yields to no idealist in his magnificent contempt for material things, when these are made to seem more important than the needs of personal life which it is their proper function to satisfy. His economic theory expresses, at every turn, the loftiest humanism, and the most complete disregard of all apparent advantages which do not really benefit individuals.

[1] *Political Economy*, p. 6.

This is the meaning of his suggestion of the need for a criticism of consumption, and for a proper appreciation of the relative value of things. He does not look with unqualified approval on the mere desire of wealth. This "haste to be rich," and the stimulus to production which it gives, are not in themselves good; and they do not even afford any real security for the realisation of ethical or economic ideals. Mill's point of view is that of a moralist, whose humanism teaches him to look below the surface of things, and not to accept blindly the thoughtless estimates either of the populace or of a scientific cult. He sees in the commercial life of England, and in the very mood of its industrial prosperity, an ambition that defeats itself, and a materialism whose doom is already sealed. "In England," he says, "it is not the desire of wealth that needs to be taught, but the use of wealth, and appreciation of the objects of desire which wealth cannot purchase, or for attaining which it is not required. Every real improvement in the character of the English, whether it consists in giving them higher aspirations, or only a juster estimate of the value of their present objects of desire, must necessarily moderate the ardour of their devotion to the pursuit of wealth."[1]

For his own part, he is "not charmed with the ideal of life held out by those who think that the normal state of human beings is that of struggling to get on;"[2] he finds, in the scramble for riches, and all its results, only "the disagreeable symptoms of one of the phases of industrial progress;"[2] and he suggests that "the best state for human nature is that in which, while no one is poor, no one desires to be richer, nor has any reason to fear being thrust back, by the efforts of others to push themselves forward."[2] He admits, indeed, that competition stimulates and increases production; but the mere increase of material wealth does not appear to him to be absolutely or necessarily good. "It is only in the backward countries of the world that increased production is still an important object: in those most advanced, what is economically needed is a better distribution;"[3] and economy in production will only secure real advantages when "civilization and improvement shall have so far advanced, that what is a benefit

---

[1] Political Economy, p. 65. [2] Ibid., p. 453.
[3] Ibid., p. 454.

to the whole shall be a benefit to each individual composing it."[1] Unproductive and not productive use of wealth is the ultimate end of the whole economic process; and it is not the amount but the misapplication of unproductively consumed wealth that calls for criticism.[2] Material wealth is, in fact, of secondary importance for Mill. "A stationary condition of capital and population implies no stationary state of human improvement."[3] On the contrary, the true ends of conduct can all be realised even when purely material progress is not going on. Moral and social advance, and the improvement of the art of living, do not depend on unlimited increase of material wealth; and they are hindered, rather than furthered, by the engrossment of men in "the art of getting on." If men's minds were free from this purely selfish occupation, then, "instead of serving no purpose but the increase of wealth, industrial improvements would produce their legitimate effect, that of abridging human labour."[4] Every economic condition, in fact, depends, for its worth, upon its effect on

---

[1] Political Economy, p. 461. [2] Ibid., pp. 33, 34.
[3] Ibid., p. 454. [4] Ibid., p. 455.

personal life. It is only in virtue of its use by conscious persons that wealth is good; and it is good simply in so far as it lends itself to their purposes.

This conception of value is profoundly ethical. Against the attempt to crush or overshadow the human spirit, or to silence its claims by the worship of outward prosperity and the deification of material wealth, Mill affirms the supreme worth of personal life, and its moral superiority to all impersonal things; and, in this assertion of the personal source of all value, he joins himself to those whose estimate is most worthy of heed. This is the ethical way of conceiving value; and it is this which makes hedonism an ethical theory.

This idea, however, that all worth is relative to personal ends, gives fundamental ethical importance to the mode in which personality is conceived. We have already seen that the degree in which Mill's ethical theory is affected by his individualistic idea of personality commits him to a view of the moral end, which separates it from the acts in which it is realised, and makes it only an external effect of them. This dislocation of the moral end from action leads, as we have seen, to real difficulties within hedonism itself; and a further difficulty arises in the attempt to pass from the egoism, which is involved in the theory that all desire is for personal pleasure, to the universalism of the utilitarian conception of the moral end. Mill partly evades this difficulty by a recognition of the social character of personality, which serves to justify his ethical universalism, but which is not consistent with his attempt to derive morality from an individualistic theory of desire.

While he does not "conceive life to be so rich in enjoyments, that it can afford to forego the cultivation of all those which address themselves to what M. Comte terms the egoistic propensities,"[1] and while he makes pleasure itself a good, Mill yet affirms that enjoyments need to be moralised; and he makes their " moralisation " consist " in cultivating the habitual wish to share them with others, and with all others, and scorning to desire anything for oneself which is incapable of being so shared."[2]

The social conception of morality could not but come naturally to a disciple of Bentham.

[1] Auguste Comte and Positivism, p. 145.   [2] Ibid.

Bentham's "morals" were of a political kind, meant to serve as a basis for legislation; and an ethical system intended primarily to guide the work of a legislator could hardly fail to be determined by the idea of a "common good." But Bentham's conception of conduct was not of a kind that made it possible for him to regard the general happiness as an end or object of desire for the individuals who make up society. It is an end, on his theory, for the community or for the legislator; but it is not desired by individuals; and the function of government is to use penal sanctions of various kinds in such a way as to establish an external connection between the private pleasure of individuals and the general good. The social character of morality is thus conceived by Bentham in a very imperfect way. The common good, or the greatest happiness of the greatest number, is not really made a moral end, because it cannot be desired by the individual agent.

While Mill's recognition of the social character of morality is really a development of Bentham's political or legislative conception of it, he does more than Bentham to justify such a conception, because he regards personal life as itself social, and makes social relationships natural to man. His assertion that the moral end is a common good connects itself with his idea of the individual as a member of society; and this revised idea of the individual, which considers his actual nature to be in some degree the embodiment of social relations, makes the common good a possible object of desire for him. The moralisation of desire — its identification with a common interest—is rendered possible by the pressure of society upon its members, and by the degree in which their nature is formed by their social relations.

"To do as one would be done by, and to love one's neighbour as oneself, constitute the ideal perfection of utilitarian morality;"[1] and the realisation of this ideal morality can be best approached by such a development of social institutions, and of public opinion, as will tend to identify private with general interests.[1] Social interests do not, on Mill's theory, require to be implanted in man artificially. "The deeply rooted conception which every individual even

[1] Utilitarianism, p. 25.

now has of himself as a social being, tends to make him feel it one of his natural wants that there should be harmony between his feelings and aims and those of his fellow-creatures." [1] The "feeling of unity with our fellow-creatures" does indeed require education and cultivation; but it is capable of becoming "as deeply rooted in our character, and to our own consciousness as completely a part of our nature, as the horror of crime is in an ordinarily well-brought-up young person;" [2] and this is possible because it is not an external law but a natural feeling.

This naturalness of the social interests constitutes the possibility of that action for the general good in which morality consists; but, in itself, it is a mere potentiality of moral life; and morality only grows up under the influence of forces which tend to identify public and private good. Society is the great educator of moral life. Its wellbeing depends on the power of unselfish interests: [3] its very existence is only possible by a discipline of selfish propensities "which consists in subordinating them to a common system of

---

[1] Utilitarianism, p. 50.   [2] Ibid., p. 40.
[3] Representative Government, p. 29.

opinions;"[1] and this dependence of society upon the power of combined action, which its members have, makes its development a growth in individuals of those qualities which unite their interests, so that "there is not a more accurate test of the progress of civilization than the progress of the power of co-operation."[2] The qualities which social life requires are thus wrought into the characters of men; and the exigencies of society produce such a development of their personal aptitudes that "what is lost in the separate efficiency of each, is far more than made up by the greater capacity of united action. In proportion as they put off the qualities of the savage, they become amenable to discipline; capable of adhering to plans concerted beforehand, and about which they may not have been consulted: of subordinating their individual caprice to a preconceived determination, and performing severally the parts allotted to them in a combined undertaking."[3] Civilisation is, in fact, "a struggle against the animal instincts."[4]

---

[1] Logic, p. 605.

[2] Dissertations and Discussions, vol. i. p. 165.

[3] Political Economy, p. 423.   [4] Ibid., p. 226.

This effect of social life upon the moral tendencies is largely due to the power of public opinion. The "feeling of unity with our fellow-creatures" shows itself in sensitiveness and responsiveness to their esteem. "All experience shows that the mass of mankind never judge of moral questions for themselves, never see anything to be right or wrong until they have been frequently told it." [1] The modern civilised man finds much of the work of moral judgment "done to his hand," [2] and inherits an experience on which "all the prudence, as well as all the morality of life, is dependent." [2] Bentham's underestimate of this accumulated experience is an aspect of his individualism which Mill singles out for criticism; [3] and Mill himself is keenly aware of its importance. Not only "when it succeeds in enforcing a servile conformity to itself," [4] but still more when it forms a steadying pressure against reforming zeal, the public opinion which embodies the traditions and experiences of hu-

[1] Political Economy, p. 226.
[2] Utilitarianism, p. 34.
[3] Dissertations and Discussions, vol. i. pp. 351, 352.
[4] Representative Government, p. 207, cf. p. 116.

manity is a powerful and wholesome influence upon character.[1] Society corrects, by this and other means, the one-sidedness of individuals;[2] and all interaction with others, whether within or beyond the limits of a single nationality, develops a breadth of character and interests, by which individuals are redeemed from their isolation, and the idea of a common good is made possible.[3] Both by the activities which its relations produce, and by the opinions and feelings which arise out of its needs, social life tends to identify the felt interests of each individual with those of others.

This moral power of society is so essential an element in its very nature, that Mill makes the moral effect of social institutions a test of their worth. "Human beings owe to each other help to distinguish the better from the worse, and encouragement to choose the former and avoid the latter. They should be for ever stimulating each other to increased exercise of their higher faculties, and increased direction of their feelings and aims towards wise instead of foolish, elevat-

---

[1] Representative Government, p. 207; cf. p. 116.
[2] Ibid., p. 300.   [3] Cf. Political Economy, pp. 351, 352.

ing instead of degrading, objects and pursuits." [1]
Even when Mill is most sceptical of the possibility of giving moral help, and most critical of
undue interference, he never suggests that the
claim of human beings on the moral support of
their fellows is less valid than any of their other
rights.   It is thus not surprising that he makes
the moral effect of social relations the main
criterion of their value.

This, for example, is one of his chief arguments
for a reform of marriage laws and of the relations
which they regulate.   No doubt much of Mill's
contention in this matter is a demand for " better
bread than can be made of wheat ; " and many of
his suggestions indicate, not so much a serious
appreciation of the facts of the case, as the im-
patience of that untold and tragic yearning for a
perfected human life, which lends so much of
pathos and dignity to his intellectual work.   But
however little he may be thought to contribute
to the actual question of what is or is not
involved in the distinction of sex, there is no
mistaking the ground on which he argues for
legal equality of married persons, as " the only

---

[1] Liberty, p. 44.

means of rendering the daily life of mankind, in any high sense, a school of moral cultivation." [1] He demands a reform of the relation of men and women, because he sees how much that relation means for the moral health of society: because family life determines the moral directions of men, the position of woman, which gives family life its character and its power for good or evil, has an importance which Mill finds it impossible to overrate. The main significance of the whole question, for him, is in the effect of the marriage relation upon character, and in the special power, which that relation has, of forming and developing moral ideas. [2]

In the same way, the value of all other social arrangements consists in their moral usefulness: their justification is their tendency to make the common good the interest of individuals. Penal laws exist in order to enforce that conduct which is for the general advantage; [3] and their legitimacy depends, for Mill, upon their serving this

---

[1] Subjection of Women, p. 78.
[2] Cf. Subjection of Women, esp. pp. 79-82, 148-152, 159, 177-180.
[3] Political Economy. p. 583.

purpose. "The proper end of government" is to reduce the waste of energy occasioned by injurious conduct, so that the whole efforts of mankind may be "turned to the legitimate employment of the human faculties, that of compelling the powers of nature to be more and more subservient to physical and moral good."[1] The protection which society affords to its members and their interests is valuable chiefly as the condition on which alone the development of industry and frugality is possible.[2] "Insecurity of person and property, is as much as to say, uncertainty of the connection between all human exertion or sacrifice, and the attainment of the ends for which they are undergone;"[3] and the obligation of society to enforce security arises from the fatal effect which this uncertainty has upon the development of character. The State is thus a moral institution. Its function is to maintain those conditions in which character can develop.

Mill's faith in democracy is rooted in the same moral idea of the value of institutions. It belongs to his conviction that society ought to

---

[1] Political Economy, p. 591.   [2] Ibid., p. 422.

[3] Ibid., p. 531.

serve the moral interests of its members; and it expresses his belief in the educative effect of popular government, rather than any blind confidence in the wisdom or goodness of the masses. The worth of popular institutions consists largely in their tendency to make each member of society "feel himself one of the public, and whatever is for their benefit to be for his benefit."[1]   They are a "school of public spirit;"[1] and without them the development of character cannot be complete.

Moral life cannot be perfected in isolation: no matter how well able the individual may be to conduct his life in solitude, the highest moral excellence is only possible for him as a member of society; and "the aim of improvement should be not solely to place human beings in a condition in which they will be able to do without one another, but to enable them to work with or for one another in relations not involving dependence."[2]   The effect of a state of society upon character is "in itself the most interesting phenomenon which that state of society

---

[1] Representative Government, p. 68.

[2] Political Economy, p. 461.

can possibly present;"[1] for there are certain
personal qualities which can only be developed
in society; and these, on the utilitarian theory,
are of the very essence of morality. The value
of social life is thus ethical—it consists in an
effect on character: society has its "perfect
work" in producing those moral qualities which
cannot exist apart from it and on which its
own stability depends. The end of society is
realised in the production of that type of character which is fitted for social life — in the
identification of the interests of individuals
with the general good.

Mill's theory of the relation of morality to
social life thus forms a highly important element
in his ethics. It constitutes a real advance upon
Bentham's external way of conceiving the relation; and it suggests, although not in a way
altogether consistent with Mill's explicit theory
of desire, how a common good or general happiness may come to be desired by individuals.
It is of more importance, however, for understanding Mill's ethical theory, to observe that
the way in which he connects the moral life

[1] *Logic*, p. 590.

with society modifies his hedonism in two respects.

In the first place, the moral standard, in reference to which Mill criticises social conditions,
is not strictly hedonistic. Too much, certainly,
might be made of this point; since it may be
argued that, while the tendency of social conditions to promote good character is the best
criterion of their value, the goodness of character itself is determined by its hedonic worth.
While, however, this objectivity of the standard
actually applied by Mill-to social relations does
not, I think, warrant us in suggesting that he
abandons the hedonistic point of view, it is yet
not without interest. It indicates at least that
other, and more objective, criteria can be applied
to the phenomena in question more readily than
the hedonistic standard; and it leads naturally
to the conclusion that good character is related,
in no merely external way, to the moral end.

It is still more important, however, to remark
that Mill's whole assertion, that the moral end
must be a " common good," contains the admission (which, indeed, he explicitly makes) that
pleasure requires " moralisation " — that mere

satisfaction does not realise the moral end, but that the very idea of morality requires a criticism of desires.

Mill is, in fact, aware of the slight extent to which men's actual desires afford them moral guidance, and of the inadequacy of their subjective feelings as a clue to their real good. He recognises that "life could not go on if it were not admitted that impulses must be controlled, and that reason ought to govern our actions;"[1] and he maintains that "the duty of man is the same in respect to his own nature as in respect to the nature of all other things, namely, not to follow but to amend it."[2] Inclinations cannot be assumed to be a safe guide for conduct: they "may be the expression not of the divine will, but of the fetters which impede its free action; and to take hints from these for the guidance of our own conduct may be falling into a trap laid by the enemy."[3]

The actual desires of men do not, in fact, represent their real needs : the greatest misfortunes —such as "ignorance and want of culture"—are

[1] Essays on Religion, p. 45.   [2] Ibid., p. 54.
[3] Ibid., p. 55.

P

those "of which the persons suffering from them
are apt to be least aware."[1] The real value of
things is not always represented in the desire
felt for them. There are things "of the worth of
which the demand of the market is by no means
a test; things of which the utility does not consist in ministering to inclinations, nor in serving
the daily uses of life, and the want of which is
least felt where the need is greatest. This is
peculiarly true of those things which are chiefly
useful as tending to raise the character of human
beings. The uncultivated cannot be competent
judges of cultivation. Those who most need to
be made wiser and better, usually desire it least,
and if they desired it, would be incapable of finding the way to it by their own lights."[2] The
utility which Mill makes his moral principle is
"utility in the largest sense, grounded on the
permanent interests of a man as a progressive
being."[3]

This sense of the limitations of subjective feeling as a guide for conduct determines one of
Mill's most significant differences from Bentham.

[1] Dissertations and Discussions, vol. i. p. 28.
[2] Political Economy, p. 575.   [3] Liberty, p. 6.

Bentham had denied all qualitative distinction between pleasures: pleasures differed, for him, only in quantity—in their intensity, that is to say, and in their duration. They differed also, when regarded as motives, in their nearness or remoteness, and their certainty or uncertainty. Considered as furnishing a criterion for conduct, they could also be compared in respect of their tendency to be followed by pleasant and not to be followed by painful feelings—their fecundity and purity; and when they were considered in relation to a number or community of persons, it became necessary to ask by how many they could be enjoyed. But all this is, for Bentham, a purely quantitative estimate of pleasure.[1]

Mill, on the other hand, maintains that "it is quite compatible with the principle of utility to recognise the fact, that some *kinds* of pleasure are more desirable and more valuable than others."[2] "It would be absurd," he says, "that ... the estimation of pleasures should be supposed to depend on quantity alone."[3] He points to the fact that "there is no known Epicurean

[1] Bentham's Principles of Morals and Legislation, chap. iv.
[2] Utilitarianism, p. 11.   [3] Ibid., p. 12.

theory of life which does not assign to the pleasures of the intellect, of the feelings and imagination, and of the moral sentiments, a much higher value as pleasures than to those of mere sensation;"[1] and he asserts that "the feelings and judgment of the experienced" "declare the pleasures derived from the higher faculties to be preferable *in kind*, apart from the question of intensity, to those of which the animal nature, disjoined from the higher faculties, is susceptible."[2] This reference to the "feelings and judgment of the experienced" is Mill's ground for the distinction between "higher" and "lower" pleasures, and for the preference which the very act of distinguishing them gives to the higher. "On a question," he says, "which is the best worth having of two pleasures, or which of two modes of existence is the most grateful to the feelings, apart from its moral attributes and from its consequences, the judgment of those who are qualified by knowledge of both, or, if they differ, that of the majority among them, must be admitted as final."[3] He asserts that only those whose higher

---

[1] Utilitarianism, p. 11.　　　[2] Ibid., p. 16.　　　[3] Ibid., p. 15.

faculties have been trained are capable of estimating the relative value of different kinds of
pleasure; and he commits the judgment of the
worth of things to the wise and good so completely that it would not " be easy, even for an
unbeliever, to find a better translation of the rule
of virtue from the abstract into the concrete,
than to endeavour so to live that Christ would
approve our life."[1]

The mode in which Mill proposes to test the
relative value of different classes of pleasure
suggests the real nature of those distinctions of
kind which he asserts to exist among them. It
indicates that he is serious in distinguishing
those differences of kind from any merely quantitative variations such as Bentham's theory had
considered: it implies that pleasures are distinguished by another criterion than that of pleasantness alone.

It is hardly possible to suspect Mill of author-
ising one man to judge what is actually most
pleasant for another. In respect of their mere
pleasantness to him, each man must be allowed
to be the best judge of his own enjoyments: so

[1] Essays on Religion, p. 255.

much of liberty can hardly be refused even to
the most foolish; and if the saint or the sage
professed to compare the pleasantness of higher
and lower enjoyments, he might lay himself open
to the retort that he did not adequately appreciate
the joys of cock-fighting or alcoholic intoxication.
The " experienced " have, indeed, no special authority to pronounce impartially upon the pleasantness of different feelings; for it is the very privi-
lege of virtue not to crave for vice, and not to
desire its joys.   The authority of the wise is in a
different sphere.   Mill's appeal to their judgment
is indeed not to be gainsaid : it has its credentials
not only in Plato and Aristotle, and in Stoicism,
but, under more or less disguise, in all ethical
theory that keeps contact with the issues of the
moral life ; it expresses the human personal
quality of all moral judgment, which has no value
as a dead code but only as a living intuition.
But the judgment of the experienced applies
to pleasure only because pleasure is not what
hedonism sometimes takes it to be—an isolated
mental state, unrelated to personal qualities, and
capable of being fully calculated in time and
intensity.   The judgment of the wise, and indeed

the moral judgment, applies to pleasures in
respect not of their mere pleasantness, but of
other relations from which their moral significance is really derived: it applies to them as
satisfactions of desire, or as results of conduct,
and, in either case, as related to the character
which action and desire express.

This is implied in Mill's own contention that the
judgment of the wise approves the type of character which is also that required for the general
happiness:[1] it is not a set of pleasures, but a
kind of person, that is preferred by " the feelings
and judgment of the experienced;" and the preference is thus not simply hedonistic.   The same
view of the distinction of kind among pleasures
is conveyed in Mill's insistence on the relativity
of pleasures to character and faculty;[2] and it is
even more evident in the judgment that "it is
better to be a human being dissatisfied than a pig
satisfied; better to be Socrates dissatisfied than a
fool satisfied."[3]   In such a statement, "better,"
plainly, does not mean more pleasant.   The idea of
pleasure or happiness as the end has given place
to a criterion of another kind.   The desire that

[1] *Utilitarianism*, p. 16.   [2] Ibid., p. 11.   [3] Ibid., p. 14.

is satisfied by the "sense of dignity" or personal worth is a desire that depends on the individual's consciousness of himself as a moral agent and a member of society.[1]

The same sense of the inadequacy of simple hedonism determines Mill's assertion of the necessity for estimating conduct in its "æsthetic" and "sympathetic," as well as in its "moral" or utilitarian aspect.[2] He criticises Bentham's omission, from his theory of conduct, of all regard for anything except its outward consequences; and he insists on the applicability of other criteria, which express the worth of conduct in relation, not to its consequences, but to the character from which it proceeds.

The actual development, then, of Mill's ethical theory makes large inroads upon his official hedonism. His universalistic conception of the moral end, and his recognition of a distinction of kind among pleasures, are two qualifications of his general theory of moral good, which are identical in principle, and which are inconsistent no less with the logical use than

---

[1] Utilitarianism, p. 13; cf. p. 18.

[2] Dissertations and Discussions. vol. i. pp. 386-388.

with the psychological basis of the hedonistic
criterion.

In regarding the "greatest happiness of the
greatest number" as the end which should determine conduct, he makes the moral good of the
individual agent consist not in the enjoyment
but in the production of pleasure; and, however
much he may be disposed to believe in the actual
coincidence of private and general happiness, he
does not hesitate, in case of conflict, to make the
common good the criterion of conduct.   This,
however, is to make the moral good of the
individual consist, not in a state of feeling, but in
a kind of activity or personal character.   Similarly, the distinction of kind among pleasures
depends upon their relation to the objective life
of character; and by this distinction, and by the
non-hedonistic preference of higher to lower
pleasures, the good, whether of single individuals
or of the greatest number, is made to consist not
in pleasure or satisfaction but in qualities of
personal life.   This conception of the moral end
derives no support from the doctrine that only
pleasure is desired; it may rather be said to be
inconsistent with that doctrine, and to depend

for its legitimacy upon a less abstract notion of desire.

The far-reaching qualification of hedonism, which is conveyed in making the moral end for individuals a common good, and in establishing qualitative differences among pleasures, is fatal also to that logical use of the hedonistic principle, as a moral calculus, which largely determined Mill's belief in its scientific value. If moral good depends upon character, and if their relation to character determines the worth of pleasures themselves, then the detail of the moral life cannot be regulated by mere calculation of pleasant feelings in the abstract.

We have already seen that it is this conception of moral good, as a state of character, which Mill actually employs as a criterion of economic conditions and of social institutions; and the same idea of the moral end determines his appreciation of individuality and independence of character. He regards strength of disposition and character as itself a good. "Desires and impulses are as much a part of a perfect human being, as beliefs and restraints;" [1] and "strong impulses are but

[1] *Liberty*, p. 35.

another name for energy."[1] The vigorous and
active character is not only <u>most powerful for
good as well as for evil,</u> but is also that which is
most likely to develop breadth of interests, and
the capacity for adapting itself to the conditions,
of life:[2] it is "not only intrinsically the best, but
is the likeliest to acquire all that is really excellent or desirable in the opposite type."[3]

The worth of individuality thus consists in its
being <u>the condition of self-development</u>; and the
supreme value of character is also the reason why
"mankind are greater gainers by suffering each
other to live as seems good to themselves, than
by compelling each to live as seems good to the
rest."[4] Mill's belief that, "among the works of
man, . . . the first in importance surely is man
himself,"[5] is the motive that leads him to defend
that "circle around every individual human
being, which no government, be it that of one, of
a few, or of the many, ought to be permitted to
overstep."[6] Interference with the liberty of any
human being is only warranted by the interests

[1] Liberty, p. 35.   [2] Representative Government, pp. 60 ff.
[3] Ibid., p. 63.   [4] Liberty, p. 8.   [5] Ibid., p. 34.
[6] Political Economy, p. 569.

of others: it is justified because "all that makes existence valuable to any one, depends on the enforcement of restraints upon the actions of other people;"[1] and its limits are set by the same ethical principle from which it derives its authority. Wherever no interests but those of the agent are involved, interference with freedom of action becomes not only needless but hurtful;[2] for "human nature is not a machine to be built after a model, and set to do exactly the work prescribed for it, but a tree, which requires to grow and develop itself on all sides, according to the tendency of the inward forces which make it a living thing."[3] The character of each individual member of society is not simply a means to social prosperity, and a part of the social whole: it is this, but it is also itself a whole, with its own laws and qualities, and its own ends determined by these. On this account, "if a person possesses any tolerable amount of common-sense and experience, his own mode of laying out his existence is the best, not

---

[1] Liberty, p. 3.

[2] Cf. Liberty, esp. pp. 3 ff. and pp. 32 ff.; Political Economy, p. 569.

[3] Liberty, p. 34.

because it is the best in itself, but because it is his own mode." [1] /

Liberty is, indeed, defended by Mill on hedon-istic grounds. Differences of individual tempera-ment must condition differences in the sources of pleasure, and each man is therefore likely to be best able to secure his own happiness; [2] freedom itself, too, is the most essential of human satis-factions, and nothing can compensate for its absence; [3] but the chief moral necessity for it consists in the fact that all development and all individuality of personal character depend upon it; [4] and it is because these are threatened, by the despotism of government and public opinion, that Mill insists on the need for "a great social support for ideas and opinions different from those of the mass." [5]

Mill's argument for liberty, vitiated as it may

---

[1] Liberty, p. 39 ; cf. Subjection of Women, pp. 159 ff.

[2] Liberty, p. 40.

[3] Cf. Subjection of Women, p. 178 and p. 182 ; Political Economy, pp. 129 ff.

[4] Political Economy, p. 570 ; Liberty, esp. pp. 36, 37, and 41 ; Representative Government, p. 48.

[5] Dissertations and Discussions, vol. ii. p. 73 ; cf. vol. i. pp. 188, 380.

be in some respects by an abstract individualism, is thus, in the main, a claim for all possible
freedom of action, on the ground that such freedom affords the only hope of moral development.
His conviction of the worth of human personality is the idea which guides that sober strenuous liberalism, of which he is the philosopher
as well as the "saint."[1]   He sees, in human
character and conduct, possibilities of worth such
as belong to nothing else; and with magnificent
hopefulness, he regards these possibilities as the
promise of a perfect life in a perfect society: he
finds in their development the highest human
task, and in their realisation the supreme good.

Such realisation, however, is not to be brought
about by external forces and influences: it can
only come as a spontaneous growth from within.
All that can be done to develop character from
without is to remove the obstructions that arise
from bad conditions, physical or moral.   In itself
the realisation of the moral end—the perfecting
of personal life—must be self-realisation: it can

[1] "I used familiarly to call him the Saint of Rationalism,"—
Mr Gladstone, in a letter quoted in Mr W. L. Courtney's 'Life
of John Stuart Mill,' p. 142.

be nothing else; for character cannot be manufactured, and its perfection is essentially its own growth.

Mill is therefore one of those who find in personal life, rightly understood, its own law. He regards the self-development of character as the moral end. We have seen by what vague and partly incoherent hints he suggests this conclusion; but it is a conclusion which at all events represents his real ethics better than the hedonism, which is generally regarded as his theory of moral good. His modifications of the doctrine that pleasure is the end of conduct are so large and so significant as to deprive that doctrine of any consistent influence on his thinking. His idea of self-consciousness and its relation to character does not, indeed, authorise any ethical theory which asserts the inner unity of conduct with its end; but it is hardly possible to avoid suggesting that "self-realisation" is the most fitting interpretation for utility "grounded on the permanent interests of a man as a progressive being."

CHAPTER XI

MILL'S intellectual work is so deeply influenced by philosophical ideas, that it is surprising to discover how little of a metaphysician he really is. He never raises metaphysical problems independently, and on their own account; and, even in his logical discussions, he takes pains to evade metaphysical issues whenever he can do so. His interest is in the concrete relations of things, rather than in their ultimate meaning; and metaphysical construction is alien to his mental habit. There are probably few other thinkers whose intellectual attitude is so directly dependent upon philosophical theories, and who have, at the same time, done so little in the way of discussing philosophical principles.

This is all the more singular because Mill's speculation contains two elements which raise the problem of metaphysic in the most definite way. It develops, on the one hand, the idea of an order of natural relations, and, on the other hand, a real sense of practical and moral interests. Now these are the two leading factors in the metaphysical problem; and the extent to which they occupy Mill's mind makes his abstinence from metaphysical discussion hard to be understood.

In the first place, Mill's consciousness of an order of nature is more than nominal. There is nothing to invalidate it in his "psychological" conception of matter, as merely "permanent possibilities of sensation"; and, while it is not easy to see how the idea of a system of natural relations can be reconciled with the doctrine that causality is only invariable or unvarying sequence, yet the conception of the causal relation which underlies Mill's theory of Induction — that of unconditional dependence — defines, as well as asserts, the reality of nature. Mill entertains and investigates the idea of the natural order, which the explanations of physical science imply: his theory of Induction expresses that conception of Nature which makes it objective and capable of being known.

It is still more significant, as a motive for metaphysical speculation, that, for Mill, man himself, no less than the conditions of his life, is part of the natural order, and a real object of knowledge: the fact that human knowledge and conduct form his main topic implies the presence in his theory of metaphysical issues; and their presence is all the more obvious because he discusses the value as well as the nature of mental facts.

His consciousness of nature, as a system of objective relations, and of man's place within that system, does nothing to weaken his ideal interests, or to impair his sense of the moral issues that are involved in human character and conduct. " It is only to a very vulgar type of mind," he says, " that a grand or beautiful object loses its charm when it loses some of its mystery, through the unveiling of a part of the process by which it is created in the secret recesses of Nature."[1] He recognises that the notion, "that

<hr/>

[1] Dissertations and Discussions, vol. iii. p. 111.

no causes can give rise to products of a more precious or elevated kind than themselves," "is at variance with the known analogies of Nature."[1] He distinguishes sharply, too, between the natural and the moral order; and he does not allow the actual or "natural" relations or things to fashion his idea of the relations that ought to obtain. The claims of ideal interests have never found a more convinced or more strenuous advocate than Mill of their validity and independence.

Now, the ideal interests and the effort that they symbolise are the chief motive of philosophy: philosophy depends on the unceasing contest between human intelligence and the dulness of earthly fact. In whatever degree all the details of human life may have been fashioned by the forces and pressures of nature, it is yet never without determination by the consciousness of ideals; and because it is, in this way, an effort, it is also an enigma. He who "seeks a country" must "confess that he is a stranger." The earth is a riddle to man, just in proportion as his affections are "set on things above." The world

[1] *Essays on Religion*, p. 152.

suggests a good that it does not realise; it
rouses anticipations that it does not satisfy; and
so it becomes a problem. The fact that Mill
recognises the ideal as well as the natural aspect
of things might lead us to expect more interest
in this problem that he actually shows.

All theory is based on practice. Our traffic
with the world gives us experiences and defines
our wants; and, both to satisfy our wants and
to combine our experiences, we are impelled to
theorise. Our conduct burdens us with the need
of asking what things are, or how they behave.
We ask these questions about the things that we
have to do with; and the answers that we find
make up the sciences of these things.

But the fact that experience comes to us in the
course of an effort imposes on us the necessity
of asking a further question about things—of
asking not only what they are but also what
they mean. It must not be supposed that this,
which is the problem of philosophy, can be
separated in any absolute sense from that inquiry into the nature of things which is prose-
cuted by the special sciences. The investigation
of the meaning of things implies that there is

a meaning which is positively and objectively theirs, and which is not a mere play of fancy on their surface. Philosophy assumes that things form in themselves an intelligible unity; and its problem is to discover the principle on which this unity depends. That meaning of things which philosophy investigates is thus not alien to their nature: it is simply the things themselves, understood in their fulness, or in the system of their relations to one another. On the other hand, in so far as the special sciences investigate certain abstracted elements or aspects of reality, they are prevented from giving a complete account of things: their function is to analyse things, and to express them in terms of their parts; but mere analysis can never give a complete explanation—for, even if carried to the furthest extent, it cannot render things perfectly intelligible. The meaning of things is their relation to the system to which they belong; and they can only be explained in terms of the principle by which that system is determined. Ultimate explanation is not of the whole by the parts, but of the part by the whole.

The demand for this kind of explanation, and with it the problem of philosophy, originates in the fact that experience is conditioned by activity and by the attempt to realise ideals. It is from these that experience derives its meaning: in proportion as it lends itself to them, it is significant; and in proportion as it fails to realise them, it is a problem which impels us to philosophise. In man's consciousness of ideals, and in the effort wherein he daily disowns anew that supremacy over him which things seem to claim, is the motive of his wonder — the mystery of his fate. For if personal life culminates in ideals, they limit even while they affirm its worth. They are our only clue to the explanation of reality; but, even while we affirm ourselves in them, in them also we become aware of our inadequacy — of the very partial and limited character of that satisfaction which we are in a position to demand. They assert, even while they seem to abrogate, human finitude. They affirm that man has a meaning for himself; but none the less clearly do they mark the fact that that meaning is partly hid from him; and so they generate philosophy.

The singleness of conscious life determines us to look for system in the world of our experiences: we inevitably demand system; our search for it is expressed in our ideas of worth; and the failure of things, as we know them, to correspond to these ideas— our inability to discern system in things—impels us in two directions.

In the first place, we cannot but objectify our ideal conceptions. The demands that we make upon things possess for us a reality which is in a certain sense greater than that of anything else. The system, of which these demands express our consciousness, is a necessity of thought. Failing to find it in the world of our experiences, we make it an object in itself; and we do so the more inevitably the more our search for it is foiled in things. The idea of it rouses feelings in us, impels us to activities, determines our relation to the objects of our knowledge. Religious experience knows it, and names it "God." Thinking it in terms of our ideals, and of whatever experiences answer best to them, and most inevitably in terms of that self-consciousness which determines our demand for it, we set it over against the things that

fail to belong to our idea of it. Faith becomes
" the evidence of things not seen ": the unyield-
ing strength of our demand upon nature compels
us to the recognition of a reality which—for us,
at least—the world does not altogether contain.

But this attitude, inevitable as it may be, is
not the whole effect of our attempt to unify
experience. System remains not only the object
of religious faith, but also a problem ; and the
making it a problem is what constitutes philosophy. Philosophy is a search for system in the
world of real things. We may, or we may not,
believe that we fully know the principle that
determines things. Perhaps philosophy means
that we do not; " for that which a man seeth
why doth he yet hope for ? " But only in so
far as we are in search of a principle in reality
can we be said to philosophise. Philosophy must
always be the effort to think things as a unity,
or to find in them that system which our ideal
demands upon reality in some degree express.
To abandon the idea of system is to abandon
philosophy itself; and the system that philosophy seeks is a system of real relations.

It appears, then, that the problem of philo-

sophy, while in a sense it expresses nothing but
reason's own nature, and the inevitable demand
for a corresponding system, does, at the same
time, arise from a deep-seated contradiction. It
has its roots in the opposition of human personality to the world of nature. It originates in
the antithesis of worth and fact, of that which
ought to be and that which actually is. Now
this opposition, which belongs to the very texture
of experience, since experience is essentially an
attempt to discern unity in things, is most
obvious in the relation of moral life to the
conditions in which it must be realised. The
opposition is indeed evident in all knowledge, so
long as the failure of things to appear as a consistent unity rouses a sense of contradictions
that must be resolved; but it is more definitely
apparent in the antagonism between the purely
theoretic view of things and the practical way
of regarding them as means to an end; and it
grows into an acute contrast, when the single
subject-matter of human conduct is made the
topic, at once of a science which regards it simply
as experienced fact, to be theoretically explained,
and of judgments which criticise it in relation to

an end or law which it ought to realise. The problem of philosophy is thus more directly raised by the opposition of the ethical and psychological conceptions of conduct than by any other form of dualism; and the impossibility of evading this problem specially reveals itself in the vital connection which exists between the terms of the opposition in question.

On the one hand, Psychology — the study of actual human conduct — involves the ethical point of view. The implication of selfhood in mental states can only be understood ethically. Their existence, their positive and special nature, is determined by their relation to the freedom or self-distinction of personal life; but this is only intelligible or real in relation to the end or law which ideally determines it; and it is thus more evident in the case of mental phenomena than of any others that they are only understood when they are conceived in relation to an end. Until they are so conceived, they remain what we call "mere" phenomena—appearances and not reality.

On the other hand, it is nowhere more plain than in the moral judgment of conduct that ends

only maintain their character as ends, in virtue
of their relation to the positive nature of things.
Teleology implies, as Lotze and Wundt show, an
absolute causal sequence in the world of events:
" a universe which had no necessary connections
between its parts could have no definite or significant structure as a whole." [1] In the case of ethics,
it is specially evident that selfhood, freedom, and
conformity to moral law can only be significant
or intelligible in relation to those mental facts
which they characterise. Every ethical system
involves a psychology of conduct, and depends
for its development upon its idea of what conduct actually is. The possibility of a science of
ethics depends upon the discovery, in human
character, of elements that can be made the
means to a realisation of the moral end; and the
denial of such elements invalidates the moral
judgment: an ethic without psychology "swims
in the air." The actual and the ideal aspects of
conduct are thus related no less by mutual implication than by mere antithesis: whichever we
may attempt to isolate involves us in the other.
The problem of philosophy, regarded as the in-

[1] Mr Bosanquet's Logic, vol. ii. p. 82.

terpretation of experience, is nowhere forced upon us more definitely or more persistently than in the relations of psychology and ethics.

Mill's abstinence from metaphysical discussion is thus something of an anomaly. He is mainly occupied with ethical and psychological questions; he is by no means unaware of the radical distinction between the points of view which determine them; he is concerned with the practical difficulties which are involved in that distinction; and, both in the acceptance and in the partial surrender of his heritage of individualism, he is deeply influenced by metaphysical theories. His neglect of the metaphysical problem demands explanation.

It has already been suggested that this absence of purely metaphysical discussion is simply the negative aspect of Mill's naturalism, and belongs, in this way, to the practical aim and character of his intellectual work. It belongs hardly less to other qualities of his mind — to the sobriety which characterises his speculative more perhaps than his practical tendencies — to his freedom from that craving for systematic unity and completeness which he finds to be so fatally conspicuous in the dogmatic Positivism of Comte.[1] It connects itself, too, we may suppose, with the absence of all religious elements from his early education. He is "one of the very few examples, in this country, of one who has, not thrown off religious belief, but never had it;"[2] and his attitude towards religious problems gives the impression of a sincere but unsuccessful attempt to understand the religious consciousness. This absence from his mind of the religious idea has real significance for his conception of philosophy. His view of religion suggests, in a striking way, his limitations in this respect.

Mill does not, indeed, maintain a consistent notion of what religious experience essentially is. He wavers, as Mr Morley shows,[3] between the idea that religion implies a supernatural object, and the view that its demands are capable of being satisfied within the known order of things: he does not decide between the idealisation and the abandonment of earthly life. He wavers no less between the notion that religion

[1] Auguste Comte and Positivism, esp. pp. 15 and 141.
[2] Autobiography, p. 43.
[3] Critical Miscellanies, 2d Series (1877), pp. 296 ff.

is simply ethical, and the conception of it as a knowledge or experience that reflects the presence of a real object; and he makes, indeed he attempts, no synthesis of these elements in the religious consciousness.

On the one hand, he finds "the essence of religion" in "strong and earnest direction of the emotions and desires towards an ideal object, recognised as of the highest excellence, and as rightfully paramount over all selfish objects of desire;"[1] and he sees "the principal worth of all religions whatever" in the "ideal conception of a Perfect Being" to which men may "habitually refer as the guide of their conscience."[2] But this idea of religion, as an imaginative or poetic reflection upon ideals of personal and especially of moral life, is replaced in Mill's polemical criticism of Hamilton and Mansel by a different conception of it. We find him regarding it as an experience of facts, or a way of conceiving the nature of things. "Whatever relates to God," he says, "I hold to be matter of inference; I would add, of inference *à posteriori*."[3] He maintains,

---

[1] Essays on Religion, p. 109.   [2] Autobiography, p. 46.
[3] Examination of Hamilton, p. 47.

against Hamilton's Agnosticism, the possibility of knowing God positively as "a concrete reality."[1] He asserts that the denial of all knowledge of God depends upon a deliberate abstraction from positive and known facts. He contends that God is known, not indeed "in himself," but just as men and nature are known, relatively or phenomenally, "by his action on the creation, as known through my senses and my rational faculty."[2]

Mill's contention that "all proofs of religion, natural or revealed, must be derived either from the testimony of the senses, or from internal feelings of the mind, or from reasonings of which one or other of these sources supplied the premises,"[3] leads him to a conception of religion as itself a theory, and capable of complete theoretic expression. It becomes, for him, simply an opinion, capable of proof and disproof; and his humanistic idea of it is replaced by a set of arguments which result in a somewhat vague and insecure Deism. In this less ethical development of his theory of religion, he regards God primarily

---

[1] Examination of Hamilton, p. 60.
[2] Ibid., p. 125.   [3] Ibid., p. 168.

as the Author of Nature; he makes an individualistic separation of the divine life from the ideal
experiences of men; and he leaves the validity of
religious experience wholly problematic, as indeed
such a conception of it must inevitably do.

In this mode of conceiving religious experience,
Mill accepts the traditions of his English predecessors. His whole idea of the way in which
religion is to be authenticated recalls Berkeley's
more mystical notion of a "Visible God"—a God
whose very nature is revealed in the facts of the
world and the order in which they affect us. The
method, too, of his inquiry into religion has a good
deal in common with that of Paley's much less
critical investigation. Mill is not, indeed, directed
from the outset, as Paley is, by a preconceived
notion of the conclusion to be reached. His
argument is more free and less conclusive than
that of the famous 'Natural Theology.' But in
Mill's Essays on "Nature" and "Theism," just
as in Paley's work, there is an attempt to base
the idea of God entirely upon a study of his
doings in the world; and it is significant of
this agreement in method that both Paley and
Mill exalt that teleological proof which "is the

oldest, the clearest, and that most in conformity with the common reason of humanity." [1]

Now, this attempt to make the idea of God represent simply the facts of nature must be admitted to have real validity and usefulness as a theological method. On the other hand, it is apt to involve neglect of the special interest and point of view of the religious consciousness; and, as a matter of fact, Mill fails to investigate the idea that determines religious experience. He identifies religion alternately with morality and with purely cognitive results; and he never shows how it is to be distinguished from these: he gives no account of the "form" which characterises every detail of religious doctrine and practice. Where he makes religion merely an imaginative treatment of morality, he treats the idea of God as accidental, and external to religion; and he is thus left to conceive moral experience, on the one hand, and, on the other, the idea of God attested by natural facts, in a mutual isolation, which deprives both of any definitely religious character.

---

[1] Kant's Critique of Pure Reason (Meiklejohn's trans.), p. 383; cf. Mill's Essays on Religion, pp. 139, 174, 175.

R

The same indifference to the metaphysical
interest, which appears in Mill's failure to investigate the idea of God, is illustrated also by
his neglect of the distinction between science
and philosophy. Philosophy, he tells us, is "the
scientific knowledge of Man as an intellectual,
moral, and social being;"[1] and "the philosophy
of a Science thus comes to mean the science
itself, considered not as to its results, the truths
which it ascertains, but as to the processes by
which the mind attains them, the marks by
which it recognises them, and the co-ordinating
and methodising of them with a view to the
greatest clearness of conception and the fullest
and readiest availability for use: in one word,
the logic of the science."[1] Now this is a view
of philosophy which entirely fails to distinguish
it from analytical science: it reduces philosophy
to logic, conceived not as a science of truth or
reality but as a statement of mental processes.
It is, indeed, a significant fact that Mill is one
of those writers who can never be trusted not
to mean "psychology" when they say "metaphysics." The idea of explanation as analysis

[1] *Auguste Comte and Positivism*, p. 53.

— and generally analysis into ideas — is one which he not only defends, but really acts on and makes use of; and his failure to distinguish the problems of science and philosophy is due to this inadequate idea of explanation: Mill sees in metaphysic nothing but an abstract statement of the results of analysis. Now, while it is important to remember the scientific character of philosophy, and even the essential unity of the philosophical problem with those of the special sciences on whose results it is based, yet to reduce interpretation to mere analysis, and to identify the meaning of things with the process by which we come to know them, is to abandon the hope of real explanation. In so far as Mill omits to mark the distinctive problem of philosophy, he imposes on himself a limitation which is fatal to the thoroughness of his speculative work.

But Mill's neglect of metaphysics does not mean that he denies the significance of nature. His application of ideal criteria is not limited to human conduct and character: it seems reasonable to him to look for the value of all actual things; and he institutes a moral demand upon the natural order. His doing so is rooted in his recognition of man's presence within that order. It is because things are related to human wants and ideals that Mill regards them as significant: it is this relation that makes their meaning a problem. Mill's moral criticism of nature points, in fact, to the transition which is made in the development of his empiricism—the transition from the idea of man as a mere subject, isolated from nature, to that which makes him an object of knowledge, determined by concrete relations in the system of reality.

The impossibility of the individualistic assumption is a lesson which empiricism is not taught from without, but learns and develops from within. Its point of view is not really corrected by the half-truths of criticism. These may suggest an unfinished knowledge; but, at the best, they are apt to breed that Agnosticism which expresses the speculative man's sense of sin. Empiricism remains, despite their force, strong in the sullen maintenance of its hold upon facts—in its contact with the real world. "The sword that gave the wound must heal it:" experience must correct its own errors.

Empiricism owes its development to the fact

that our knowledge of nature changes its character as we deepen it. We see at first facts that follow one another in an endless and unmeaning series; and our sense of tragic issues—of a worth and meaning in ourselves—all but gives way as we regard the settled sequence of fact upon fact in a world of continual change. But the growth of our knowledge of things makes all this different; for it involves the habit of regarding nature's laws as things that practically concern us, of reckoning with its forces, and shaping our conduct to its requirements; and this, which is the very mood of empiricism, leads to the discovery of a significance in nature. The attempt to know nature is essentially practical in its motive; and the practical attitude towards nature is itself an admission of man's membership in nature's kingdom. Just because his life depends on nature, natural events are significant for him; and it is their significance for him which requires him to know them.

Little by little, we are compelled to face the inclusion of human beings within the world of natural events. As we grow intimate with nature, we find it to be not merely man's birthplace and

his home, but his very life. He becomes for us,
in very truth, part of the order of the world. In
every detail, his personal life derives its content
from natural sources. The attempt to isolate from
nature the larger issues of human growth is but
a temporary shift. It may be required for a
time, to justify that objective and unconcerned
way of regarding nature which the growth of
experience demands ; but it is a way of thinking
which cannot be permanent, and whose doom is
fixed from the first.

But this dependence of man upon nature—
this inclusion in it of all his interests—recasts
the conception of it. So long as we sever man
from the natural order, it remains possible to regard that order as a mere train of consequences,
which reveals no worth, and of which we need not
devise any explanation. But it appears that man
is not thus abruptly dissociated from his world :
his mental life, and his moral faiths, and his
social institutions are all found to be rooted in
the order of material events ; and nature derives
a significance from man's presence within it
which it could not otherwise have had. When

we regard human life as continuous with, or an
element in, the natural order, we seem to concede
all that empiricism claims; in point of fact, we
make its further development consist merely in
the discovery of these concrete facts in which
man is bound up with the world. But when
man is seen as part of nature, nature remains no
longer meaningless, or dead, or unspiritual: the
significance which man has for himself is im-
parted to it. The demand which he makes upon
his own life is transferred or extended to the
whole order of which that life is seen to be a
part: nature becomes a means to an end. Mill
formulates, if he does not satisfy, the demand for
an interpretation of nature; and his doing so is
the result of his strong sense of the connection
between human personality and the world of
non-human nature.

It must be remembered that, in making this demand upon nature—in assuming that it is a significant system and that its significance belongs to
man's presence in it—Mill does not merely reflect
the results of those theories to which we naturally
refer such a point of view: his work is prior to

the influences by which our idea of the interpretation of nature is mainly formed. Our conception of nature as a system, and of man's place in it, owes its most important development to the theory of organic evolution; and the whole idea of philosophical interpretation has been transformed by the influence of critical idealism. Mill's endeavour to interpret the natural order, in relation to self-consciousness, is unaffected by these two factors, which have most to do with our way of conceiving the problem : neither the idea of evolution nor the critical account of experience possessed any central importance for his mind. His attempt is thus all the more significant of his own speculative tendency.

On the one hand, we have already seen that he interprets all good or worth in an ethical sense. He means by it a contribution to the development of personal life, or a realisation of personal ideals ; and it is in this sense that he asks whether, or how far, the facts of nature justify belief in its worth as a system or suggest the beneficence of its Author. He makes the human ideals no less objective and valid than the experience of facts. This is the meaning of his demand that the goodness of God shall not be conceived as opposite to human excellence.[1]

On the other hand, it is no less characteristic of Mill that he looks for all worth, and so for an intelligible system, in things themselves. He does not content himself with the idea of a perfection separate from the experienced facts of the real world. He owes it to his empiricism that he never deserts the realm of facts and events to construct an ideal existence from merely ethical data. In this respect, his is a genuinely philosophical enterprise. Determined, as it is, by the consciousness of worth, it is also regulated by the facts of experience. It is thus, so far as it goes, a real attempt to explain things, or to find an interpretation of them which belongs to their actual nature.

In all this, Mill gives effect to the abiding interest of philosophy. It is no more open to philosophy to ignore the nature of things than to find its term of explanation in anything external to self - consciousness: it is a surrender of the problem of philosophy to neglect experience, just as it is to use principles of explanation that do

[1] Examination of Hamilton, pp. 128, 129, &c.

not express the nature of self-conscious thought.
Mill's problem—the problem of the relation of
Nature to human ideals—is one which the development of knowledge does nothing to super-
sede; and the whole issue of the relation of Nature
and Spirit is involved in the question whether the
world in which man lives can be made a means to
his spiritual ends. Mill's failure to develop this
wider issue is due to the limitation of his interest
to human affairs. That limitation is not allowed
to suppress the demand for an interpretation of
nature in relation to human ideals, because
Mill's consciousness both of these ideals and of
the system of nature renders the demand inevitable for him; but it is sufficiently operative
to confine his inquiry to the relation of nature to
the moral life of man.

The answer to this question, which Mill finds
in the facts of Nature, is of a very tentative and
dubious kind. "The net results of Natural
Theology" yield only the idea of "a Being of
great but limited power, how or by what limited
we cannot even conjecture; of great, and perhaps
unlimited intelligence, but perhaps, also, more
narrowly limited than his power; who desires,

and pays some regard to, the happiness of his creatures, but who seems to have other motives of action which he cares more for, and who can hardly be supposed to have created the universe for that purpose alone."[1] This result is entirely based upon that examination of the facts of nature which forms, as we have already seen, the ground of Mill's idea of God; for Mill refuses to allow that the existence of ideals can prove "the reality of a corresponding object;"[2] and he points out that the optimism, which makes human demands an evidence of the reality of their objects, assumes, and cannot be made to authenticate, belief in God.[3]

When he comes to examine the natural order, Mill finds its relation to morality hard to make out. He sees "no shadow of justice in the general arrangements of Nature."[4] He maintains that nature is an incessant performance of acts which would be condemned as immoral if done by a human agent, and that it cannot be made a law or example for human conduct: "nearly all the things which men are hanged or

---

[1] Essays on Religion, p. 194. [2] Ibid., p. 140.
[3] Ibid., p. 166. [4] Ibid., p. 191.

imprisoned for doing to one another, are nature's everyday performances."[1]　Nature is reckless, cruel, and destructive. The natural order is a source of misery no less than of happiness; and its distribution of pain and pleasure cannot be shown either to secure a balance of well-being, or to have any tendency to promote virtue: it "is constructed with even less regard to the requirements of justice than to those of benevolence."[2]

Nature, as it appears in human character, has no more authority for conduct than non-human nature has. "Nearly every respectable attribute of humanity is the result not of instinct, but of a victory over instinct;"[3] and "there is hardly a single point of excellence belonging to human character, which is not decidedly repugnant to the untutored feelings of human nature."[3] Even such rudiments of virtue as courage, cleanliness, self-control, and justice are all unnatural or artificial, in the sense of requiring for their development a discipline of natural inclinations. They are only established as the result of an effort: in

[1] Essays on Religion, p. 28.　　　[2] Ibid., p. 37.
[3] Ibid., p. 46.

so far as man is distinguished from nature, they are of human and not of natural origin.[1]

In this way, "conformity to nature has no connection whatever with right and wrong;"[2] and the fact "that a feeling is bestowed on us by Nature, does not necessarily legitimate all its promptings."[3] Divine government is carried on, "not by the mere indulgence of our natural tendencies, but by the regulation and control of them;"[4] and "the duty of man is the same in respect to his own nature as in respect to the nature of all other things, namely, not to follow but to amend it."[5] In fact, Mill's whole indictment of nature is meant to show that nature is not the source of moral law. When nature is taken to mean the whole system of things, including man, it is idle to enjoin conformity to natural laws or to give them "moral" meaning; and when human efforts and ideals are excluded from nature, then nature ceases to be a reliable guide. "While human

---

[1] Essays on Religion, pp. 46-53. [2] Ibid., p. 62.
[3] Utilitarianism, p. 62.
[4] Examination of Hamilton, p. 171.
[5] Essays on Religion, p. 54.

action cannot help conforming to Nature in the
one meaning of the term, the very aim and
object of action is to alter and improve Nature
in the other meaning." [1]

The significance of Mill's criticism of nature
appears in this conclusion. Moral good is relative to human needs, and it depends no less on
human exertions. The demand which man makes
upon nature returns upon himself. That limitation of the power of the divine beneficence, by
which Mill expresses rather than explains the
mysterious failure of nature, leaves something
for man to do. Apart from man, nature realises
no end, and is capable of no explanation. Mill's
criticism thus proves itself to be double-edged.
Even when it seems to weaken the authority of
moral ideals by finding no ground for them in
nature, it becomes at the same time, in Mill's
hands, an additional necessity for the moral life.
Man can expect nothing from nature on this
theory. Nature is, at best, only the opportunity
of goodness; and morality will not exist unless
the effort of men originates it. Nor is this all.
Nature's failure to realise that divine end, which

[1] Essays on Religion, p. 19.

is manifest in the facts of the world as well as in man's spiritual life, leaves the burden of the world upon man himself. Only his effort can give to nature that meaning which he himself demands in it: only his obedience and faith can realise the divine purpose, and work out those ends in relation to which alone the world is intelligible. "The earnest expectation of the creature waiteth for the manifestation of the sons of God:" the moral life is a divine neces-sity — a claim which the purpose revealed in things makes upon the character and person-ality of men. In this, as in other aspects of his philosophy, Mill betrays his profoundly ethical interest.[1]

On the other hand, this essentially religious conception of the moral life of man can hardly be reconciled with the individualistic Deism which is expressed in Mill's natural theology. It contains a view of man's relations, both to the natural world and to the Divine Spirit, which seems to count for nothing in the more official attempt to define those relations. In so far as human effort is the vehicle or instrument

_____
[1] Cf. Essays on Religion, pp. 37 ff., 256, &c.

of the Divine Spirit, it constitutes a revelation of divine ends to which Mill gives little heed when he sets out explicitly to collect evidence for his theodicy; and, in so far as it is capable of re-deeming the natural order from complete failure, it must belong to that order in such a way as to turn the edge of Mill's criticism, and make it impossible to convict nature of unspirituality.

Mill's assertion that the divine power is limited, and the indictment of nature on which that assertion is based, are made in forgetfulness of his own recognition of man's membership in the natural order. There is, indeed, nothing in that order, taken by itself, which can be called "moral," except by a figure of speech. Things must always be without moral significance, ex-cept in so far as they enter into experience, and become related to self-consciousness. Further, it may appear that the net result of nature, so far as experience has access to it, is pain; and this, if it be the case, condemns nature absolutely from a hedonistic point of view.) It may appear, too, that moral failure, no less than virtue, has its roots in nature; and this would make it impos-sible to regard nature as a moral example, however far the natural pedigree of man's moralities might be traced back. But that very relation of man to nature, which makes it possible to criticise natural laws and facts as means to an end, renders the criticism of nature, taken in abstraction from human life, irrelevant and futile. In so far as nature can be criticised, it must include all the human facts; since it is the presence of man in nature that makes nature significant. But when the world is seen as the sphere and opportunity and potency of human life, with its ideal interests and its divine significance, things are no longer outside the divine purpose, so far as that purpose is open to human comprehension. It is true that our experience only gives effect, in an inadequate and partial way, even to our most limited ideas of good; and it can never be forgotten how little likely these ideas are to exhaust the demand that might be made upon things. But the inclusion of man in nature is fatal to that perverse cleavage of reality which makes the world independent of God.

Man himself, dependent on nature for his very life, and yet for himself, and first, and finally, neither machine, nor brute, but spirit, is the

s

living refutation of all attempts to fix an absolute gulf between the natural order and the spiritual interests. So long as he lives by bread, and hungers still for every word that comes out of the mouth of God, so long will it be impossible to persuade him that nature is unspiritual; and it is because Mill's topic is human life, that the bonds of Deism cannot wholly restrain him from the attempt to interpret the natural world in terms of self-conscious reason.

THE END

PRINTED BY WILLIAM BLACKWOOD AND SONS.

Catalogue

of

Messrs Blackwood & Sons'

Publications

PHILOSOPHICAL CLASSICS FOR ENGLISH READERS.

EDITED BY WILLIAM KNIGHT, LL.D.,

Professor of Moral Philosophy in the University of St Andrews.

In crown 8vo Volumes, with Portraits, price 3s. 6d.

Contents of the Series.

DESCARTES, by Professor Mahaffy, Dublin.—BUTLER, by Rev. W. Lucas Collins, M.A.—BERKELEY, by Professor Campbell Fraser.—FICHTE, by Professor Adamson, Owens College, Manchester. — KANT, by Professor Wallace, Oxford.—HAMILTON, by Professor Veitch, Glasgow. — HEGEL, by the Master of Balliol. — LEIBNIZ, by J. Theodore Merz.—VICO, by Professor Flint, Edinburgh.—HOBBES, by Professor Croom Robertson.—HUME, by the Editor.—SPINOZA, by the Very Rev. Principal Caird, Glasgow. — BACON: Part I. The Life, by Professor Nichol.—BACON: Part II. Philosophy, by the same Author.—LOCKE, by Professor Campbell Fraser.

FOREIGN CLASSICS FOR ENGLISH READERS.

EDITED BY MRS OLIPHANT.

In crown 8vo, 2s. 6d.

Contents of the Series.

DANTE, by the Editor.—VOLTAIRE, by General Sir E. B. Hamley, K.C.B. —PASCAL, by Principal Tulloch.—PETRARCH, by Henry Reeve, C.B.—GOETHE, by A. Hayward, Q.C.—MOLIÈRE, by the Editor and F. Tarver, M.A.—MONTAIGNE, by Rev. W. L. Collins, M.A.—RABELAIS, by Walter Besant, M.A.—CALDERON, by E. J. Hasell.—SAINT SIMON, by Clifton W. Collins, M.A.—CERVANTES, by the Editor. — CORNEILLE AND RACINE, by Henry M. Trollope. — MADAME DE SÉVIGNÉ, by Miss Thackeray.—LA FONTAINE, AND OTHER FRENCH FABULISTS, by Rev. W. Lucas Collins, M.A.—SCHILLER, by James Sime, M.A., Author of 'Lessing, his Life and Writings.'—TASSO, by E. J. Hasell. — ROUSSEAU, by Henry Grey Graham.— ALFRED DE MUSSET, by C. F. Oliphant.

ANCIENT CLASSICS FOR ENGLISH READERS.

EDITED BY THE REV. W. LUCAS COLLINS, M.A.

Complete in 28 Vols. crown 8vo, cloth, price 2s. 6d. each. And may also be had in 14 Volumes, strongly and neatly bound, with calf or vellum back, £3, 10s.

Contents of the Series.

HOMER: THE ILIAD, by the Editor.—HOMER: THE ODYSSEY, by the Editor.—HERODOTUS, by George C. Swayne, M.A.—XENOPHON, by Sir Alexander Grant, Bart., LL.D.—EURIPIDES, by W. B. Donne.—ARISTOPHANES, by the Editor.—PLATO, by Clifton W. Collins, M.A.—LUCIAN, by the Editor.—ÆSCHYLUS, by the Right Rev. the Bishop of Colombo.—SOPHOCLES, by Clifton W. Collins, M.A.—HESIOD AND THEOGNIS, by the Rev. J. Davies, M.A.—GREEK ANTHOLOGY, by Lord Neaves.—VIRGIL, by the Editor.—HORACE, by Sir Theodore Martin, K.C.B.—JUVENAL, by Edward Walford, M.A.—PLAUTUS AND TERENCE, by the Editor—THE COMMENTARIES OF CÆSAR, by Anthony Trollope.—TACITUS, by W. B. Donne.—CICERO, by the Editor. — PLINY'S LETTERS, by the Rev. Alfred Church, M.A., and the Rev. W. J. Brodribb, M.A. — LIVY, by the Editor.—OVID, by the Rev. A. Church, M.A. — CATULLUS, TIBULLUS, AND PROPERTIUS, by the Rev. Jas. Davies, M.A.—DEMOSTHENES, by the Rev. W. J. Brodribb, M.A.—ARISTOTLE, by Sir Alexander Grant, Bart., LL.D.—THUCYDIDES, by the Editor.—LUCRETIUS, by W. H. Mallock, M.A.—PINDAR, by the Rev. F. D. Morice, M.A.

Saturday Review.—"It is difficult to estimate too highly the value of such a series as this in giving 'English readers' an insight, exact as far as it goes, into those olden times which are so remote, and yet to many of us so close."

CATALOGUE

OF

MESSRS BLACKWOOD & SONS'

PUBLICATIONS.

ALISON.
History of Europe. By Sir ARCHIBALD ALISON, Bart., D.C.L.
1. From the Commencement of the French Revolution to
the Battle of Waterloo.
LIBRARY EDITION, 14 vols., with Portraits. Demy 8vo, £10, 10s.
ANOTHER EDITION, in 20 vols. crown 8vo, £6.
PEOPLE'S EDITION, 13 vols. crown 8vo, £2, 11s.

2. Continuation to the Accession of Louis Napoleon.
LIBRARY EDITION, 8 vols. 8vo, £6, 7s. 6d.
PEOPLE'S EDITION, 8 vols. crown 8vo, 34s.

Epitome of Alison's History of Europe. Thirtieth Thou-
sand, 7s. 6d.
Atlas to Alison's History of Europe. By A. Keith Johnston.
LIBRARY EDITION, demy 4to, £3, 3s.
PEOPLE'S EDITION, 31s. 6d.
Life of John Duke of Marlborough. With some Account of
his Contemporaries, and of the War of the Succession. Third Edition. 2 vols.
8vo. Portraits and Maps, 30s.
Essays: Historical, Political, and Miscellaneous. 3 vols.
demy 8vo, 45s.

ACROSS FRANCE IN A CARAVAN: BEING SOME ACCOUNT
OF A JOURNEY FROM BORDEAUX TO GENOA IN THE "ESCARGOT," taken in the Winter
1889-90. By the Author of 'A Day of my Life at Eton.' With fifty Illustrations
by John Wallace, after Sketches by the Author, and a Map. Cheap Edition,
demy 8vo, 7s. 6d.

ACTA SANCTORUM HIBERNIÆ; Ex Codice Salmanticensi.
Nunc primum integre edita opera CAROLI DE SMEDT et JOSEPHI DE BACKER, e
Soc. Jesu, Hagiographorum Bollandianorum; Auctore et Sumptus Largiente
JOANNE PATRICIO MARCHIONE BOTHAE. In One handsome 4to Volume, bound in
half roxburghe, £2, 2s.; in paper cover, 31s. 6d.

ADOLPHUS. Some Memories of Paris. By F. ADOLPHUS.
Crown 8vo, 6s.

AIKMAN.
Manures and the Principles of Manuring. By C. M. AIKMAN,
D.Sc., F.R.S.E., &c., Professor of Chemistry, Glasgow Veterinary College;
Examiner in Chemistry, University of Glasgow, &c. Crown 8vo, 6s. 6d.
Farmyard Manure: Its Nature, Composition, and Treatment.
Crown 8vo, 1s. 6d.

AIRD. Poetical Works of Thomas Aird. Fifth Edition, with
Memoir of the Author by the Rev. JARDINE WALLACE, and Portrait. Crown 8vo,
7s. 6d.

ALLARDYCE.

The City of Sunshine. By ALEXANDER ALLARDYCE, Author of 'Earlscourt,' 'Balmoral: A Romance of the Queen's Country,' &c. New and Revised Edition. Crown 8vo, 6s.

Memoir of the Honourable George Keith Elphinstone, K.B., Viscount Keith of Stonehaven, Marischal, Admiral of the Red. 8vo, with Portrait, Illustrations, and Maps, 21s.

ALMOND. Sermons by a Lay Head-master. By HELY HUTCH-INSON ALMOND, M.A. Oxon., Head-master of Loretto School. Crown 8vo, 5s.

ANCIENT CLASSICS FOR ENGLISH READERS. Edited by Rev. W. LUCAS COLLINS, M.A. Price 2s. 6d. each. *For List of Vols., see p. 2.*

ANDERSON. Daniel in the Critics' Den. A Reply to Dean Farrar's 'Book of Daniel.' By ROBERT ANDERSON, LL.D., Barrister-at-Law, Assistant Commissioner of Police of the Metropolis; Author of 'The Coming Prince,' 'Human Destiny,' &c. Post 8vo, 4s. 6d.

AYTOUN.

Lays of the Scottish Cavaliers, and other Poems. By W. EDMONDSTOUNE AYTOUN, D.C.L., Professor of Rhetoric and Belles-Lettres in the University of Edinburgh. New Edition. Fcap. 8vo, 3s. 6d.
ANOTHER EDITION. Fcap. 8vo, 7s. 6d.
CHEAP EDITION. 1s. Cloth, 1s. 3d.

An Illustrated Edition of the Lays of the Scottish Cavaliers. From designs by Sir NOEL PATON. Cheaper Edition. Small 4to, 10s. 6d.

Bothwell : a Poem. Third Edition. Fcap., 7s. 6d.

Poems and Ballads of Goethe. Translated by Professor AYTOUN and Sir THEODORE MARTIN, K.C.B. Third Edition. Fcap., 6s.

Bon Gaultier's Book of Ballads. By the SAME. Fifteenth Edition. With Illustrations by Doyle, Leech, and Crowquill. Fcap. 8vo, 5s.

The Ballads of Scotland. Edited by Professor AYTOUN. Fourth Edition. 2 vols. fcap. 8vo, 12s.

Memoir of William E. Aytoun, D.C.L. By Sir THEODORE MARTIN, K.C.B. With Portrait. Post 8vo, 12s.

BACH.

On Musical Education and Vocal Culture. By ALBERT B. BACH. Fourth Edition. 8vo, 7s. 6d.

The Principles of Singing. A Practical Guide for Vocalists and Teachers. With Course of Vocal Exercises. Second Edition. With Portrait of the Author. Crown 8vo, 6s.

The Art Ballad : Loewe and Schubert. With Musical Illustrations. With a Portrait of LOEWE. Third Edition. Small 4to, 5s.

BAIRD LECTURES.

Theism. By Rev. Professor FLINT, D.D., Edinburgh. Eighth Edition. Crown 8vo, 7s. 6d.

Anti-Theistic Theories. By the SAME. Fifth Edition. Crown 8vo, 10s. 6d.

The Inspiration of the Holy Scriptures. By Rev. ROBERT JAMIESON, D.D. Crown 8vo, 7s. 6d.

The Early Religion of Israel. As set forth by Biblical Writers and modern Critical Historians. By Rev. Professor ROBERTSON, D.D., Glasgow. Fourth Edition. Crown 8vo, 10s. 6d.

The Mysteries of Christianity. By Rev. Professor CRAWFORD, D.D. Crown 8vo, 7s. 6d.

Endowed Territorial Work : Its Supreme Importance to the Church and Country. By Rev. WILLIAM SMITH, D.D. Crown 8vo, 6s.

BALLADS AND POEMS. By MEMBERS OF THE GLASGOW BALLAD CLUB. Crown 8vo, 7s. 6d.

BELLAIRS.
The Transvaal War, 1880-81. Edited by Lady BELLAIRS.
With a Frontispiece and Map. 8vo, 15s.
Gossips with Girls and Maidens, Betrothed and Free. New
Edition. Crown 8vo, 3s. 6d. Cloth, extra gilt edges, 5s.
BELLESHEIM. History of the Catholic Church of Scotland.
From the Introduction of Christianity to the Present Day. By ALPHONS BEL-
LESHEIM, D.D., Canon of Aix-la-Chapelle. Translated, with Notes and Additions,
by D. OSWALD HUNTER BLAIR, O.S.B., Monk of Fort Augustus. Cheap Edition.
Complete in 4 vols. demy 8vo, with Maps. Price 21s. net.
BENTINCK. Racing Life of Lord George Cavendish Bentinck,
M.P., and other Reminiscences. By JOHN KENT, Private Trainer to the Good-
wood Stable. Edited by the Hon. FRANCIS LAWLEY. With Twenty-three full-
page Plates, and Facsimile Letter. Third Edition. Demy 8vo, 25s.
BESANT.
The Revolt of Man. By Sir WALTER BESANT. Tenth Edition.
Crown 8vo, 3s. 6d.
Readings in Rabelais. Crown 8vo, 7s. 6d.
BEVERIDGE.
Culross and Tulliallan; or Perthshire on Forth. Its History
and Antiquities. With Elucidations of Scottish Life and Character from the
Burgh and Kirk-Session Records of that District. By DAVID BEVERIDGE. 2 vols.
8vo, with Illustrations, 42s.
Between the Ochils and the Forth; or, From Stirling Bridge
to Aberdour. Crown 8vo 6s.
BICKERDYKE. A Banished Beauty. By JOHN BICKERDYKE,
Author of 'Days in Thule, with Rod, Gun, and Camera,' 'The Book of the All-
Round Angler,' 'Curiosities of Ale and Beer,' &c. With Illustrations. Crown
8vo, 6s.
BIRCH.
Examples of Stables, Hunting-Boxes, Kennels, Racing Estab-
lishments, &c. By JOHN BIRCH, Architect, Author of 'Country Architecture,'
&c. With 30 Plates. Royal 8vo, 7s.
Examples of Labourers' Cottages, &c. With Plans for Im-
proving the Dwellings of the Poor in Large Towns. With 34 Plates. Royal 8vo,
7s.
Picturesque Lodges. A Series of Designs for Gate Lodges,
Park Entrances, Keepers', Gardeners', Bailiffs', Grooms', Upper and Under Ser-
vants' Lodges, and other Rural Residences. With 16 Plates. 4to, 12s. 6d.
BLACK. Heligoland and the Islands of the North Sea. By
WILLIAM GEORGE BLACK. Crown 8vo, 4s.
BLACKIE.
John Stuart Blackie: A Biography. By ANNA M. STODDART.
With 3 Plates. Third Edition. 2 vols. demy 8vo, 21s.
Lays and Legends of Ancient Greece. By JOHN STUART
BLACKIE, Emeritus Professor of Greek in the University of Edinburgh. Second
Edition. Fcap. 8vo, 5s.
The Wisdom of Goethe. Fcap. 8vo. Cloth, extra gilt, 6s.
Scottish Song: Its Wealth, Wisdom, and Social Significance.
Crown 8vo. With Music. 7s. 6d.
A Song of Heroes. Crown 8vo, 6s.
BLACKMORE. The Maid of Sker. By R. D. BLACKMORE,
Author of 'Lorna Doone,' &c. New Edition. Crown 8vo, 6s. Cheaper Edi-
tion. Crown 8vo, 3s. 6d.
BLACKWOOD.
Blackwood's Magazine, from Commencement in 1817 to Sep-
tember 1895. Nos. 1 to 959, forming 158 Volumes.
Index to Blackwood's Magazine. Vols. 1 to 50. 8vo, 15s.

BLACKWOOD.

Tales from Blackwood. First Series. Price One Shilling each,
in Paper Cover. Sold separately at all Railway Bookstalls.
They may also be had bound in 12 vols., cloth, 18s. Half calf, richly gilt, 30s. Or the 12 vols. in 6, roxburghe, 21s. Half red morocco, 28s.

Tales from Blackwood. Second Series. Complete in Twenty-
four Shilling Parts. Handsomely bound in 12 vols., cloth, 30s. In leather back, roxburghe style, 37s. 6d. Half calf, gilt, 52s. 6d. Half morocco, 55s.

Tales from Blackwood. Third Series. Complete in Twelve
Shilling Parts. Handsomely bound in 6 vols., cloth, 15s.; and in 12 vols., cloth, 18s. The 6 vols. in roxburghe, 21s. Half calf, 25s. Half morocco, 28s.

Travel, Adventure, and Sport. From 'Blackwood's Magazine.'
Uniform with 'Tales from Blackwood.' In Twelve Parts, each price 1s. Handsomely bound in 6 vols., cloth, 15s. And in half calf, 25s.

New Educational Series. *See separate Catalogue.*

New Uniform Series of Novels (Copyright).
Crown 8vo, cloth. Price 3s. 6d. each. Now ready:—

THE MAID OF SKER. By R. D. Blackmore.
WENDERHOLME. By P. G. Hamerton.
THE STORY OF MARGRÉDEL. By D. Storrar Meldrum.
MISS MARJORIBANKS. By Mrs Oliphant.
THE PERPETUAL CURATE, and THE RECTOR. By the Same.
SALEM CHAPEL, and THE DOCTOR'S FAMILY. By the Same.
A SENSITIVE PLANT. By E. D. Gerard.
LADY LEE'S WIDOWHOOD. By General Sir E. B. Hamley.
KATIE STEWART, and other Stories. By Mrs Oliphant.
VALENTINE, AND HIS BROTHER. By the Same.
SONS AND DAUGHTERS. By the Same.
MARMORNE. By P. G. Hamerton.

REATA. By E. D. Gerard.
BEGGAR MY NEIGHBOUR. By the Same.
THE WATERS OF HERCULES. By the Same.
FAIR TO SEE. By L. W. M. Lockhart.
MINE IS THINE. By the Same.
DOUBLES AND QUITS. By the Same.
ALTIORA PETO. By Laurence Oliphant.
PICCADILLY. By the Same. With Illustrations.
THE REVOLT OF MAN. By Walter Besant.
LADY BABY. By D. Gerard.
THE BLACKSMITH OF VOE. By Paul Cushing.
THE DILEMMA. By the Author of 'The Battle of Dorking.'
MY TRIVIAL LIFE AND MISFORTUNE. By A Plain Woman.
POOR NELLIE. By the Same.

Others in preparation.

Standard Novels. Uniform in size and binding. Each
complete in one Volume.

FLORIN SERIES, Illustrated Boards. Bound in Cloth, 2s. 6d.

TOM CRINGLE'S LOG. By Michael Scott.
THE CRUISE OF THE MIDGE. By the Same.
CYRIL THORNTON. By Captain Hamilton.
ANNALS OF THE PARISH. By John Galt.
THE PROVOST, &c. By the Same.
SIR ANDREW WYLIE. By the Same.
THE ENTAIL. By the Same.
MISS MOLLY. By Beatrice May Butt.
REGINALD DALTON. By J. G. Lockhart.

PEN OWEN. By Dean Hook.
ADAM BLAIR. By J. G. Lockhart.
LADY LEE'S WIDOWHOOD. By General Sir E. B. Hamley.
SALEM CHAPEL. By Mrs Oliphant.
THE PERPETUAL CURATE. By the Same.
MISS MARJORIBANKS. By the Same.
JOHN: A Love Story. By the Same.

SHILLING SERIES, Illustrated Cover. Bound in Cloth, 1s. 6d

THE RECTOR, and THE DOCTOR'S FAMILY. By Mrs Oliphant.
THE LIFE OF MANSIE WAUCH. By D. M. Moir.
PENINSULAR SCENES AND SKETCHES. By F. Hardman.

SIR FRIZZLE PUMPKIN, NIGHTS AT MESS, &c.
THE SUBALTERN.
LIFE IN THE FAR WEST. By G. F. Ruxton.
VALERIUS: A Roman Story. By J. G. Lockhart.

BON GAULTIER'S BOOK OF BALLADS. Fifteenth Edi-
tion. With Illustrations by Doyle, Leech, and Crowquill. Fcap. 8vo, 5s.

BONNAR. Biographical Sketch of George Meikle Kemp, Archi-
tect of the Scott Monument, Edinburgh. By THOMAS BONNAR, F.S.A. Scot., Author of 'The Present Art Revival,' &c. With Three Portraits and numerous Illustrations. Post 8vo, 7s. 6d.

BRADDON. Thirty Years of Shikar. By Sir EDWARD BRADDON, K.C.M.G. With Illustrations by G. D. Giles, and Map of Oudh Forest Tracts and Nepal Terai Demy 8vo, 18s.

BROUGHAM. Memoirs of the Life and Times of Henry Lord Brougham. Written by HIMSELF. 3 vols. 8vo, £2, 8s. The Volumes are sold separately, price 16s. each.

BROWN. The Forester: A Practical Treatise on the Planting and Tending of Forest-trees and the General Management of Woodlands. By JAMES BROWN, LL.D. Sixth Edition, Enlarged. Edited by JOHN NISBET, D.Œc., Author of 'British Forest Trees,' &c. In 2 vols. royal 8vo, with 350 Illustrations, 42s. net.

BROWN. Stray Sport. By J. MORAY BROWN, Author of 'Shikar Sketches,' 'Powder, Spur, and Spear,' 'The Days when we went Hog-Hunting.' 2 vols. post 8vo, with Fifty Illustrations, 21s.

BROWN. A Manual of Botany, Anatomical and Physiological. For the Use of Students. By ROBERT BROWN, M.A., Ph.D. Crown 8vo, with numerous Illustrations, 12s. 6d.

BRUCE.
In Clover and Heather. Poems by WALLACE BRUCE. New and Enlarged Edition. Crown 8vo, 4s. 6d.
A limited number of Copies of the First Edition, on large hand-made paper 12s. 6d.

Here's a Hand. Addresses and Poems. Crown 8vo, 5s. Large Paper Edition, limited to 100 copies, price 21s.

BUCHAN. Introductory Text-Book of Meteorology. By ALEXANDER BUCHAN, LL.D., F.R.S.E., Secretary of the Scottish Meteorological Society, &c. New Edition. Crown 8vo, with Coloured Charts and Engravings.
[In preparation.

BURBIDGE.
Domestic Floriculture, Window Gardening, and Floral Decorations. Being practical directions for the Propagation, Culture, and Arrangement of Plants and Flowers as Domestic Ornaments. By F. W. BURBIDGE. Second Edition. Crown 8vo, with numerous Illustrations 7s. 6d.

Cultivated Plants: Their Propagation and Improvement. Including Natural and Artificial Hybridisation, Raising from Seed, Cuttings, and Layers, Grafting and Budding, as applied to the Families and Genera in Cultivation. Crown 8vo, with numerous Illustrations, 12s. 6d.

BURGESS. The Viking Path. A Tale of the White Christ. By J. J. HALDANE BURGESS, Author of 'Rasmie's Büddie,' 'Shetland Sketches,' &c. Crown 8vo, 6s.

BURROWS.
Commentaries on the History of England, from the Earliest Times to 1865. By MONTAGU BURROWS, Chichele Professor of Modern History in the University of Oxford; Captain R.N.; F.S.A., &c.; "Officier de l'Instruction Publique," France. Crown 8vo, 7s. 6d.

The History of the Foreign Policy of Great Britain. Demy 8vo, 12s.

BURTON.
The History of Scotland: From Agricola's Invasion to the Extinction of the last Jacobite Insurrection. By JOHN HILL BURTON, D.C.L., Historiographer-Royal for Scotland. New and Enlarged Edition, 8 vols., and Index. Crown 8vo, £3, 3s.

History of the British Empire during the Reign of Queen Anne. In 3 vols. 8vo. 36s.

The Scot Abroad. Third Edition. Crown 8vo, 10s. 6d.

The Book-Hunter. By JOHN HILL BURTON. New Edition. With Portrait. Crown 8vo, 7s. 6d.

BUTE.

The Roman Breviary: Reformed by Order of the Holy Œcumenical Council of Trent; Published by Order of Pope St Pius V.; and Revised by Clement VIII. and Urban VIII.; together with the Offices since granted. Translated out of Latin into English by JOHN, Marquess of Bute, K.T. In 2 vols. crown 8vo, cloth boards, edges uncut. £2, 2s.

The Altus of St Columba. With a Prose Paraphrase and Notes. In paper cover, 2s. 6d.

BUTT.

Theatricals: An Interlude. By BEATRICE MAY BUTT. In 1 vol. crown 8vo. [In the press.

Miss Molly. Cheap Edition, 2s.

Eugenie. Crown 8vo, 6s. 6d.

Elizabeth, and other Sketches. Crown 8vo, 6s.

Delicia. New Edition. Crown 8vo, 2s. 6d.

CAIRD.

Sermons. By JOHN CAIRD, D.D., Principal of the University of Glasgow. Seventeenth Thousand. Fcap. 8vo, 5s.

Religion in Common Life. A Sermon preached in Crathie Church, October 14, 1855, before Her Majesty the Queen and Prince Albert. Published by Her Majesty's Command. Cheap Edition, 3d.

CALDER. Chaucer's Canterbury Pilgrimage. Epitomised by WILLIAM CALDER. With Photogravure of the Pilgrimage Company, and other Illustrations, Glossary, &c. Crown 8vo, gilt edges, 4s. Cheaper Edition without Photogravure Plate. Crown 8vo, 2s. 6d.

CALDWELL. Schopenhauer's System in its Philosophical Significance (the Shaw Fellowship Lectures, 1893). By WILLIAM CALDWELL, M.A., D.Sc., Professor of Moral and Social Philosophy, North Western University, U.S.A.; formerly Assistant to the Professor of Logic and Metaphysics, Edin.; and Examiner in Philosophy in the University of St Andrews. 1 vol. demy 8vo. [In the press.

CAMPBELL. Critical Studies in St Luke's Gospel: Its Demonology and Ebionitism. By COLIN CAMPBELL, D.D., Minister of the Parish of Dundee, formerly Scholar and Fellow of Glasgow University. Author of the 'Three First Gospels in Greek, arranged in parallel columns.' Post 8vo, 7s. 6d.

CAMPBELL. Sermons Preached before the Queen at Balmoral. By the Rev. A. A. CAMPBELL, Minister of Crathie. Published by Command of Her Majesty. Crown 8vo, 4s. 6d.

CAMPBELL. Records of Argyll. Legends, Traditions, and Recollections of Argyllshire Highlanders, collected chiefly from the Gaelic. With Notes on the Antiquity of the Dress, Clan Colours, or Tartans of the Highlanders. By Lord ARCHIBALD CAMPBELL. Illustrated with Nineteen full-page Etchings. 4to, printed on hand-made paper, £3, 3s.

CANTON. A Lost Epic, and other Poems. By WILLIAM CANTON. Crown 8vo, 5s.

CARSTAIRS.

Human Nature in Rural India. By R. CARSTAIRS. Crown 8vo, 6s.

British Work in India. Crown 8vo, 6s.

CAUVIN. A Treasury of the English and German Languages. Compiled from the best Authors and Lexicographers in both Languages. By JOSEPH CAUVIN, LL.D. and Ph.D., of the University of Göttingen, &c. Crown 8vo, 7s. 6d.

CHARTERIS. Canonicity; or, Early Testimonies to the Existence and Use of the Books of the New Testament. Based on Kirchhoffer's 'Quellensammlung.' Edited by A. H. CHARTERIS, D.D., Professor of Biblical Criticism in the University of Edinburgh. 8vo, 18s.

CHENNELLS. Recollections of an Egyptian Princess. By her English Governess (Miss E. CHENNELLS). Being a Record of Five Years' Residence at the Court of Ismael Pasha, Khédive. Second Edition. With Three Portraits. Post 8vo, 7s. 6d.

CHESNEY. The Dilemma. By General Sir GEORGE CHESNEY, K.C.B., M.P., Author of 'The Battle of Dorking,' &c. New Edition. Crown 8vo, 3s. 6d.

CHRISTISON. Life of Sir Robert Christison, Bart., M.D., D.C.L. Oxon., Professor of Medical Jurisprudence in the University of Edinburgh. Edited by his Sons. In 2 vols. 8vo. Vol. I.—Autobiography. 16s. Vol. II.—Memoirs. 16s.

CHURCH. Chapters in an Adventurous Life. Sir Richard Church in Italy and Greece. By E. M. CHURCH. With Photogravure Portrait. Demy 8vo, 10s. 6d.

CHURCH SERVICE SOCIETY.

A Book of Common Order : being Forms of Worship issued by the Church Service Society. Sixth Edition. Crown 8vo, 6s. Also in 2 vols. crown 8vo, 6s. 6d.

Daily Offices for Morning and Evening Prayer throughout the Week. Crown 8vo, 3s. 6d.

Order of Divine Service for Children. Issued by the Church Service Society. With Scottish Hymnal. Cloth, 3d.

CLOUSTON. Popular Tales and Fictions : their Migrations and Transformations. By W. A. CLOUSTON, Editor of 'Arabian Poetry for English Readers,' &c. 2 vols. post 8vo, roxburghe binding, 25s.

COCHRAN. A Handy Text-Book of Military Law. Compiled chiefly to assist Officers preparing for Examination ; also for all Officers of the Regular and Auxiliary Forces. Comprising also a Synopsis of part of the Army Act. By Major F. COCHRAN, Hampshire Regiment Garrison Instructor, North British District. Crown 8vo, 7s. 6d.

COLQUHOUN. The Moor and the Loch. Containing Minute Instructions in all Highland Sports, with Wanderings over Crag and Corrie, Flood and Fell. By JOHN COLQUHOUN. Cheap Edition. With Illustrations. Demy 8vo, 10s. 6d.

COLVILE. Round the Black Man's Garden. By Lady Z. COLVILE, F.R.G.S. With 2 Maps and 50 Illustrations from Drawings by the Author and from Photographs. Demy 8vo, 16s.

CONSTITUTION AND LAW OF THE CHURCH OF SCOTLAND. With an Introductory Note by the late Principal Tulloch. New Edition, Revised and Enlarged. Crown 8vo, 3s. 6d.

COTTERILL. Suggested Reforms in Public Schools. By C. C. COTTERILL, M.A. Crown 8vo, 3s. 6d.

CRANSTOUN.

The Elegies of Albius Tibullus. Translated into English Verse, with Life of the Poet, and Illustrative Notes. By JAMES CRANSTOUN, LL.D., Author of a Translation of 'Catullus.' Crown 8vo, 6s. 6d.

The Elegies of Sextus Propertius. Translated into English Verse, with Life of the Poet, and Illustrative Notes. Crown 8vo, 7s. 6d.

CRAWFORD. An Atonement of East London, and other Poems. By HOWARD CRAWFORD, M.A. Crown 8vo, 5s.

CRAWFORD. Saracinesca. By F. MARION CRAWFORD, Author of 'Mr Isaacs,' &c., &c. Eighth Edition. Crown 8vo, 6s

CRAWFORD.

The Doctrine of Holy Scripture respecting the Atonement. By the late THOMAS J. CRAWFORD, D.D., Professor of Divinity in the University of Edinburgh. Fifth Edition. 8vo, 12s.

CRAWFORD.
The Fatherhood of God, Considered in its General and Special
Aspects. Third Edition, Revised and Enlarged. 8vo, 9s.
The Preaching of the Cross, and other Sermons. 8vo, 7s. 6d.
The Mysteries of Christianity. Crown 8vo, 7s. 6d.

CROSS. Impressions of Dante, and of the New World ; with a
Few Words on Bimetallism. By J. W. CROSS, Editor of 'George Eliot's Life, as
related in her Letters and Journals.' Post 8vo, 6s.

CUMBERLAND. Sport on the Pamirs and Turkistan Steppes.
By Major C. S. CUMBERLAND. With Map and Frontispiece. Demy 8vo, 10s. 6d.

CURSE OF INTELLECT. Third Edition. Fcap 8vo, 2s. 6d. net.

CUSHING.
The Blacksmith of Voe. By PAUL CUSHING, Author of 'The
Bull i' th' Thorn,' 'Cut with his own Diamond.' Cheap Edition. Crown 8vo, 3s. 6d.

DAVIES.
Norfolk Broads and Rivers ; or, The Waterways, Lagoons,
and Decoys of East Anglia. By G. CHRISTOPHER DAVIES. Illustrated with
Seven full-page Plates. New and Cheaper Edition. Crown 8vo, 6s.
Our Home in Aveyron. Sketches of Peasant Life in Aveyron
and the Lot. By G. CHRISTOPHER DAVIES and Mrs BROUGHALL. Illustrated
with full-page Illustrations. 8vo, 15s. Cheap Edition, 7s. 6d.

DE LA WARR. An Eastern Cruise in the 'Edeline.' By the
Countess DE LA WARR. In Illustrated Cover. 2s.

DESCARTES. The Method, Meditations, and Principles of Philo-
sophy of Descartes. Translated from the Original French and Latin. With a
New Introductory Essay, Historical and Critical, on the Cartesian Philosophy.
By Professor VEITCH, LL.D., Glasgow University. Tenth Edition. 6s. 6d.

DOGS, OUR DOMESTICATED : Their Treatment in reference
to Food, Diseases, Habits, Punishment, Accomplishments. By 'MAGENTA.'
Crown 8vo, 2s. 6d.

DOUGLAS. John Stuart Mill. A Study of his Philosophy.
By CHARLES DOUGLAS, M.A., D.Sc., Lecturer in Moral Philosophy, and Assistant
to the Professor of Moral Philosophy, in the University of Edinburgh. Crown
8vo, 4s. 6d. net.

DOUGLAS. Chinese Stories. By ROBERT K. DOUGLAS. With
numerous Illustrations by Parkinson, Forestier, and others. New and Cheaper
Edition. Small demy 8vo, 5s.

DU CANE. The Odyssey of Homer, Books I.-XII. Translated
into English Verse. By Sir CHARLES DU CANE, K.C.M.G. 8vo, 10s. 6d.

DUDGEON. History of the Edinburgh or Queen's Regiment
Light Infantry Militia, now 3rd Battalion The Royal Scots ; with an Account of
the Origin and Progress of the Militia, and a Brief Sketch of the Old Royal
Scots. By Major R. C. DUDGEON, Adjutant 3rd Battalion the Royal Scots.
Post 8vo, with Illustrations, 10s. 6d.

DUNCAN. Manual of the General Acts of Parliament relating
to the Salmon Fisheries of Scotland from 1828 to 1882. By J. BARKER DUNCAN.
Crown 8vo, 5s.

DUNSMORE. Manual of the Law of Scotland as to the Rela-
tions between Agricultural Tenants and the Landlords, Servants, Merchants, and
Bowers. By W. DUNSMORE. 8vo, 7s. 6d.

ELIOT.

George Eliot's Life, Related in Her Letters and Journals.
Arranged and Edited by her husband, J. W. CROSS. With Portrait and other Illustrations. Third Edition. 3 vols. post 8vo, 42s.

George Eliot's Life. (Cabinet Edition.) With Portrait and other Illustrations. 3 vols. crown 8vo, 15s.

George Eliot's Life. With Portrait and other Illustrations.
New Edition, in one volume. Crown 8vo, 7s. 6d.

Works of George Eliot (Standard Edition). 21 volumes, crown 8vo. In buckram cloth, gilt top, 2s. 6d. per vol.; or in Roxburghe binding, 3s. 6d. per vol.

Ready.

ADAM BEDE. 2 vols.—THE MILL ON THE FLOSS. 2 vols.—FELIX HOLT, the Radical. 2 vols.—ROMOLA. 2 vols.—SCENES OF CLERICAL LIFE. 2 vols.—MIDDLEMARCH. 3 vols.—DANIEL DERONDA. 3 vols.

In preparation.

SILAS MARNER, and JUBAL. 2 vols.—THE SPANISH GIPSY, and ESSAYS. 2 vols.—THEOPHRASTUS SUCH. 1 vol.

Works of George Eliot (Cabinet Edition). 21 volumes, crown 8vo, price £5, 5s. Also to be had handsomely bound in half and full calf. The Volumes are sold separately, bound in cloth, price 5s. each.

Novels by George Eliot. Cheap Edition.
Adam Bede. Illustrated. 3s. 6d., cloth.—The Mill on the Floss. Illustrated. 3s. 6d., cloth.—Scenes of Clerical Life. Illustrated. 3s., cloth.—Silas Marner: the Weaver of Raveloe. Illustrated. 2s. 6d., cloth.—Felix Holt, the Radical. Illustrated. 3s. 6d., cloth.—Romola. With Vignette. 3s. 6d., cloth.

Middlemarch. Crown 8vo, 7s. 6d.

Daniel Deronda. Crown 8vo, 7s. 6d.

Essays. New Edition. Crown 8vo, 5s.

Impressions of Theophrastus Such. New Edition. Crown 8vo, 5s.

The Spanish Gypsy. New Edition. Crown 8vo, 5s.

The Legend of Jubal, and other Poems, Old and New.
New Edition. Crown 8vo, 5s.

Wise, Witty, and Tender Sayings, in Prose and Verse. Selected from the Works of GEORGE ELIOT. New Edition. Fcap. 8vo, 3s. 6d.

The George Eliot Birthday Book. Printed on fine paper, with red border, and handsomely bound in cloth, gilt. Fcap. 8vo, 3s. 6d. And in French morocco or Russia, 5s.

ESSAYS ON SOCIAL SUBJECTS. Originally published in the 'Saturday Review.' New Edition. First and Second Series. 2 vols. crown 8vo, 6s. each.

FAITHS OF THE WORLD, The. A Concise History of the Great Religious Systems of the World. By various Authors. Crown 8vo, 5s.

FALKNER. The Lost Stradivarius. By J. MEADE FALKNER. Crown 8vo, 6s.

FERGUSON. Sir Samuel Ferguson in the Ireland of his Day.
By LADY FERGUSON, Author of 'The Irish before the Conquest,' 'Life of William Reeves, D.D., Lord Bishop of Down, Connor, and Dromore,' &c., &c. 2 vols. post 8vo. [*In the press.*

FERRIER.
Philosophical Works of the late James F. Ferrier, B.A.
Oxon., Professor of Moral Philosophy and Political Economy, St Andrews. New Edition. Edited by Sir ALEXANDER GRANT, Bart., D.C.L., and Professor LUSHINGTON. 3 vols. crown 8vo, 34s. 6d.

FERRIER.
Institutes of Metaphysic. Third Edition. 10s. 6d.
Lectures on the Early Greek Philosophy. 4th Edition. 10s. 6d.
Philosophical Remains, including the Lectures on Early
Greek Philosophy. New Edition. 2 vols. 24s.

FITZROY. Dogma and the Church of England. By A. I.
FitzRoy. Post 8vo, 7s. 6d.

FLINT.
Historical Philosophy in France and French Belgium and
Switzerland. By Robert Flint, Corresponding Member of the Institute of
France, Hon. Member of the Royal Society of Palermo, Professor in the Univer-
sity of Edinburgh, &c. 8vo, 21s.
Agnosticism. Being the Croall Lecture for 1887-88.
[*In the press.*
Theism. Being the Baird Lecture for 1876. Eighth Edition,
Revised. Crown 8vo, 7s. 6d.
Anti-Theistic Theories. Being the Baird Lecture for 1877.
Fifth Edition. Crown 8vo 10s. 6d.

FOREIGN CLASSICS FOR ENGLISH READERS. Edited
by Mrs Oliphant. Price 2s. 6d. *For List of Volumes, see page 2.*

FOSTER. The Fallen City, and other Poems. By Will Foster.
Crown 8vo, 6s.

FRANCILLON. Gods and Heroes ; or, The Kingdom of Jupiter.
By R. E. Francillon. With 8 Illustrations. Crown 8vo, 5s.

FRASER. Philosophy of Theism. Being the Gifford Lectures
delivered before the University of Edinburgh in 1894-95. First Series. By
Alexander Campbell Fraser, D.C.L., Oxford ; Emeritus Professor of Logic
and Metaphysics in the University of Edinburgh. Post 8vo, 7s. 6d. net.

FULLARTON.
Merlin : A Dramatic Poem. By Ralph Macleod Fullar-
ton. Crown 8vo, 5s.
Tanhäuser. Crown 8vo, 6s.
Lallan Sangs and German Lyrics. Crown 8vo, 5s.

GALT.
Novels by John Galt. With General Introduction and
Prefatory Notes by S. R. Crockett. The Text Revised and Edited by D.
Storrar Meldrum, Author of 'The Story of Margrédel.' With Photogravure
Illustrations from Drawings by John Wallace. Fcap. 8vo, 3s. net each vol.
Annals of the Parish, and The Ayrshire Legatees. 2 vols.
Sir Andrew Wylie. 2 vols.
The Entail. 2 vols.
The Provost, and The Last of the Lairds. 2 vols. [*In the press.*
See also Standard Novels, *p.* 6.

GENERAL ASSEMBLY OF THE CHURCH OF SCOTLAND.
Scottish Hymnal, With Appendix Incorporated. Published
for use in Churches by Authority of the General Assembly. 1. Large type,
cloth, red edges, 2s. 6d.; French morocco, 4s. 2. Bourgeois type, limp cloth, 1s.;
French morocco, 2s. 3. Nonpareil type, cloth, red edges, 6d.; French morocco,
1s. 4d. 4. Paper covers, 3d. 5. Sunday-School Edition, paper covers, 1d.,
cloth, 2d. No. 1, bound with the Psalms and Paraphrases, French morocco, 8s.
No. 2, bound with the Psalms and Paraphrases, cloth, 2s.; French morocco, 3s.
Prayers for Social and Family Worship. Prepared by a
Special Committee of the General Assembly of the Church of Scotland. Entirely
New Edition, Revised and Enlarged. Fcap. 8vo, red edges, 2s.

GENERAL ASSEMBLY OF THE CHURCH OF SCOTLAND.
Prayers for Family Worship. A Selection of Four Weeks'
Prayers. New Edition. Authorised by the General Assembly of the Church of
Scotland Fcap. 8vo, red edges, 1s. 6d.
One Hundred Prayers. Prepared by a Committee of the General Assembly of the Church of Scotland. 16mo, cloth limp, 6d.

GERARD.
Reata: What's in a Name. By E. D. GERARD. Cheap
Edition. Crown 8vo, 3s. 6d.
Beggar my Neighbour. Cheap Edition. Crown 8vo, 3s. 6d.
The Waters of Hercules. Cheap Edition. Crown 8vo, 3s. 6d.
A Sensitive Plant. Crown 8vo, 3s. 6d.

GERARD.
A Foreigner. An Anglo-German Study. By E. GERARD. In
1 vol. crown 8vo. *[In the press.*
The Land beyond the Forest. Facts, Figures, and Fancies
from Transylvania. With Maps and Illustrations. 2 vols. post 8vo, 25s.
Bis: Some Tales Retold. Crown 8vo, 6s.
A Secret Mission. 2 vols. crown 8vo, 17s.

GERARD.
The Wrong Man. By DOROTHEA GERARD. Crown 8vo, 6s.
Lady Baby. Cheap Edition. Crown 8vo, 3s. 6d.
Recha. Second Edition. Crown 8vo, 6s.
The Rich Miss Riddell. Second Edition. Crown 8vo, 6s.

GERARD. Stonyhurst Latin Grammar. By Rev. JOHN GERARD.
Second Edition. Fcap. 8vo, 3s.

GILL.
Free Trade: an Inquiry into the Nature of its Operation.
By RICHARD GILL. Crown 8vo, 7s. 6d.
Free Trade under Protection. Crown 8vo, 7s. 6d.

GOETHE. Poems and Ballads of Goethe. Translated by Professor AYTOUN and Sir THEODORE MARTIN, K.C.B. Third Edition. Fcap. 8vo, 6s.

GOETHE'S FAUST. Translated into English Verse by Sir
THEODORE MARTIN, K.C.B. Part I. Second Edition, crown 8vo, 6s. Ninth Edition, fcap., 3s. 6d. Part II. Second Edition, Revised. Fcap. 8vo, 6s.

GORDON CUMMING.
At Home in Fiji. By C. F. GORDON CUMMING. Fourth
Edition, post 8vo. With Illustrations and Map. 7s. 6d.
A Lady's Cruise in a French Man-of-War. New and Cheaper
Edition. 8vo. With Illustrations and Map. 12s. 6d.
Fire-Fountains. The Kingdom of Hawaii: Its Volcanoes,
and the History of its Missions. With Map and Illustrations. 2 vols. 8vo, 25s.
Wanderings in China. New and Cheaper Edition. 8vo, with
Illustrations, 10s.
Granite Crags: The Yō-semité Region of California. Illustrated with 8 Engravings. New and Cheaper Edition. 8vo, 8s. 6d.

GRAHAM. Manual of the Elections (Scot.) (Corrupt and Illegal
Practices) Act, 1890. With Analysis, Relative Act of Sederunt, Appendix containing the Corrupt Practices Acts of 1883 and 1885, and Copious Index. By J.
EDWARD GRAHAM, Advocate. 8vo, 4s. 6d.

GRAND.
A Domestic Experiment. By SARAH GRAND, Author of
'The Heavenly Twins,' 'Ideala: A Study from Life.' Crown 8vo, 6s.
Singularly Deluded. Crown 8vo, 6s.

GRANT. Bush-Life in Queensland. By A. C. GRANT. New
Edition. Crown 8vo, 6s.

GRANT. Life of Sir Hope Grant. With Selections from his
Correspondence. Edited by Henry Knollys, Colonel (H.P.) Royal Artillery,
his former A.D.C., Editor of 'Incidents in the Sepoy War;' Author of 'Sketches
of Life in Japan,' &c. With Portraits of Sir Hope Grant and other Illustrations. Maps and Plans. 2 vols. demy 8vo, 21s.

GRIER. In Furthest Ind. The Narrative of Mr Edward Car-
lyon of Ellswether, in the County of Northampton, and late of the Honourable
East India Company's Service, Gentleman. Wrote by his own hand in the year
of grace 1697. Edited, with a few Explanatory Notes, by Sydney C. Grier.
Post 8vo, 6s.

GUTHRIE-SMITH. Crispus: A Drama. By H. Guthrie-
Smith. Fcap. 4to, 5s.

HAGGARD. Under Crescent and Star. By Lieut.-Col. Andrew
Haggard, D.S.O., Author of 'Dodo and I,' 'Tempest Torn,' &c. With a
Portrait. Crown 8vo, 6s.

HALDANE. Subtropical Cultivations and Climates. A Handy
Book for Planters, Colonists, and Settlers. By R. C. Haldane. Post 8vo, 9s.

HAMERTON.
Wenderholme: A Story of Lancashire and Yorkshire Life.
By P. G. Hamerton, Author of 'A Painter's Camp.' New Edition. Crown
8vo, 3s. 6d.

Marmorne. New Edition. Crown 8vo, 3s. 6d.

HAMILTON.
Lectures on Metaphysics. By Sir William Hamilton,
Bart., Professor of Logic and Metaphysics in the University of Edinburgh.
Edited by the Rev. H. L. Mansel, B.D., LL.D., Dean of St Paul's; and John
Veitch, M.A., LL.D., Professor of Logic and Rhetoric, Glasgow. Seventh
Edition. 2 vols. 8vo, 24s.

Lectures on Logic. Edited by the Same. Third Edition,
Revised. 2 vols., 24s.

Discussions on Philosophy and Literature, Education and
University Reform. Third Edition. 8vo, 21s.

Memoir of Sir William Hamilton, Bart., Professor of Logic
and Metaphysics in the University of Edinburgh. By Professor Veitch, of the
University of Glasgow. 8vo, with Portrait, 18s.

Sir William Hamilton: The Man and his Philosophy. Two
Lectures delivered before the Edinburgh Philosophical Institution, January and
February 1883. By Professor Veitch. Crown 8vo, 2s.

HAMLEY.
The Life of General Sir Edward Bruce Hamley, K.C.B.,
K.C.M.G. By Alexander Innes Shand. With two Photogravure Portraits and
other Illustrations. 2 vols. demy 8vo, 21s.

The Operations of War Explained and Illustrated. By
General Sir Edward Bruce Hamley, K.C.B., K.C.M.G. Fifth Edition, Revised
throughout. 4to, with numerous Illustrations, 30s.

National Defence; Articles and Speeches. Post 8vo, 6s.

Shakespeare's Funeral, and other Papers. Post 8vo, 7s. 6d.

Thomas Carlyle: An Essay. Second Edition. Crown 8vo,
2s. 6d.

On Outposts. Second Edition. 8vo, 2s.

Wellington's Career; A Military and Political Summary.
Crown 8vo, 2s.

Lady Lee's Widowhood. New Edition. Crown 8vo, 3s. 6d.
Cheaper Edition, 2s. 6d.

Our Poor Relations. A Philozoic Essay. With Illustrations,
chiefly by Ernest Griset. Crown 8vo, cloth gilt, 3s. 6d.

HARE. Down the Village Street: Scenes in a West Country
Hamlet. By Christopher Hare. Crown 8vo, 6s.

HARRADEN. In Varying Moods : Short Stories. By BEATRICE
HARRADEN, Author of 'Ships that Pass in the Night.' Eleventh Edition.
Crown 8vo, 3s. 6d.

HARRIS.
Tafilet. The Narrative of a Journey of Exploration to the
Atlas Mountains and the Oases of the North-West Sahara. By WALTER B.
HARRIS, F.R.G.S., Author of 'The Land of an African Sultan ; Travels in
Morocco,' &c. With Illustrations by Maurice Romberg from Sketches and
Photographs by the Author, and Two Maps. Demy 8vo, 12s.

A Journey through the Yemen, and some General Remarks
upon that Country. With 3 Maps and numerous Illustrations by Forestier and
Wallace from Sketches and Photographs taken by the Author. Demy 8vo, 16s.

Danovitch, and other Stories. Crown 8vo, 6s.

HAWKER. The Prose Works of Rev. R. S. HAWKER, Vicar of
Morwenstow. Including 'Footprints of Former Men in Far Cornwall.' Re-edited,
with Sketches never before published. With a Frontispiece. Crown 8vo, 3s. 6d.

HAY. The Works of the Right Rev. Dr George Hay, Bishop of
Edinburgh. Edited under the Supervision of the Right Rev. Bishop STRAIN.
With Memoir and Portrait of the Author. 5 vols. crown 8vo, bound in extra
cloth, £1, 1s. The following Volumes may be had separately—viz. :
The Devout Christian Instructed in the Law of Christ from the Written
Word. 2 vols., 8s.—The Pious Christian Instructed in the Nature and Practice
of the Principal Exercises of Piety. 1 vol., 3s.

HEATLEY.
The Horse-Owner's Safeguard. A Handy Medical Guide for
every Man who owns a Horse. By G. S. HEATLEY, M.R.C.V.S. Crown 8vo, 5s.

The Stock-Owner's Guide. A Handy Medical Treatise for
every Man who owns an Ox or a Cow. Crown 8vo, 4s. 6d.

HEDDERWICK. Lays of Middle Age ; and other Poems. By
JAMES HEDDERWICK, LL.D., Author of 'Backward Glances.' Price 3s. 6d.

HEMANS.
The Poetical Works of Mrs Hemans. Copyright Editions.
Royal 8vo, 5s. The Same with Engravings, cloth, gilt edges, 7s. 6d.

Select Poems of Mrs Hemans. Fcap., cloth, gilt edges, 3s.

HERKLESS. Cardinal Beaton : Priest and Politician. By
JOHN HERKLESS, Professor of Church History, St Andrews. With a Portrait.
Post 8vo, 7s. 6d.

HEWISON. The Isle of Bute in the Olden Time. With Illus-
trations, Maps, and Plans. By JAMES KING HEWISON, M.A., F.S.A. (Scot.),
Minister of Rothesay. Vol. I., Celtic Saints and Heroes. Crown 4to, 15s. net.
Vol. II., The Royal Stewards and the Brandanes. Crown 4to, 15s. net.

HOME PRAYERS. By Ministers of the Church of Scotland
and Members of the Church Service Society. Second Edition. Fcap. 8vo, 3s.

HOMER.
The Odyssey. Translated into English Verse in the Spen-
serian Stanza. By PHILIP STANHOPE WORSLEY. New and Cheaper Edition.
Post 8vo, 7s. 6d. net.

The Iliad. Translated by P. S. WORSLEY and Professor CON-
INGTON. 2 vols. crown 8vo, 21s.

HUTCHINSON. Hints on the Game of Golf. By HORACE G.
HUTCHINSON. Eighth Edition, Enlarged. Fcap. 8vo, cloth, 1s.

HYSLOP. The Elements of Ethics. By JAMES H. HYSLOP,
Ph.D., Instructor in Ethics, Columbia College, New York, Author of 'The
Elements of Logic.' Post 8vo, 7s. 6d. net.

IDDESLEIGH.
Lectures and Essays. By the late EARL of IDDESLEIGH,
G.C.B., D.C.L., &c. 8vo, 16s.

Life, Letters, and Diaries of Sir Stafford Northcote, First
Earl of Iddesleigh. By ANDREW LANG. With Three Portraits and a View of
Pynes. Third Edition. 2 vols. post 8vo, 31s. 6d.

INDEX GEOGRAPHICUS: Being a List, alphabetically arranged, of the Principal Places on the Globe, with the Countries and Subdivisions of the Countries in which they are situated, and their Latitudes and Longitudes. Imperial 8vo, pp. 676, 21s.

JEAN JAMBON. Our Trip to Blunderland; or, Grand Excursion to Blundertown and Back. By JEAN JAMBON. With Sixty Illustrations designed by CHARLES DOYLE, engraved by DALZIEL. Fourth Thousand. Cloth, gilt edges, 6s. 6d. Cheap Edition, cloth, 3s. 6d. Boards, 2s. 6d.

JEBB. A Strange Career. The Life and Adventures of JOHN GLADWYN JEBB. By his Widow. With an Introduction by H. RIDER HAGGARD, and an Electrogravure Portrait of Mr Jebb. Third Edition. Demy 8vo, 10s. 6d. CHEAP EDITION. With Illustrations by John Wallace. Crown 8vo, 3s. 6d.

JENNINGS. Mr Gladstone : A Study. By LOUIS J. JENNINGS, M.P., Author of 'Republican Government in the United States,' 'The Croker Memoirs,' &c. Popular Edition. Crown 8vo, 1s.

JERNINGHAM.
Reminiscences of an Attaché. By HUBERT E. H. JERNINGHAM. Second Edition. Crown 8vo, 5s.

Diane de Breteuille. A Love Story. Crown 8vo, 2s. 6d.

JOHNSTON.
The Chemistry of Common Life. By Professor J. F. W. JOHNSTON. New Edition, Revised. By ARTHUR HERBERT CHURCH, M.A. Oxon.; Author of 'Food : its Sources, Constituents, and Uses,' &c. With Maps and 102 Engravings. Crown 8vo, 7s. 6d.

Elements of Agricultural Chemistry. An entirely New Edition from the Edition by Sir CHARLES A. CAMERON, M.D., F.R.C.S.I., &c. Revised and brought down to date by C. M. AIKMAN, M.A., B.Sc., F.R.S.E., Professor of Chemistry, Glasgow Veterinary College. Crown 8vo, 6s. 6d.

Catechism of Agricultural Chemistry. An entirely New Edition from the Edition by Sir CHARLES A. CAMERON. Revised and Enlarged by C. M. AIKMAN, M.A., &c. 92d Thousand. With numerous Illustrations. Crown 8vo, 1s.

JOHNSTON. Agricultural Holdings (Scotland) Acts, 1883 and 1889 ; and the Ground Game Act, 1880. With Notes, and Summary of Procedure, &c. By CHRISTOPHER N. JOHNSTON, M.A., Advocate. Demy 8vo, 5s.

JOKAI. Timar's Two Worlds. By MAURUS JOKAI. Authorised Translation by Mrs HEGAN KENNARD. Cheap Edition. Crown 8vo, 6s.

KEBBEL. The Old and the New : English Country Life By T. E. KEBBEL, M.A., Author of 'The Agricultural Labourers,' 'Essays in History and Politics,' 'Life of Lord Beaconsfield.' Crown 8vo, 5s.

KERR. St Andrews in 1645-46. By D. R. KERR. Crown 8vo, 2s. 6d.

KING. The Metamorphoses of Ovid. Translated in English Blank Verse. By HENRY KING, M.A., Fellow of Wadham College, Oxford, and of the Inner Temple, Barrister-at-Law. Crown 8vo, 10s. 6d.

KINGLAKE.
History of the Invasion of the Crimea. By A. W. KINGLAKE. Cabinet Edition, Revised. With an Index to the Complete Work. Illustrated with Maps and Plans. Complete in 9 vols., crown 8vo, at 6s. each.

History of the Invasion of the Crimea. Demy 8vo. Vol. VI. Winter Troubles. With a Map, 16s. Vols. VII. and VIII. From the Morrow of Inkerman to the Death of Lord Raglan. With an Index to the Whole Work. With Maps and Plans. 28s.

Eothen. A New Edition, uniform with the Cabinet Edition of the 'History of the Invasion of the Crimea.' 6s.

KIRBY. In Haunts of Wild Game : A Hunter-Naturalist's Wanderings from Kahlamba to Libombo. By FREDERICK VAUGHAN KIRBY, F.Z.S. (Maqaqamba). With numerous Illustrations by Charles Whymper, and a Map. 1 vol. large demy 8vo. [*In the press.*]

KLEIN. Among the Gods. Scenes of India, with Legends by
the Way. By AUGUSTA KLEIN. With 22 Full-page Illustrations. Demy 8vo, 15s.

KNEIPP. My Water-Cure. As Tested through more than
Thirty Years, and Described for the Healing of Diseases and the Preservation of
Health. By SEBASTIAN KNEIPP, Parish Priest of Wörishofen (Bavaria). With a
Portrait and other Illustrations. Authorised English Translation from the
Thirtieth German Edition, by A. de F. Cheap Edition. With an Appendix, con-
taining the Latest Developments of Pfarrer Kneipp's System, and a Preface by
E. Gerard. Crown 8vo, 3s. 6d.

KNOLLYS. The Elements of Field-Artillery. Designed for
the Use of Infantry and Cavalry Officers. By HENRY KNOLLYS, Colonel Royal
Artillery; Author of 'From Sedan to Saarbrück,' Editor of 'Incidents in the
Sepoy War,' &c. With Engravings. Crown 8vo, 7s. 6d.

LAMINGTON. In the Days of the Dandies. By the late Lord
LAMINGTON. Crown 8vo. Illustrated cover, 1s.; cloth, 1s. 6d.

LANG. Life, Letters, and Diaries of Sir Stafford Northcote,
First Earl of Iddesleigh. By ANDREW LANG. With Three Portraits and a View
of Pynes. Third Edition. 2 vols. post 8vo, 31s. 6d.
POPULAR EDITION. With Portrait and View of Pynes. Post 8vo, 7s. 6d.

LEES. A Handbook of the Sheriff and Justice of Peace Small
Debt Courts. With Notes, References, and Forms. By J. M. LEES, Advocate,
Sheriff of Stirling, Dumbarton, and Clackmannan. 8vo, 7s. 6d.

LINDSAY. The Progressiveness of Modern Christian Thought.
By the Rev. JAMES LINDSAY, M.A., B.D., B.Sc., F.R.S.E., F.G.S., Minister of
the Parish of St Andrew's, Kilmarnock. Crown 8vo, 6s.

LOCKHART.
Doubles and Quits. By LAURENCE W. M. LOCKHART. New
Edition. Crown 8vo, 3s. 6d.
Fair to See. New Edition. Crown 8vo, 3s. 6d.
Mine is Thine. New Edition. Crown 8vo, 3s. 6d.

LOCKHART.
The Church of Scotland in the Thirteenth Century. The
Life and Times of David de Bernham of St Andrews (Bishop), A.D. 1239 to 1253.
With List of Churches dedicated by him, and Dates. By WILLIAM LOCKHART,
A.M., D.D., F.S.A. Scot., Minister of Colinton Parish. 2d Edition. 8vo, 6s.
Dies Tristes : Sermons for Seasons of Sorrow. Crown 8vo, 6s.

LORIMER.
The Institutes of Law : A Treatise of the Principles of Juris-
prudence as determined by Nature. By the late JAMES LORIMER, Professor of
Public Law and of Nature and Nations in the University of Edin-
burgh. New Edition, Revised and much Enlarged. 8vo, 18s.
The Institutes of the Law of Nations. A Treatise of the
Jural Relation of Separate Political Communities. In 2 vols. 8vo. Volume I.,
price 16s. Volume II., price 20s.

LUGARD. The Rise of our East African Empire : Early Efforts
in Uganda and Nyasaland. By F. D. LUGARD, Captain Norfolk Regiment.
With 130 Illustrations from Drawings and Photographs under the personal
superintendence of the Author, and 14 specially prepared Maps. In 2 vols. large
demy 8vo, 42s.

M'CHESNEY. Kathleen Clare: Her Book, 1637-41. Edited by
DORA GREENWELL M'CHESNEY. With Frontispiece, and five full-page Illustrations by James A. Shearman. Crown 8vo, 6s.

M'COMBIE. Cattle and Cattle-Breeders. By WILLIAM M'COMBIE,
Tillyfour. New Edition, Enlarged, with Memoir of the Author by JAMES
MACDONALD, F.R.S.E., Secretary Highland and Agricultural Society of Scotland,
Crown 8vo, 3s. 6d.

M'CRIE.
Works of the Rev. Thomas M'Crie, D.D. Uniform Edition.
4 vols. crown 8vo, 24s.
Life of John Knox. Crown 8vo, 6s. Another Edition, 3s. 6d.
Life of Andrew Melville. Crown 8vo, 6s.
History of the Progress and Suppression of the Reformation
in Italy in the Sixteenth Century. Crown 8vo, 4s.
History of the Progress and Suppression of the Reformation
in Spain in the Sixteenth Century. Crown 8vo, 3s. 6d.

M'CRIE. The Public Worship of Presbyterian Scotland. Histori-
cally treated. With copious Notes, Appendices, and Index. The Fourteenth
Series of the Cunningham Lectures. By the Rev. CHARLES G. M'CRIE, D.D.
Demy 8vo, 10s. 6d.

MACDONALD. A Manual of the Criminal Law (Scotland) Procedure Act, 1887. By NORMAN DORAN MACDONALD. Revised by the LORD
JUSTICE-CLERK. 8vo, 10s. 6d.

MACDONALD.
Stephens' Book of the Farm. Fourth Edition. Revised and
in great part Rewritten by JAMES MACDONALD, F.R.S.E., Secretary, Highland
and Agricultural Society of Scotland. Complete in 3 vols., bound with leather
back, gilt top, £3, 3s. In Six Divisional Vols., bound in cloth, each 10s. 6d.
Stephens' Catechism of Practical Agriculture. New Edition.
Revised by JAMES MACDONALD. With numerous Illustrations. Crown 8vo, 1s.
Pringle's Live Stock of the Farm. Third Edition. Revised
and Edited by JAMES MACDONALD. Crown 8vo, 7s. 6d.
M'Combie's Cattle and Cattle - Breeders. New Edition,
Enlarged, with Memoir of the Author by JAMES MACDONALD. Crown 8vo, 3s. 6d.
History of Polled Aberdeen and Angus Cattle. Giving an
Account of the Origin, Improvement, and Characteristics of the Breed. By JAMES
MACDONALD and JAMES SINCLAIR. Illustrated with numerous Animal Portraits.
Post 8vo, 12s. 6d.

MACDOUGALL AND DODDS. A Manual of the Local Govern-
ment (Scotland) Act, 1894. With Introduction, Explanatory Notes, and Copious
Index. By J. PATTEN MACDOUGALL, Legal Secretary to the Lord Advocate, and
J. M. DODDS. Tenth Thousand, Revised. Crown 8vo, 2s. 6d. net.

MACINTYRE. Hindu - Koh : Wanderings and Wild Sports on
and beyond the Himalayas. By Major-General DONALD MACINTYRE, V.C., late
Prince of Wales' Own Goorkhas, F.R.G.S. *Dedicated to H.R.H. The Prince of
Wales.* New and Cheaper Edition, Revised, with numerous Illustrations. Post
8vo, 3s. 6d.

MACKAY.
A Manual of Modern Geography ; Mathematical, Physical,
and Political. By the Rev. ALEXANDER MACKAY, LL.D., F.R.G.S. 11th
Thousand, Revised to the present time. Crown 8vo, pp. 688, 7s. 6d.
Elements of Modern Geography. 55th Thousand, Revised to
the present time. Crown 8vo, pp. 300, 3s.
The Intermediate Geography. Intended as an Intermediate
Book between the Author's 'Outlines of Geography' and 'Elements of Geo-
graphy.' Seventeenth Edition, Revised. Crown 8vo, pp. 238, 2s.
Outlines of Modern Geography. 191st Thousand, Revised to
the present time. 18mo, pp. 128, 1s.
First Steps in Geography. 105th Thousand. 18mo, pp. 56.
Sewed, 4d. ; cloth, 6d.
Elements of Physiography. New Edition. Rewritten and
Enlarged. With numerous Illustrations. Crown 8vo. [*In the press.*

MACKENZIE. Studies in Roman Law. With Comparative
Views of the Laws of France, England, and Scotland. By Lord MACKENZIE,
one of the Judges of the Court of Session in Scotland. Sixth Edition, Edited
by JOHN KIRKPATRICK, M.A., LL.B., Advocate, Professor of History in the
University of Edinburgh. 8vo, 12s.

MACPHERSON. Glimpses of Church and Social Life in the
Highlands in Olden Times. By ALEXANDER MACPHERSON, F.S.A. Scot. With
6 Photogravure Portraits and other full-page Illustrations. Small 4to, 25s.

M'PHERSON. Golf and Golfers. Past and Present. By J.
GORDON M'PHERSON, Ph.D., F.R.S.E. With an Introduction by the Right Hon.
A. J. BALFOUR, and a Portrait of the Author. Fcap. 8vo, 1s. 6d.

MACRAE. A Handbook of Deer-Stalking. By ALEXANDER
MACRAE, late Forester to Lord Henry Bentinck. With Introduction by Horatio
Ross, Esq. Fcap. 8vo, with 2 Photographs from Life. 3s. 6d.

MAIN. Three Hundred English Sonnets. Chosen and Edited
by DAVID M. MAIN. Fcap. 8vo, 6s.

MAIR. A Digest of Laws and Decisions, Ecclesiastical and
Civil, relating to the Constitution, Practice, and Affairs of the Church of Scot-
land. With Notes and Forms of Procedure. By the Rev. WILLIAM MAIR, D.D.,
Minister of the Parish of Earlston. New Edition, Revised. Crown 8vo, 9s. *net*.

MARCHMONT AND THE HUMES OF POLWARTH. By
One of their Descendants. With numerous Portraits and other Illustrations.
Crown 4to, 21s. net.

MARSHMAN. History of India. From the Earliest Period to
the present time. By JOHN CLARK MARSHMAN, C.S.I. Third and Cheaper
Edition. Post 8vo, with Map, 6s.

MARTIN.
Goethe's Faust. Part I. Translated by Sir THEODORE MARTIN,
K.C.B. Second Edition, crown 8vo, 6s. Ninth Edition, fcap. 8vo, 3s. 6d.
Goethe's Faust. Part II. Translated into English Verse.
Second Edition, Revised. Fcap. 8vo, 6s.
The Works of Horace. Translated into English Verse, with
Life and Notes. 2 vols. New Edition. Crown 8vo, 21s.
Poems and Ballads of Heinrich Heine. Done into English
Verse. Third Edition. Small crown 8vo, 5s.
The Song of the Bell, and other Translations from Schiller,
Goethe, Uhland, and Others. Crown 8vo, 7s. 6d.
Madonna Pia: A Tragedy; and Three Other Dramas. Crown
8vo, 7s. 6d.
Catullus. With Life and Notes. Second Edition, Revised
and Corrected. Post 8vo, 7s. 6d.
The 'Vita Nuova' of Dante. Translated, with an Introduction
and Notes. Third Edition. Small crown 8vo, 5s.
Aladdin: A Dramatic Poem. By ADAM OEHLENSCHLAEGER.
Fcap. 8vo, 5s.
Correggio: A Tragedy. By OEHLENSCHLAEGER. With Notes.
Fcap. 8vo, 3s.

MARTIN. On some of Shakespeare's Female Characters. By
HELENA FAUCIT, Lady MARTIN. Dedicated by permission to Her Most Gracious
Majesty the Queen. Fifth Edition. With a Portrait by Lehmann. Demy
8vo, 7s. 6d.

MARWICK. Observations on the Law and Practice in regard
to Municipal Elections and the Conduct of the Business of Town Councils and
Commissioners of Police in Scotland. By Sir JAMES D. MARWICK, LL.D.,
Town-Clerk of Glasgow. Royal 8vo, 30s.

MATHESON.
Can the Old Faith Live with the New? or, **The Problem of**
Evolution and Revelation. By the Rev. GEORGE MATHESON, D.D. Third Edition. Crown 8vo, 7s. 6d.
The Psalmist and the Scientist; or, **Modern Value of the Reli-**
gious Sentiment. Third Edition. Crown 8vo, 5s.
Spiritual Development of St Paul. Third Edition. Cr. 8vo, 5s.
The Distinctive Messages of the Old Religions. Second Edi-
tion. Crown 8vo, 5s.
Sacred Songs. New and Cheaper Edition. Crown 8vo, 2s. 6d.
MAURICE. The Balance of Military Power in Europe. An
Examination of the War Resources of Great Britain and the Continental States.
By Colonel MAURICE, R.A., Professor of Military Art and History at the Royal
Staff College. Crown 8vo, with a Map, 6s.
MAXWELL.
A Duke of Britain. A Romance of the Fourth Century.
By Sir HERBERT MAXWELL, Bart., M.P., F.S.A., &c., Author of 'Passages in
the Life of Sir Lucian Elphin.' Fourth Edition. Crown 8vo, 6s.
Life and Times of the Rt. Hon. William Henry Smith, M.P.
With Portraits and numerous Illustrations by Herbert Railton, G. L. Seymour,
and Others. 2 vols. demy 8vo, 25s.
POPULAR EDITION. With a Portrait and other Illustrations. Crown 8vo, 3s. 6d.
Scottish Land Names : Their Origin and Meaning. Being
the Rhind Lectures in Archæology for 1893. Post 8vo, 6s.
Meridiana : Noontide Essays. Post 8vo, 7s. 6d.
Post Meridiana : Afternoon Essays. Post 8vo, 6s.
MELDRUM.
The Story of Margrédel : Being a Fireside History of a Fife-
shire Family. By D. STORRAR MELDRUM. Cheap Edition. Crown 8vo, 3s. 6d.
Grey Mantle and Gold Fringe. 1 vol. crown 8vo. [*In the press*
MICHEL. A Critical Inquiry into the Scottish Language. With
the view of Illustrating the Rise and Progress of Civilisation in Scotland. By
FRANCISQUE-MICHEL, F.S.A. Lond. and Scot., Correspondant de l'Institut de
France, &c. 4to, printed on hand-made paper, and bound in roxburghe, 66s.
MICHIE.
The Larch : Being a Practical Treatise on its Culture and
General Management. By CHRISTOPHER Y. MICHIE, Forester, Cullen House.
Crown 8vo, with Illustrations. New and Cheaper Edition, Enlarged, 5s.
The Practice of Forestry. Crown 8vo, with Illustrations. 6s.
MIDDLETON. The Story of Alastair Bhan Comyn; or, **The**
Tragedy of Dunphail. A Tale of Tradition and Romance. By the Lady MIDDLE-
TON. Square 8vo, 10s. Cheaper Edition, 5s.
MINTO.
A Manual of English Prose Literature, Biographical and
Critical : designed mainly to show Characteristics of Style. By W. MINTO,
M.A., Hon. LL.D. of St Andrews ; Professor of Logic in the University of Aber-
deen. Third Edition, Revised. Crown 8vo, 7s. 6d.
Characteristics of English Poets, from Chaucer to Shirley.
New Edition, Revised. Crown 8vo, 7s. 6d.
Plain Principles of Prose Composition. Crown 8vo, 1s. 6d.
The Literature of the Georgian Era. Edited, with a Bio-
graphical Introduction, by Professor KNIGHT, St Andrews. Post 8vo, 6s.

MOIR. Life of Mansie Wauch, Tailor in Dalkeith. By D. M.
Moir. With Cruikshank's Illustrations. Cheaper Edition. Crown 8vo, 2s. 6d.
Another Edition, without Illustrations, fcap. 8vo, 1s. 6d.

MOLE. For the Sake of a Slandered Woman. By MARION
Mole. Fcap. 8vo, 2s. 6d. net.

MOMERIE.

Defects of Modern Christianity, and other Sermons. By
Alfred Williams Momerie, M.A., D.Sc., LL.D. Fifth Edition. Crown
8vo, 5s.

The Basis of Religion. Being an Examination of Natural
Religion. Third Edition. Crown 8vo, 2s. 6d.

The Origin of Evil, and other Sermons. Eighth Edition,
Enlarged. Crown 8vo, 5s.

Personality. The Beginning and End of Metaphysics, and
a Necessary Assumption in all Positive Philosophy. Fifth Edition, Revised.
Crown 8vo, 3s.

Agnosticism. Fourth Edition, Revised. Crown 8vo, 5s.

Preaching and Hearing ; and other Sermons. Fourth Edition,
Enlarged. Crown 8vo, 5s.

Belief in God. Third Edition. Crown 8vo, 3s.

Inspiration ; and other Sermons. Second Edition, Enlarged.
Crown 8vo, 5s.

Church and Creed. Third Edition. Crown 8vo, 4s. 6d.

The Future of Religion, and other Essays. Second Edition.
Crown 8vo, 3s. 6d.

MONCREIFF. The X Jewel. A Scottish Romance of the Days
of James VI. By the Hon. Frederick Moncreiff. In 1 vol. crown 8vo.
[*In the press.*

MONTAGUE. Military Topography. Illustrated by Practical
Examples of a Practical Subject. By Major-General W. E. Montague, C.B.,
P.S.C., late Garrison Instructor Intelligence Department, Author of 'Campaign-
ing in South Africa.' With Forty-one Diagrams. Crown 8vo, 5s.

MONTALEMBERT. Memoir of Count de Montalembert. A
Chapter of Recent French History. By Mrs Oliphant, Author of the 'Life of
Edward Irving,' &c. 2 vols. crown 8vo, £1, 4s.

MORISON.

Doorside Ditties. By Jeanie Morison. With a Frontispiece. Crown 8vo, 3s. 6d.

Æolus. A Romance in Lyrics. Crown 8vo, 3s.

There as Here. Crown 8vo, 3s.
   ₊ *A limited impression on hand-made paper, bound in vellum, 7s. 6d.*

Selections from Poems. Crown 8vo, 4s. 6d.

Sordello. An Outline Analysis of Mr Browning's Poem.
Crown 8vo, 3s.

Of "Fifine at the Fair," "Christmas Eve and Easter Day,"
and other of Mr Browning's Poems. Crown 8vo, 3s.

The Purpose of the Ages. Crown 8vo, 9s.

Gordon : An Our-day Idyll. Crown 8vo, 3s.

Saint Isadora, and other Poems. Crown 8vo, 1s. 6d.

Snatches of Song. Paper, 1s. 6d. ; Cloth, 3s.

Pontius Pilate. Paper, 1s. 6d. ; Cloth, 3s.

Mill o' Forres. Crown 8vo, 1s.

Ane Booke of Ballades. Fcap. 4to, 1s.

MOZLEY. Essays from 'Blackwood.' By the late ANNE MOZLEY, Author of 'Essays on Social Subjects'; Editor of 'The Letters and Correspondence of Cardinal Newman,' 'Letters of the Rev. J. B. Mozley,' &c. With a Memoir by her Sister, FANNY MOZLEY. Post 8vo, 7s. 6d.

MUNRO. Rambles and Studies in Bosnia-Herzegovina and Dalmatia. With an Account of the Proceedings of the Congress of Archæologists and Anthropologists held at Sarajevo in 18 4. By ROBERT MUNRO, M.A., M.D , F.R.S.E., Author of 'The Lake-Dwellings of Europe,' &c. With numerous Illustrations. 1 vol. demy 8vo. *[In the press.*

MUNRO. On Valuation of Property. By WILLIAM MUNRO, M.A., Her Majesty's Assessor of Railways and Canals for Scotland. Second Edition, Revised and Enlarged. 8vo, 3s. 6d.

MURDOCH. Manual of the Law of Insolvency and Bankruptcy: Comprehending a Summary of the Law of Insolvency, Notour Bankruptcy, Composition-contracts, Trust-deeds, Cessios, and Sequestrations; and the Winding-up of Joint-Stock Companies in Scotland; with Annotations on the various Insolvency and Bankruptcy Statutes; and with Forms of Procedure applicable to these Subjects. By JAMES MURDOCH, Member of the Faculty of Procurators in Glasgow. Fifth Edition, Revised and Enlarged. 8vo, 12s. net.

MY TRIVIAL LIFE AND MISFORTUNE: A Gossip with no Plot in Particular. By A PLAIN WOMAN. Cheap Edition. Crown 8vo, 3s. 6d.

By the SAME AUTHOR.

POOR NELLIE. Cheap Edition. Crown 8vo, 3s. 6d.

MY WEATHER-WISE COMPANION. Presented by B. T. Fcap. 8vo, 1s. net.

NAPIER. The Construction of the Wonderful Canon of Logarithms. By JOHN NAPIER of Merchiston. Translated, with Notes, and a Catalogue of Napier's Works, by WILLIAM RAE MACDONALD. Small 4to, 15s. *A few large-paper copies on Whatman paper,* 30s.

NEAVES.

Songs and Verses, Social and Scientific. By An Old Contributor to 'Maga.' By the Hon. Lord NEAVES. Fifth Edition. Fcap. 8vo, 4s.

The Greek Anthology. Being Vol. XX. of 'Ancient Classics for English Readers.' Crown 8vo, 2s. 6d.

NICHOLSON.

A Manual of Zoology, for the use of Students. With a General Introduction on the Principles of Zoology. By HENRY ALLEYNE NICHOLSON, M.D. D.Sc., F.L.S., F.G.S., Regius Professor of Natural History in the University of Aberdeen. Seventh Edition, Rewritten and Enlarged. Post 8vo, pp. 956, with 555 Engravings on Wood, 18s.

Text-Book of Zoology, for Junior Students. Fifth Edition, Rewritten and Enlarged. Crown 8vo, with 358 Engravings on Wood, 10s. 6d.

Introductory Text-Book of Zoology, for the use of Junior Classes. Sixth Edition, Revised and Enlarged, with 166 Engravings, 3s.

Outlines of Natural History, for Beginners: being Description of a Progressive Series of Zoological Types. Third Edition, with Engravings, 1s. 6d.

A Manual of Palæontology, for the use of Students. With a General Introduction on the Principles of Palæontology. By Professor H. ALLEYNE NICHOLSON and RICHARD LYDEKKER, B.A. Third Edition, entirely Rewritten and greatly Enlarged. 2 vols. 8vo, £3, 3s.

The Ancient Life-History of the Earth. An Outline of the Principles and Leading Facts of Palæontological Science. Crown 8vo, with 276 Engravings, 10s. 6d.

On the "Tabulate Corals" of the Palæozoic Period, with Critical Descriptions of Illustrative Species. Illustrated with 15 Lithographed Plates and numerous Engravings. Super-royal 8vo, 21s.

NICHOLSON.
Synopsis of the Classification of the Animal Kingdom. 8vo,
with 106 Illustrations, 6s.
On the Structure and Affinities of the Genus Monticulipora
and its Sub-Genera, with Critical Descriptions of Illustrative Species. Illustrated
with numerous Engravings on Wood and Lithographed Plates. Super-royal
8vo, 18s.
NICHOLSON.
Thoth. A Romance. By JOSEPH SHIELD NICHOLSON, M.A.,
D.Sc., Professor of Commercial and Political Economy and Mercantile Law in
the University of Edinburgh. Third Edition. Crown 8vo, 4s. 6d.
A Dreamer of Dreams. A Modern Romance. Second Edi-
tion. Crown 8vo, 6s.
NICOLSON AND MURE. A Handbook to the Local Govern-
ment (Scotland) Act, 1889. With Introduction, Explanatory Notes, and Index.
By J. BADENACH NICOLSON, Advocate, Counsel to the Scotch Education
Department, and W. J. MURE, Advocate, Legal Secretary to the Lord Advocate
for Scotland. Ninth Reprint. 8vo, 5s.

OLIPHANT.
Masollam : A Problem of the Period. A Novel. By LAURENCE
OLIPHANT. 3 vols. post 8vo, 25s. 6d.
Scientific Religion ; or, Higher Possibilities of Life and
Practice through the Operation of Natural Forces. Second Edition. 8vo, 16s.
Altiora Peto. Cheap Edition. Crown 8vo, boards, 2s. 6d. ;
cloth, 3s. 6d. Illustrated Edition. Crown 8vo, cloth, 6s.
Piccadilly. With Illustrations by Richard Doyle. New Edi-
tion, 3s. 6d. Cheap Edition, boards, 2s. 6d.
Traits and Travesties ; Social and Political. Post 8vo, 10s. 6d.
Episodes in a Life of Adventure ; or, Moss from a Rolling
Stone. Cheaper Edition. Post 8vo, 3s. 6d.
Haifa : Life in Modern Palestine. Second Edition. 8vo, 7s. 6d.
The Land of Gilead. With Excursions in the Lebanon.
With Illustrations and Maps. Demy 8vo, 21s.
Memoir of the Life of Laurence Oliphant, and of Alice
Oliphant, his Wife. By Mrs M. O. W. OLIPHANT. Seventh Edition. 2 vols.
post 8vo, with Portraits. 21s.
POPULAR EDITION. With a New Preface. Post 8vo, with Portraits. 7s. 6d.
OLIPHANT.
Who was Lost and is Found. By Mrs OLIPHANT. Second
Edition. Crown 8vo, 6s.
Miss Marjoribanks. New Edition. Crown 8vo, 3s. 6d.
The Perpetual Curate, and The Rector. New Edition. Crown
8vo, 3s. 6d.
Salem Chapel, and The Doctor's Family. New Edition.
Crown 8vo, 3s. 6d.
Katie Stewart, and other Stories. New Edition. Crown 8vo,
cloth, 3s. 6d.
Valentine and his Brother. New Edition. Crown 8vo, 3s. 6d.
Sons and Daughters. Crown 8vo, 3s. 6d.
Katie Stewart. Illustrated boards, 2s. 6d.
Two Stories of the Seen and the Unseen. The Open Door
—Old Lady Mary. Paper covers, 1s.
OLIPHANT. Notes of a Pilgrimage to Jerusalem and the Holy
Land. By F. R. OLIPHANT. Crown 8vo, 3s. 6d.
OSWALD. By Fell and Fjord ; or, Scenes and Studies in Ice-
land. By E. J. OSWALD. Post 8vo, with Illustrations. 7s. 6d.

PAGE.

Introductory Text-Book of Geology. By DAVID PAGE, LL.D., Professor of Geology in the Durham University of Physical Science, Newcastle, and Professor LAPWORTH of Mason Science College, Birmingham. With Engravings and Glossarial Index. Twelfth Edition, Revised and Enlarged. 3s. 6d.

Advanced Text-Book of Geology, Descriptive and Industrial. With Engravings, and Glossary of Scientific Terms. New Edition, by Professor LAPWORTH. [*In preparation.*

Introductory Text-Book of Physical Geography. With Sketch-Maps and Illustrations. Edited by Professor LAPWORTH, LL.D., F.G.S., &c., Mason Science College, Birmingham. Thirteenth Edition, Revised and Enlarged. 2s. 6d.

Advanced Text-Book of Physical Geography. Third Edition. Revised and Enlarged by Professor LAPWORTH. With Engravings. 5s.

PATON.

Spindrift. By Sir J. NOEL PATON. Fcap., cloth, 5s.

Poems by a Painter. Fcap., cloth, 5s.

PATON. Body and Soul. A Romance in Transcendental Pathology. By FREDERICK NOEL PATON. Third Edition. Crown 8vo, 1s.

PATRICK. The Apology of Origen in Reply to Celsus. A Chapter in the History of Apologetics. By the Rev. J. PATRICK, B.D. Post 8vo, 7s. 6d.

PAUL. History of the Royal Company of Archers, the Queen's Body-Guard for Scotland. By JAMES BALFOUR PAUL, Advocate of the Scottish Bar. Crown 4to, with Portraits and other Illustrations. £2, 2s.

PEILE. Lawn Tennis as a Game of Skill. By Lieut.-Col. S. C. F. PEILE, B.S.C. Revised Edition. Fcap., cloth, 1s.

PETTIGREW. The Handy Book of Bees, and their Profitable Management. By A. PETTIGREW. Fifth Edition, Enlarged, with Engravings. Crown 8vo, 3s. 6d.

PFLEIDERER. Philosophy and Development of Religion. Being the Edinburgh Gifford Lectures for 1894. By OTTO PFLEIDERER, D.D., Professor of Theology at Berlin University. In 2 vols. post 8vo, 15s. net.

PHILOSOPHICAL CLASSICS FOR ENGLISH READERS. Edited by WILLIAM KNIGHT, LL.D., Professor of Moral Philosophy, University of St Andrews. In crown 8vo volumes, with Portraits, price 3s. 6d. [*For List of Volumes, see page 2.*

POLLARD. A Study in Municipal Government : The Corporation of Berlin. By JAMES POLLARD, C.A., Chairman of the Edinburgh Public Health Committee, and Secretary of the Edinburgh Chamber of Commerce. Second Edition, Revised. Crown 8vo, 3s. 6d.

POLLOK. The Course of Time : A Poem. By ROBERT POLLOK, A.M. Cottage Edition, 32mo, 8d. The Same, cloth, gilt edges, 1s. 6d. Another Edition, with Illustrations by Birket Foster and others, fcap., cloth, 3s. 6d., or with edges gilt, 4s.

PORT ROYAL LOGIC. Translated from the French ; with Introduction, Notes, and Appendix. By THOMAS SPENCER BAYNES, LL.D., Professor in the University of St Andrews. Tenth Edition, 12mo, 4s.

POTTS AND DARNELL.

Aditus Faciliores : An Easy Latin Construing Book, with Complete Vocabulary. By A. W. POTTS, M.A., LL.D., and the Rev. C. DARNELL, M.A., Head-Master of Cargilfield Preparatory School, Edinburgh. Tenth Edition, fcap. 8vo, 3s. 6d.

POTTS AND DARNELL.
Aditus Faciliores Graeci. An Easy Greek Construing Book,
with Complete Vocabulary. Fifth Edition, Revised. Fcap. 8vo, 3s.

POTTS. School Sermons. By the late ALEXANDER WM. POTTS,
LL.D., First Head-Master of Fettes College. With a Memoir and Portrait
Crown 8vo, 7s. 6d.

PRINGLE. The Live - Stock of the Farm. By ROBERT O.
PRINGLE. Third Edition. Revised and Edited by JAMES MACDONALD. Crown
8vo, 7s. 6d.

PRYDE. Pleasant Memories of a Busy Life. By DAVID PRYDE,
M.A., LL.D., Author of 'Highways of Literature,' 'Great Men in European History,' 'Biographical Outlines of English Literature,' &c. With a Mezzotint Portrait. Post 8vo, 6s.

PUBLIC GENERAL STATUTES AFFECTING SCOTLAND
from 1707 to 1847, with Chronological Table and Index. 3 vols. large 8vo, £3, 3s.

PUBLIC GENERAL STATUTES AFFECTING SCOTLAND,
COLLECTION OF. Published Annually, with General Index.

RAE. The Syrian Church in India. By GEORGE MILNE RAE,
M.A., D.D., Fellow of the University of Madras; late Professor in the Madras
Christian College. With 6 full-page Illustrations. Post 8vo, 10s. 6d.

RAMSAY. Scotland and Scotsmen in the Eighteenth Century.
Edited from the MSS. of JOHN RAMSAY, Esq. of Ochtertyre, by ALEXANDER
ALLARDYCE, Author of 'Memoir of Admiral Lord Keith, K.B.,' &c. 2 vols.
8vo, 31s. 6d.

RANKIN. The Zambesi Basin and Nyassaland. By DANIEL J.
RANKIN, F.R.S.G.S., M.R.A.S. With 3 Maps and 10 full-page Illustrations.
Post 8vo, 10s. 6d.

RANKIN.
A Handbook of the Church of Scotland. By JAMES RANKIN,
D.D., Minister of Muthill; Author of 'Character Studies in the Old Testament,
&c. An entirely New and much Enlarged Edition. Crown 8vo, with 2 Maps,
7s. 6d.

The First Saints. Post 8vo, 7s. 6d.

The Creed in Scotland. An Exposition of the Apostles'
Creed. With Extracts from Archbishop Hamilton's Catechism of 1552, John
Calvin's Catechism of 1556, and a Catena of Ancient Latin and other Hymns.
Post 8vo, 7s. 6d.

The Worthy Communicant. A Guide to the Devout Obser-
vance of the Lord's Supper. Limp cloth, 1s. 3d.

The Young Churchman. Lessons on the Creed, the Com-
mandments, the Means of Grace, and the Church. Limp cloth, 1s. 3d.

First Communion Lessons. 25th Edition. Paper Cover, 2d.

RECORDS OF THE TERCENTENARY FESTIVAL OF THE
UNIVERSITY OF EDINBURGH. Celebrated in April 1884. Published under
the Sanction of the Senatus Academicus. Large 4to, £2, 12s. 6d.

ROBERTSON. The Early Religion of Israel. As set forth by
Biblical Writers and Modern Critical Historians. Being the Baird Lecture for
1888-89. By JAMES ROBERTSON, D.D., Professor of Oriental Languages in the
University of Glasgow. Fourth Edition. Crown 8vo, 10s. 6d.

ROBERTSON.
Orellana, and other Poems. By J. LOGIE ROBERTSON,
M.A. Fcap. 8vo. Printed on hand-made paper. 6s.

A History of English Literature. For Secondary Schools.
With an Introduction by Professor MASSON, Edinburgh University. Cr. 8vo, 3s.

English Verse for Junior Classes. In Two Parts. Crown 8vo.
[*In the press.*

ROBERTSON. Our Holiday among the Hills. By JAMES and
JANET LOGIE ROBERTSON. Fcap. 8vo, 3s. 6d.

ROBERTSON. Essays and Sermons. By the late W. ROBERT-
SON, B.D., Minister of the Parish of Sprouston. With a Memoir and Portrait.
Crown 8vo, 5s. 6d.

ROBINSON. The Saviour in the Newer Light : A Present Day
Study of Jesus Christ. By ALEXANDER ROBINSON, B.D., Minister of the Parish
of Kilmun. Demy 8vo, 7s. 6d. net.

RODGER. Aberdeen Doctors at Home and Abroad. The Story
of a Medical School. By ELLA HILL BURTON RODGER. Demy 8vo, 10s. 6d.

ROSCOE. Rambles with a Fishing-Rod. By E. S. ROSCOE.
Crown 8vo, 4s. 6d.

ROSS AND SOMERVILLE. Beggars on Horseback : A Riding
Tour in North Wales. By MARTIN ROSS and E. Œ. SOMERVILLE. With Illustrations by E. Œ. SOMERVILLE. Crown 8vo, 3s. 6d.

RUTLAND.
Notes of an Irish Tour in 1846. By the DUKE OF RUTLAND,
G.C.B. (Lord JOHN MANNERS). New Edition. Crown 8vo, 2s. 6d.

Correspondence between the Right Honble. William Pitt
and Charles Duke of Rutland, Lord - Lieutenant of Ireland, 1781-1787. With
Introductory Note by JOHN DUKE OF RUTLAND. 8vo, 7s. 6d.

RUTLAND.
Gems of German Poetry. Translated by the DUCHESS OF
RUTLAND (Lady JOHN MANNERS). [*New Edition in preparation.*

Impressions of Bad-Homburg. Comprising a Short Account
of the Women's Associations of Germany under the Red Cross. Crown 8vo, 1s. 6d.

Some Personal Recollections of the Later Years of the Earl
of Beaconsfield, K.G. Sixth Edition. 6d.

Employment of Women in the Public Service. 6d.

Some of the Advantages of Easily Accessible Reading and
Recreation Rooms and Free Libraries. With Remarks on Starting and Main-
taining them. Second Edition. Crown 8vo, 1s.

A Sequel to Rich Men's Dwellings, and other Occasional
Papers. Crown 8vo, 2s. 6d.

Encouraging Experiences of Reading and Recreation Rooms,
Aims of Guilds, Nottingham Social Guide, Existing Institutions, &c., &c.
Crown 8vo, 1s.

SALMON. Songs of a Heart's Surrender, and other Verse.
By ARTHUR L. SALMON. Fcap. 8vo, 2s.

SCHEFFEL. The Trumpeter. A Romance of the Rhine. By
JOSEPH VICTOR VON SCHEFFEL. Translated from the Two Hundredth German
Edition by JESSIE BECK and LOUISA LORIMER. With an Introduction by Sir
THEODORE MARTIN, K.C.B. Long 8vo, 3s. 6d.

SCHILLER. Wallenstein. A Dramatic Poem. By FRIEDRICH
VON SCHILLER. Translated by C. G. N. LOCKHART. Fcap. 8vo, 7s. 6d.

SCOTCH LOCH FISHING. By "BLACK PALMER." Crown 8vo,
interleaved with blank pages, 4s.

SCOTT. Tom Cringle's Log. By MICHAEL SCOTT. New Edition.
With 19 Full-page Illustrations. Crown 8vo, 3s. 6d.

SCOUGAL. Prisons and their Inmates ; or, Scenes from a
Silent World. By FRANCIS SCOUGAL. Crown 8vo, boards, 2s.

SELLAR'S Manual of the Acts relating to Education in Scotland. By J. EDWARD GRAHAM, B.A. Oxon., Advocate. Ninth Edition. Demy 8vo, 12s. 6d.

SETH.
Scottish Philosophy. A Comparison of the Scottish and German Answers to Hume. Balfour Philosophical Lectures, University of Edinburgh. By ANDREW SETH, LL.D., Professor of Logic and Metaphysics in Edinburgh University. Second Edition. Crown 8vo, 5s.

Hegelianism and Personality. Balfour Philosophical Lectures. Second Series. Second Edition. Crown 8vo, 5s.

SETH. A Study of Ethical Principles. By JAMES SETH, M.A., Professor of Philosophy in Brown University, U.S.A. Second Edition, Revised. Post 8vo, 10s. 6d. net.

SHADWELL. The Life of Colin Campbell, Lord Clyde. Illustrated by Extracts from his Diary and Correspondence. By Lieutenant-General SHADWELL, C.B. With Portrait, Maps, and Plans. 2 vols. 8vo, 36s.

SHAND.
The Life of General Sir Edward Bruce Hamley, K.C.B., K.C.M.G. By ALEX. INNES SHAND, Author of 'Kilcarra,' 'Against Time,' &c. With two Photogravure Portraits and other Illustrations. 2 vols. demy 8vo, 21s.

Half a Century; or, Changes in Men and Manners. Second Edition. 8vo, 12s. 6d.

Letters from the West of Ireland. Reprinted from the 'Times.' Crown 8vo, 5s.

SHARPE. Letters from and to Charles Kirkpatrick Sharpe. Edited by ALEXANDER ALLARDYCE, Author of 'Memoir of Admiral Lord Keith, K.B.,' &c. With a Memoir by the Rev. W. K. R. BEDFORD. In 2 vols. 8vo. Illustrated with Etchings and other Engravings. £2, 12s. 6d.

SIM. Margaret Sim's Cookery. With an Introduction by L. B. WALFORD, Author of 'Mr Smith: A Part of his Life,' &c. Crown 8vo, 5s.

SIMPSON. The Wild Rabbit in a New Aspect; or, Rabbit-Warrens that Pay. A book for Landowners, Sportsmen, Land Agents, Farmers, Gamekeepers, and Allotment Holders. A Record of Recent Experiments conducted on the Estate of the Right Hon. the Earl of Wharncliffe at Wortley Hall. By J. SIMPSON. Second Edition, Enlarged. Small crown 8vo, 5s.

SKELTON.
The Table-Talk of Shirley. By JOHN SKELTON, Advocate, C.B., LL.D., Author of 'The Essays of Shirley.' With a Frontispiece. Fourth Edition. Post 8vo, 7s. 6d.

Maitland of Lethington; and the Scotland of Mary Stuart. A History. Limited Edition, with Portraits. Demy 8vo, 2 vols., 28s. net.

The Handbook of Public Health. A Complete Edition of the Public Health and other Sanitary Acts relating to Scotland. Annotated, and with the Rules, Instructions, and Decisions of the Board of Supervision brought up to date with relative forms. Second Edition. With Introduction, containing the Administration of the Public Health Act in Counties. 8vo, 8s. 6d.

The Local Government (Scotland) Act in Relation to Public Health. A Handy Guide for County and District Councillors, Medical Officers, Sanitary Inspectors, and Members of Parochial Boards. Second Edition. With a new Preface on appointment of Sanitary Officers. Crown 8vo, 2s.

SKRINE. Columba: A Drama. By JOHN HUNTLEY SKRINE, Warden of Glenalmond; Author of 'A Memory of Edward Thring.' Fcap. 4to, 6s.

SMITH.
Thorndale; or, The Conflict of Opinions. By WILLIAM SMITH, Author of 'A Discourse on Ethics,' &c. New Edition. Crown 8vo, 10s. 6d.

Gravenhurst; or, Thoughts on Good and Evil. Second Edition. With Memoir and Portrait of the Author. Crown 8vo, 8s.

SMITH.
The Story of William and Lucy Smith. Edited by GEORGE
MERRIAM. Large post 8vo, 12s. 6d.

SMITH. Memoir of the Families of M'Combie and Thoms,
originally M'Intosh and M'Thomas. Compiled from History and Tradition. By
WILLIAM M'COMBIE SMITH. With Illustrations. 8vo, 7s. 6d.

SMITH. Greek Testament Lessons for Colleges, Schools, and
Private Students, consisting chiefly of the Sermon on the Mount and the Parables
of our Lord. With Notes and Essays. By the Rev. J. HUNTER SMITH, M.A.,
King Edward's School, Birmingham. Crown 8vo, 6s.

SMITH. The Secretary for Scotland. Being a Statement of the
Powers and Duties of the new Scottish Office. With a Short Historical Intro-
duction, and numerous references to important Administrative Documents. By
W. C. SMITH, LL.B., Advocate. 8vo, 6s.

"SON OF THE MARSHES, A."
From Spring to Fall ; or, When Life Stirs. By "A SON OF
THE MARSHES." Crown 8vo, 3s. 6d.
Within an Hour of London Town : Among Wild Birds and
their Haunts. Edited by J. A. OWEN. Cheap Uniform Edition. Crown 8vo,
3s. 6d.
With the Woodlanders, and By the Tide. Cheap Uniform
Edition. Crown 8vo, 3s. 6d.
On Surrey Hills. Cheap Uniform Edition. Crown 8vo, 3s. 6d.
Annals of a Fishing Village. Cheap Uniform Edition. Crown
8vo, 3s. 6d.

SORLEY. The Ethics of Naturalism. Being the Shaw Fellowship Lectures, 1884. By W. R. SORLEY, M.A., Fellow of Trinity College, Cambridge, Professor of Moral Philosophy in the University of Aberdeen. Crown
8vo, 6s.

SPEEDY. Sport in the Highlands and Lowlands of Scotland
with Rod and Gun. By TOM SPEEDY. Second Edition, Revised and Enlarged.
With Illustrations by Lieut.-General Hope Crealocke, C.B., C.M.G., and others.
8vo, 15s.

SPROTT. The Worship and Offices of the Church of Scotland.
By GEORGE W. SPROTT, D.D., Minister of North Berwick. Crown 8vo, 6s.

STATISTICAL ACCOUNT OF SCOTLAND. Complete, with
Index. 15 vols. 8vo, £16, 16s.

STEPHENS.
The Book of the Farm ; detailing the Labours of the Farmer,
Farm-Steward, Ploughman, Shepherd, Hedger, Farm-Labourer, Field-Worker,
and Cattle-man. Illustrated with numerous Portraits of Animals and Engravings
of Implements, and Plans of Farm Buildings. Fourth Edition. Revised, and
in great part Rewritten by JAMES MACDONALD, F.R.S.E., Secretary, Highland
and Agricultural Society of Scotland. Complete in Six Divisional Volumes,
bound in cloth, each 10s. 6d., or handsomely bound, in 3 volumes, with leather
back and gilt top, £3, 3s.
Catechism of Practical Agriculture. New Edition. Revised
by JAMES MACDONALD, F.R.S.E. With numerous Illustrations. Crown 8vo, 1s.
The Book of Farm Implements and Machines. By J. SLIGHT
and R. SCOTT BURN, Engineers. Edited by HENRY STEPHENS. Large 8vo, £2, 2s.

STEVENSON. British Fungi. (Hymenomycetes.) By Rev.
JOHN STEVENSON, Author of 'Mycologia Scotica,' Hon. Sec. Cryptogamic Society
of Scotland. Vols. I. and II., post 8vo, with Illustrations, price 12s. 6d. net each.

STEWART.
Advice to Purchasers of Horses. By JOHN STEWART, V.S.
New Edition. 2s. 6d.
Stable Economy. A Treatise on the Management of Horses
in relation to Stabling, Grooming, Feeding, Watering, and Working. Seventh
Edition. Fcap. 8vo, 6s. 6d.
STEWART. A Hebrew Grammar, with the Pronunciation, Syl-
labic Division and Tone of the Words, and Quantity of the Vowels. By Rev.
DUNCAN STEWART, D.D. Fourth Edition. 8vo, 3s. 6d.
STEWART. Boethius: An Essay. By HUGH FRASER STEWART,
M.A., Trinity College, Cambridge. Crown 8vo, 7s. 6d.
STODDART. Angling Songs. By THOMAS TOD STODDART.
New Edition, with a Memoir by ANNA M. STODDART. Crown 8vo, 7s. 6d.
STODDART.
John Stuart Blackie: A Biography. By ANNA M. STODDART.
With 3 Plates. Third Edition. 2 vols. demy 8vo, 21s.
Sir Philip Sidney: Servant of God. Illustrated by MARGARET
L. HUGGINS. With a New Portrait of Sir Philip Sidney. Small 4to, with a
specially designed Cover. 5s.
STORMONTH.
Etymological and Pronouncing Dictionary of the English
Language. Including a very Copious Selection of Scientific Terms. For use in
Schools and Colleges, and as a Book of General Reference. By the Rev. JAMES
STORMONTH. The Pronunciation carefully revised by the Rev. P. H. PHELP, M.A.
Cantab. Eleventh Edition, with Supplement. Crown 8vo, pp. 800. 7s. 6d.
Dictionary of the English Language, Pronouncing, Etymo-
logical, and Explanatory. Revised by the Rev. P. H. PHELP. Library Edition.
New and Cheaper Edition, with Supplement. Imperial 8vo, handsomely bound
in half morocco, 18s. net.
The School Etymological Dictionary and Word-Book. Fourth
Edition. Fcap. 8vo, pp. 254. 2s.
STORY.
Nero; A Historical Play. By W. W. STORY, Author of
'Roba di Roma.' Fcap. 8vo, 6s.
Vallombrosa. Post 8vo, 5s.
Poems. 2 vols., 7s. 6d.
Fiammetta. A Summer Idyl. Crown 8vo, 7s. 6d.
Conversations in a Studio. 2 vols. crown 8vo, 12s. 6d.
Excursions in Art and Letters. Crown 8vo, 7s. 6d.
A Poet's Portfolio: Later Readings. 18mo, 3s. 6d.
STRACHEY. Talk at a Country House. Fact and Fiction.
By Sir EDWARD STRACHEY, Bart. With a Portrait of the Author. Crown 8vo,
4s. 6d. net.
STURGIS.
John-a-Dreams. A Tale. By JULIAN STURGIS. New Edi-
tion. Crown 8vo, 3s. 6d.
Little Comedies, Old and New. Crown 8vo, 7s. 6d.
SUTHERLAND (DUCHESS OF). How I Spent my Twentieth
Year. Being a Record of a Tour Round the World, 1886-87. By the DUCHESS
OF SUTHERLAND (MARCHIONESS OF STAFFORD). With Illustrations. Crown 8vo,
7s. 6d.
SUTHERLAND. Handbook of Hardy Herbaceous and Alpine
Flowers, for General Garden Decoration. Containing Descriptions of upwards
of 1000 Species of Ornamental Hardy Perennial and Alpine Plants; along with
Concise and Plain Instructions for their Propagation and Culture. By WILLIAM
SUTHERLAND, Landscape Gardener; formerly Manager of the Herbaceous Depart-
ment at Kew. Crown 8vo, 7s. 6d.

TAYLOR. The Story of my Life. By the late Colonel
MEADOWS TAYLOR, Author of 'The Confessions of a Thug,' &c., &c. Edited by
his Daughter. New and Cheaper Edition, being the Fourth. Crown 8vo, 6s.

THOMSON.
The Diversions of a Prime Minister. By Basil Thomson.
With a Map, numerous Illustrations by J. W. CAWSTON and others, and Repro-
ductions of Rare Plates from Early Voyages of Sixteenth and Seventeenth Centuries. Small demy 8vo, 15s.

South Sea Yarns. With 10 Full-page Illustrations. Cheaper
Edition. Crown 8vo, 3s. 6d.

THOMSON.
Handy Book of the Flower-Garden : being Practical Direc-
tions for the Propagation, Culture, and Arrangement of Plants in Flower-
Gardens all the year round. With Engraved Plans. By DAVID THOMSON,
Gardener to his Grace the Duke of Buccleuch, K.T., at Drumlanrig. Fourth
and Cheaper Edition. Crown 8vo, 5s.

The Handy Book of Fruit-Culture under Glass : being a
series of Elaborate Practical Treatises on the Cultivation and Forcing of Pines,
Vines, Peaches, Figs, Melons, Strawberries, and Cucumbers. With Engravings
of Hothouses, &c. Second Edition, Revised and Enlarged. Crown 8vo, 7s. 6d.

THOMSON. A Practical Treatise on the Cultivation of the
Grape Vine. By WILLIAM THOMSON, Tweed Vineyards. Tenth Edition. 8vo, 5s.

THOMSON. Cookery for the Sick and Convalescent. With
Directions for the Preparation of Poultices, Fomentations, &c. By BARBARA
THOMSON. Fcap. 8vo, 1s. 6d.

THORBURN. Asiatic Neighbours. By S. S. THORBURN, Bengal
Civil Service, Author of 'Bannú ; or, Our Afghan Frontier,' 'David Leslie :
A Story of the Afghan Frontier,' 'Musalmans and Money-Lenders in the Pan-
jab.' With Two Maps. Demy 8vo, 10s. 6d. net.

THORNTON. Opposites. A Series of Essays on the Unpopular
Sides of Popular Questions. By LEWIS THORNTON. 8vo, 12s. 6d.

TRANSACTIONS OF THE HIGHLAND AND AGRICUL-
TURAL SOCIETY OF SCOTLAND. Published annually, price 5s.

TRAVEL, ADVENTURE, AND SPORT. From 'Blackwood's
Magazine.' Uniform with 'Tales from Blackwood.' In 12 Parts, each price 1s.
Handsomely bound in 6 vols., cloth, 15s. ; half calf, 25s.

TRAVERS. Mona Maclean, Medical Student. A Novel. By
GRAHAM TRAVERS. Eleventh Edition. Crown 8vo, 6s.

TULLOCH.
Rational Theology and Christian Philosophy in England in
the Seventeenth Century. By JOHN TULLOCH, D.D., Principal of St Mary's College in the University of St Andrews ; and one of her Majesty's Chaplains in
Ordinary in Scotland. Second Edition. 2 vols. 8vo, 16s.

Modern Theories in Philosophy and Religion. 8vo, 15s.

Luther, and other Leaders of the Reformation. Third Edition, Enlarged. Crown 8vo, 3s. 6d.

Memoir of Principal Tulloch, D.D., LL.D. By Mrs OLIPHANT,
Author of 'Life of Edward Irving.' Third and Cheaper Edition. 8vo, with
Portrait, 7s. 6d.

TWEEDIE. The Arabian Horse : His Country and People.
By Major-General W. TWEEDIE, C.S.I., Bengal Staff Corps ; for many years
H.B.M.'s Consul-General, Baghdad, and Political Resident for the Government
of India in Turkish Arabia. In one vol. royal 4to, with Seven Coloured Plates
and other Illustrations, and a Map of the Country. Price £3, 3s. net.

VEITCH.
The History and Poetry of the Scottish Border : their Main
Features and Relations. By JOHN VEITCH, LL.D., Professor of Logic and
Rhetoric in the University of Glasgow. New and Enlarged Edition. 2 vols.
demy 8vo, 16s.
Institutes of Logic. Post 8vo, 12s. 6d.
The Feeling for Nature in Scottish Poetry. From the Ear-
liest Times to the Present Day. 2 vols. fcap. 8vo, in roxburghe binding, 15s.
Merlin and other Poems. Fcap. 8vo, 4s. 6d.
Knowing and Being. Essays in Philosophy. First Series.
Crown 8vo, 5s.
Dualism and Monism ; and other Essays. Essays in Phil-
osophy. Second Series. With an Introduction by R. M. Wenley. Crown 8vo,
4s. 6d. net.

VIRGIL. The Æneid of Virgil. Translated in English Blank
Verse by G. K. RICKARDS, M.A., and Lord RAVENSWORTH. 2 vols. fcap. 8vo, 10s.

WACE. Christianity and Agnosticism. Reviews of some Recent
Attacks on the Christian Faith. By HENRY WACE, D.D., Principal of King's
College, London ; Preacher of Lincoln's Inn ; Chaplain to the Queen. Second
Edition. Post 8vo, 10s. 6d. net.

WADDELL. An Old Kirk Chronicle : Being a History of Auld-
hame, Tyninghame, and Whitekirk, in East Lothian. From Session Records,
1615 to 1850. By Rev. P. HATELY WADDELL, B.D., Minister of the United
Parish. Small Paper Edition, 200 Copies. Price £1. Large Paper Edition, 50
Copies. Price £1, 10s.

WALFORD. Four Biographies from 'Blackwood' : Jane Taylor,
Hannah More, Elizabeth Fry, Mary Somerville. By L. B. WALFORD. Crown
8vo, 5s.

WARREN'S (SAMUEL) WORKS :—
Diary of a Late Physician. Cloth, 2s. 6d. ; boards, 2s.
Ten Thousand A-Year. Cloth, 3s. 6d. ; boards, 2s. 6d.
Now and Then. The Lily and the Bee. Intellectual and
Moral Development of the Present Age. 4s. 6d.
Essays : Critical, Imaginative, and Juridical. 5s.

WEBSTER. The Angler and the Loop - Rod. By DAVID
WEBSTER. Crown 8vo, with Illustrations, 7s. 6d.

WENLEY.
Socrates and Christ : A Study in the Philosophy of Religion.
By R. M. WENLEY, M.A., D.Sc., Lecturer on Mental and Moral Philosophy in
Queen Margaret College, Glasgow; formerly Examiner in Philosophy in the
University of Glasgow. Crown 8vo, 6s.
Aspects of Pessimism. Crown 8vo, 6s.

WESTMINSTER ASSEMBLY. Minutes of the Westminster
Assembly, while engaged in preparing their Directory for Church Government,
Confession of Faith, and Catechisms (November 1644 to March 1649). Edited
by the Rev. Professor ALEX. T. MITCHELL, of St Andrews, and the Rev. JOHN
STRUTHERS, LL.D. With a Historical and Critical Introduction by Professor
Mitchell. 8vo, 15s.

WHITE.
The Eighteen Christian Centuries. By the Rev. JAMES
WHITE. Seventh Edition. Post 8vo, with Index, 6s.
History of France, from the Earliest Times. Sixth Thousand.
Post 8vo, with Index, 6s.
Archæological Sketches in Scotland—Kintyre and Knapdale.
By Colonel T. P. WHITE, R.E., of the Ordnance Survey. With numerous Illus-
trations. 2 vols. folio, £4, 4s. Vol. I., Kintyre, sold separately, £2, 2s.

WHITE. The Ordnance Survey of the United Kingdom. A Popular
Account. Crown 8vo, 5s.

WILLIAMSON. The Horticultural Handbook and Exhibitor's
Guide. A Treatise on Cultivating, Exhibiting, and Judging Plants, Flowers,
Fruits, and Vegetables. By W. WILLIAMSON, Gardener. Revised by MALCOLM
DUNN, Gardener to his Grace the Duke of Buccleuch and Queensberry, Dalkeith
Park. New and Cheaper Edition, enlarged. Crown 8vo, paper cover, 2s. ;
cloth, 2s. 6d.

WILLIAMSON. Poems of Nature and Life. By DAVID R.
WILLIAMSON, Minister of Kirkmaiden. Fcap. 8vo, 3s.

WILLIAMSON. Light from Eastern Lands on the Lives of
Abraham, Joseph, and Moses. By the Rev. ALEX. WILLIAMSON, Author of 'The
Missionary Heroes of the Pacific,' 'Sure and Comfortable Words,' 'Ask and
Receive,' &c. Crown 8vo, 3s. 6d.

WILLS. Behind an Eastern Veil. A Plain Tale of Events
occurring in the Experience of a Lady who had a unique opportunity of observ-
ing the Inner Life of Ladies of the Upper Class in Persia. By C. J. WILLS,
Author of 'In the Land of the Lion and Sun,' 'Persia as it is,' &c., &c. Cheaper
Edition. Demy 8vo, 5s.

WILLS AND GREENE. Drawing-Room Dramas for Children.
By W. G. WILLS and the Hon. Mrs GREENE. Crown 8vo, 6s.

WILSON. -
Works of Professor Wilson. Edited by his Son-in-Law,
Professor FERRIER. 12 vols. crown 8vo, £2, 8s.
Christopher in his Sporting-Jacket. 2 vols., 8s.
Isle of Palms, City of the Plague, and other Poems. 4s.
Lights and Shadows of Scottish Life, and other Tales. 4s.
Essays, Critical and Imaginative. 4 vols., 16s.
The Noctes Ambrosianæ. 4 vols., 16s.
Homer and his Translators, and the Greek Drama. Crown
8vo, 4s.

WORSLEY.
Poems and Translations. By PHILIP STANHOPE WORSLEY,
M.A. Edited by EDWARD WORSLEY. Second Edition, Enlarged. Fcap. 8vo, 6s.
Homer's Odyssey. Translated into English Verse in the
Spenserian Stanza. By P. S. Worsley. New and Cheaper Edition. Post 8vo,
7s. 6d. net.
Homer's Iliad. Translated by P. S. Worsley and Prof. Con-
ington 2 vols. crown 8vo, 21s.

YATE. England and Russia Face to Face in Asia. A Record of
Travel with the Afghan Boundary Commission. By Captain A. C. YATE, Bombay
Staff Corps. 8vo, with Maps and Illustrations, 21s.

YATE. Northern Afghanistan ; or, Letters from the Afghan
Boundary Commission. By Major C. E. YATE, C.S.I., C.M.G. Bombay Staff
Corps, F.R.G.S. 8vo, with Maps, 18s.

YULE. Fortification : For the use of Officers in the Army, and
Readers of Military History. By Colonel YULE, Bengal Engineers. 8vo, with
Numerous Illustrations, 10s.